Better Software Faster

ISBN 013008752-1

9 780130 087522

90000

The Coad Series

Peter Coad, *Series Editor*

———■———

- David Astels, Granville Miller, Miroslav Novak
  A Practical Guide to eXtreme Programming

- Andy Carmichael, Dan Haywood
  Better Software Faster

- Donald Kranz, Ronald J. Norman
  A Practical Guide to Unified Process

- Jill Nicola, Mark Mayfield, Michael Abney
  Streamlined Object Modeling: Patterns, Rules, and Implementation

- Stephen R. Palmer, John M. Felsing
  A Practical Guide to Feature-Driven Development

- Jo Ellen Perry, Jeff Micke
  How to Get the Most Out of the Together ControlCenter

About the Series

The mission statement of the Coad Series is: Improving the ways people work together. Targeted for developers, business people, and IT decision makers, this series delivers practical keys for building lasting value into business, by building people and their skills. Peter Coad personally selects authors and topics for this series and works on a strategic level with authors during the development of each book.

About the Series Editor

Peter Coad (Chairman, Founder, and Chief Strategy Officer at TogetherSoft) is known around the world as Business Strategist, Model Builder, and Thought Leader. As Business Strategist, Peter formulates the overall strategies executed at TogetherSoft (www.togethersoft.com). Previously, as CEO and President, he led in growing the company 11.6 times revenue in the span of two years, overall profitably, making TogetherSoft the momentum leader in its space. As Model Builder, Peter has built hundreds of models for nearly every business imaginable, ever focusing on building-in strategic business advantage. As Thought Leader, Peter writes books (six to date) on building better software and speaks at software-industry events worldwide; he is the Editor-in-Chief of The Coad Letter (www.thecoadletter.com) and of The Coad Series (a new series of books published by Prentice Hall); in addition, he is writing a new book on effective tech-company business strategies.

Better Software Faster

Andy Carmichael
Dan Haywood

 Prentice Hall PTR, Upper Saddle River, NJ 07458
www.phptr.com

Library of Congress Cataloging-in-Publication Data

CIP date available.

Editorial/Production Supervision: *Mary Sudul*
Page Layout: FAST*pages*
Acquisitions Editor: *Paul Petralia*
Editorial Assistant: *Richard Winkler*
Manufacturing manager: *Alexis Heydt-Long*
Art Director: *Gail Cocker-Bogusz*
Interior Series Design: *Meg Van Arsdale*
Cover Design: *Design Source*
Cover Design Direction: *Jerry Votta*

 © 2002 by Prentice Hall PTR
Prentice-Hall, Inc.
Upper Saddle River, NJ 07458

Prentice Hall books are widely used by corporations and government agencies for training, marketing, and resale.

The publisher offers discounts on this book when ordered in bulk quantities. For more information, contact Corporate Sales Department, phone: 800-382-3419; fax: 201-236-7141; email: corpsales@prenhall.com Or write Corporate Sales Department, Prentice Hall PTR, One Lake Street, Upper Saddle River, NJ 07458.

Product and company names mentioned herein are the trademarks or registered trademarks of their respective owners.

Printed in the United States of America

10 9 8 7 6 5 4 3 2 1

ISBN 0-13-008752-1

Pearson Education LTD.
Pearson Education Australia PTY, Limited
Pearson Education Singapore, Pte. Ltd.
Pearson Education North Asia Ltd.
Pearson Education Canada, Ltd.
Pearson Educación de Mexico, S.A. de C.V.
Pearson Education — Japan
Pearson Education Malaysia, Pte. Ltd.

contents

Chapter 3

The First Step: Model the Domain   45

Chapter 4

The Stakeholder Step: Specify Requirements   65

Chapter 5

The Controlling Step: Feature-Centric Management   91

Chapter 6

The Continuous Step: Measure the Quality   111

Chapter 7

The Micro Step: Design and Implement   163

Chapter 8

The Macro Step: Architecture   211

Chapter 9

The J2EE Architecture   241

Chapter 10

Appendix A

Appendix B

Appendix C

Customizing Together with .config files   293

Appendix D

Customizing Together's Templates   299

Appendix E

Customizing Together's Inspectors   303

by Edward Yourdon

Though I have spent the great majority of my IT career as a consultant and a "methodologist," several of my assignments in the past two or three years have been of a very specialized nature: working as an "expert witness" on computer-related lawsuits. And for reasons I'll explain shortly, this has given me an appreciation for the advice and guidelines in Andy Carmichael and Dan Haywood's new book, *Better Software Faster*, and a strong desire that every IT project manager should read it carefully.

Most of my assignments follow a similar pattern: an ambitious business organization decides that it needs an innovative new information system; it then contracts with an aggressive software development firm to build the system. At the beginning, the atmosphere is one of enthusiasm and optimism; the customer promises to devote resources and energy throughout the project, the vendor promises to provide high-quality, "professional" services, and both parties pledge to work in a "partnership" mode. A contract is generated and duly signed, though inevitably it turns out that the attorneys for at least one of the parties have never seen it; indeed, one often wonders whether *anyone* other than the vendor's marketing representative has actually read the document.

After a period that ranges from a few months to a couple years, things begin to turn sour. Deadlines come and go; budgets are exceeded; amendments to the contract are hurriedly negotiated and signed; and the mood gradually turns grim and hostile. Sooner or later, one of the parties abandons all hope, and terminates the contract; in most cases, it's the client who pulls the plug, complaining that the project has taken twice as long as initially promised, and has cost twice as much as originally budgeted. And to add insult to injury, the system either doesn't work at all, or is full of bugs, or runs so slowly that only 3 users can access it concurrently, instead of the 300 that had been promised.

At that point, both parties bring in their respective lawyers. Notwithstanding all of the cynical jokes you've heard about lawyers, most of them are simply trying to clean up a mess that was created by naïve business managers who let things get out of hand. But because the mess involves the mysterious technology of computers and software, "experts" like me are brought in to advise the lawyers, the judge and the jury. All of them want credible answers to some very basic questions: whose fault was it that the project failed? How did it happen? When should it have been evident that the project was in trouble? Why didn't someone, on either one side or the other, *do* something about it?

If you don't think such things can happen in the "real world," let me assure you that they do; indeed, the cost of litigation now exceeds the cost of coding for most large software development organizations. Only a small percentage of such failures actually result in lawsuits; a much greater percentage of the failures result in both parties walking away from the mess, swearing never to speak to one another again. And an even larger percentage of such failures are completely "invisible," because they involve a business department and an IT department within the same organization. Companies don't sue themselves, but IT project failures result in ruined careers, missed business opportunities, and staggering financial losses.

If you've never seen such a disaster unfold, just turn to the first chapter of *Better Software Faster*; the example may be fictionalized, but it's typical of what is happening in thousands of business organizations day in, and day out. The amazing thing is that Carmichael and Haywood summarize the strategy for *avoiding* such disasters within the first two pages of the book: "By discovering what the business imperatives are, the team can deliver enhancements to the current capabilities within the specified period while also preparing for longer term requirements. If the team follows this route, it will need a flexible and lightweight development process with rapid feedback loops to report holdups and roadblocks—and it will need to plan contingencies accordingly."

If it's as simple and obvious as that, why doesn't everyone do it? And, having glimpsed the "secret" for avoiding project disasters, why do you need to bother reading past page 2 of *Better Software Faster*? The answer to both questions, unfortunately, is that the devil is in the details. There are still some obstinate and/or stubborn business managers who insist on getting *all* of the functionality for their IT system in one fell swoop, delivered for an unrealistic amount of money on an outrageously optimistic schedule. But any IT project team with an aggregate IQ exceeding two digits already understands the concept espoused by Carmichael and Haywood right at the beginning of their book: "…there will need to be many deliveries of the software, each adding incrementally to the desired functionality. The development team's question to the business team is not so much "Which of these requirements do you not want delivered?" but "Which ones will contribute most to the business now, and therefore, which ones should be delivered first?"

The concept may be familiar and obvious, but it's the details that distinguish the winners from the losers in the IT project game; and it's the details you'll find in this excellent book by two veterans who have succeeded often enough that they truly deserve to be called "winners." One of the "details" that remains controversial, and that requires careful, detailed explanation involves the software "process" associated with the familiar activities of analysis, design, implementation and testing. For at least a decade, IT project teams have rejected the ponderous bureaucracy of the "heavy" processes that were first created in the 1970s and 1980s*; unfortunately, they have often replaced it with anarchy—no process at all. Carmichael and Haywood describe, in detail, a happy medium: just enough process, with just enough formality, and just enough documentation.

One way of accomplishing this efficiently and productively is to use an automated development environment—but one that far exceeds the kind of "programming environment" that most developers associate with languages such as Visual Basic, C++, or Java. The authors are predisposed to using the development environment from Togethersoft, which creates object-oriented analysis/design models, and keeps them continuously synchronized with the code in Java or C++. As someone who has no business relationship or involvement with Togethersoft, I can confirm that it is indeed an elegant choice; but readers should also be aware that other choices are possible. The main thing that IT project teams need to realize is that a modest investment of time and energy in "light" processes for analysis and design does *not* slow the project down, but actually speeds it up.

It's easy to say such things in the abstract; but as noted earlier, the devil is in the details. And the only way to see those details, and to be persuaded that a combination of light processes and advanced systems development tools really can prevent the project disasters that keep lawyers and juries busy, is to see a detailed example. Much of the content of *Better Software Faster* is devoted to a detailed case study; in addition to what's in the book, the authors provide additional material that you can download from their web site.

Even with an excellent book like *Better Software Faster*, one can't help wondering if it really will improve the situation in today's IT industry. If only one systems analyst on the project team reads the book, he or she might be overwhelmed by the other project team members, and/or the end-users or project stakeholders—many of whom are convinced that brute-force coding, starting on the first day of the project, is the only way to succeed. If only one person can read the book, it should be the project leader; even better results can be expected if both the project leader and the responsible customer/ user representative read it before the project begins, and reach a consensus on the contents. Ideally, everyone on the project team should read it, so that they have a shared mental model (which, as you'll see from the book, is a *colored* mental model) of the system they are developing, and their strategy for building it.

In the best of all worlds, every IT professional and every business person who wants an IT system would read *Better Software Faster*. Then there would be no more lawsuits; lawyers would have to get an honest job, and I

---

*.   To illustrate just how heavy such processes can be, metrics guru Capers Jones estimates that the U.S. Defense Department DOD-2167A software development process required an average of 400 English words of documentation for every line of source code. Thus, if you were building a medium-sized business application consisting of 50,000 lines of code, you would need an army of technical writers to generate 20 million words of documentation to explain what the code does, how it does what it does, and why it does what it does.

could go back to helping people *build* systems, rather than helping to assign blame and explain why the disaster occurred. Meanwhile, Carmichael and Haywood would grow rich and famous as they watched their book zoom to the top of the *New York Times* bestseller list, and could dream about Pulitzer Prizes and perhaps even a Hollywood rendition with famous actors and actresses.

I'll help get the process started by buying a copy of *Better Software Faster* for my own bookshelf, and a couple more copies for some project manager friends and clients. How about you?

Ed Yourdon
New York City
March 2002

There is a vast difference between a product that *forces* you to change the way you work and one that *inspires* you to work differently. Being forced to do it "their" way is uncomfortable and usually unproductive. The freedom to discover better ways of working is more enjoyable and inspires new insights into other approaches to get your work done.

The reason we wrote this book is a product called Together Control-Center and the different way of working that it enables. We didn't just write it for users of Together—users of competing development platforms or no development platform will, we hope, also find it helpful, but we admit, Together is the inspiration behind the book.

You won't often come across products that fit into the "inspirational" category, but it seems for many users that's exactly where Together fits. It is certainly revolutionary compared to the typical modeling and code-generation tools that preceded it. For us, Together ControlCenter has caused us to look again at how teams work together. So, one of the objectives of this book is to show you how Together will help you to develop software in ways that deliver the same or better quality software in a shorter timeframe—in short, how to make better software faster.

We wrote this book for software development teams, their team leaders, and their managers—particularly, small teams using Java or similar object-oriented languages as their programming language.

Small teams consist of more than a pair of developers and fewer than a dozen. A small team doesn't need subdivisions for management purposes; it has minimum administrative overhead and it consists of people who generally all know each other well—at least they do after a few months of the project! That gives small teams great advantages over large teams, even though their resources are less. The likelihood of a project failing increases significantly with the team size.[*] This is a good reason why a great deal of commercial software (if not the majority) is developed by small teams.

Small teams don't necessarily need to use a *named* software development process. Other books in this series are designed to help the practitioners of various named processes, such as FDD (Palmer & Felsing 2002), XP (Astels, Miller, & Novak 2001) and UP (Norman & Kranz, in press), to successfully apply them. This book, however, focuses more on recommending the simplest way to get things done while drawing on many of these more

---

[*]. According to research carried out by the Standish Group (Johnson 1995; see also *www.standishgroup.com*) over 30 percent of all software projects will be canceled before they are completed. The larger projects are, the more likely they are to suffer failures, such as cancellation or severe budget/schedule overruns.

formal processes for their best ideas and advice. Our aim is to give development teams maximum help with minimum overhead.

This book is written for those using Java to implement their software. We hope this won't totally deter those using C++, C# and VB.NET especially, from seeking insights in its pages, but we must apologize to them now that throughout we've used Java examples, our downloadable case study is in Java, and discussion of distributed systems and persistence draws exclusively on Java environments, especially the J2EE architecture.

We hope, of course, that this book will also be of interest to many others: those in larger teams or using other languages; those involved as business analysts, users, or testers; and indeed to students, teachers, trainers, and consultants. However, the book is for a technical (software development) audience, not a non-technical one. The best projects tend to be those in which there is a trust between the business and the technical staff as to what can be accomplished in any given timeframe. In our experience, this trust is best built up when the business representatives and users take real interest in the development process, even in some cases joining as full members of the team. We do discuss areas where business and user representatives actively participate in the development process, particularly modeling the problem domain and specification and prioritization of the requirements. In these areas and others, we hope the book contributes to increased understanding between the technical and non-technical teams. So, if you think of yourself as primarily non-technical, then we hope you learn something about what Together can do and how software can be developed more effectively by using it.

How the Book Is Organized

In Chapter 1, "Together—The Difference It Makes", we talk about why Together is an exciting technology. We are not interested in the marketing flannel here. Together does something different from other development platforms, and that opens up new possibilities. We want to look into what this is and why it can make a significant difference to a team's performance. Also in Chapter 1 we introduce four foundational themes that run through most of the other chapters:

- maintaining just one single-source model
- the minimum metamodel
- the perturbation change model
- continuous measurement of quality.

Maintaining just one single-source model is based on the idea that information about the system should be stored in only one place and maintained only once, even though it is viewed and modified in many different forms.

The minimum meta-model is a view of the essential elements in any development process that need to be defined and effectively cross-referenced—requirements, tests, design and implementation.

The perturbation change model is a way of looking at the development process in terms of moving from one valid build to the next in small iterative steps. This is not a different development process but a way of looking at most iterative evolutionary development processes.

Continuous measurement of quality is a necessary requirement for iterative evolutionary lifecycles, that put different stresses on the development activities and the tools environment compared to waterfall-style lifecycles.

After this introduction, what about the structure for the rest of the book? Many books are structured by each step in a development process from requirements to deployment, or by taking each UML diagram type in turn. But there are some snags with that approach. First, it is hard to relate the diagram types to a software development process—many diagrams are touched at different points in the software development process and with a different emphasis at each point. Second, it is artificial. Together invites you to develop your software in an organic and evolutionary way, and we wanted to write a book that invites you to read and explore similarly. Another pressing reason we decided against structuring the book by the different diagram types is because it would be rather dull—for you to read and for us to write!

Then, we were posed an interesting question: What's the least that needs to be done to deliver and use software? Well, if you have some software already (and there nearly always is some), the answer is to just deliver and use that software. You may do other steps before that, particularly if you want different or additional functionality or quality, but you must also deliver the software. Furthermore, in looking for a common way of thinking about the development process for small teams, this last step is also the starting point, since before you can add functionality to a system, you must be sure its current functionality works.

So, we decided that Chapter 2 should start here—the "last" step. That chapter is called "The Last Step: Deploy and Run!" We take the opportunity to introduce our example domain model that will be used for most of our illustrations. We also explore many of Together's capabilities with a system that actually runs—a good way to learn. The best way to read this chapter is alongside your computer where you can access the software discussed at this book's companion Web site. If you have access to the Web now, check it out at *www.bettersoftwarefaster.com*. By starting here, we can also ensure that those of you using the book with this software are starting from a valid starting point—one where the existing code and the chosen development environment run correctly and the defined tests all pass.

In Chapter 3, "The First Step: Model the Domain," we look at an important launching point for a new team. While this is also a good opportunity to discuss the essentials of the class diagram, the main emphasis is on how to build a model that will act as an effective interface between business experts who know the essence of the business and the vision for the new system and the software development team that must realize the vision. This model is also important, as it defines the vocabulary for both requirements and implementation classes, and it links too to the definitions of persistent data and user interaction. This chapter uses object modeling in color,** as defined by Peter Coad and others, which helps to bring the analysis patterns

---

**.   Some of you may be wondering how a book printed in black and white can use object modeling in color! We've annotated the diagrams to help you, but once again we'd encourage you to use the companion Web site (*www.bettersoftwarefaster.com*) to get the full picture.

and domain-neutral models to life and enhance the readability of the models (Coad, Lefebvre, & De Luca 1999).

Gaining a good understanding of the requirements is sometimes overlooked by small (and larger) teams in time-pressured projects, but this is a potentially project-fatal mistake. In Chapter 4, "The Stakeholder Step: Specify Requirements," we discuss capturing specifications using UML, particularly the use case and activity diagrams. The diagrams are simple to understand, which is essential to make them effective at this level. But building effective requirements models is by no means easy, and we discuss key issues to keep in mind, especially strategies for keeping the requirements simple and amenable to management in an agile, iterative process that small teams need.

Chapter 5, "The Controlling Step: Feature-Centric Management," is an explanation of a planning, estimating, and project control process that we recommend to teams. Our interest here is to keep planning and management as simple and as transparent as possible. Again, the question posed before is relevant: What is the least we need to do to deliver the software?—that's our goal. One key simplification introduced to improve the management of iterative lifecycles is to merge the units of planning with the units of requirements, whether these are use cases or features. We refer to development processes that make this simplification as "feature-centric"—hence the title of this chapter.

Some might interpret the goal of seeking the *least* that is needed as suggesting that we are looking for the line of least resistance, and inevitably the quality of the software will suffer. While this could be a danger, it is certainly not our meaning nor our intention. Chapter 6, "The Continuous Step: Measure the Quality," looks at how to ensure that quality is maintained throughout the development process. Our book is called *Better Software Faster*, to which the natural response is "Better than what?" This chapter looks at the techniques for measuring quality continuously so that we can compare the quality of any software build against any other and thereby objectively assess whether or not it is better. By contrast, many projects only measure quality with functional tests, and only carry this out late in the project. This is a serious mistake. We suggest a variety of ways in which the quality status of builds can be established, including testing, automated metrics, automated audits, document generation, and inspection.

Chapter 7, "The Micro Step: Design and Implement," is a look at the work of software development day by day. It considers the tasks in taking one or more requirements and adding that functionality to the current build. We also look at the techniques you will employ using Together Control-Center for designing the functional tests, the user interaction, the object interaction and persistent data, as well as documenting the code and links to the requirements. Elements of Together's Interactive Development Environment (IDE), such as its editors, GUI-builder, debugger and source-code formatter are mentioned.

Chapter 8, "The Macro Step: Architecture," considers the system at a different scale and perspective. Many different definitions of software architecture have been used since the phrase was first coined, reputedly by F. P. Brooks. For us, architecture means the principle divisions of the software and the policies and patterns used to extend the software. In small teams, architecture is not the job of a separate team, and for this reason some teams simply let it evolve. We believe, though, that architecture is too important not to be given separate consideration. In this chapter we look at how the requirements for architecture are derived from non-functional or "level of service" requirements. This chapter also gives us an opportunity to consider how the package diagram, with Together's dependency analysis, is a key weapon in the software architect's armory and how component and deployment diagrams also help.

Chapter 9, "The J2EE Architecture," looks at the specifics of architectures based on Sun's J2EE standard and how Together ControlCenter provides support for this. We also talk briefly about our favorite technique for mapping objects to databases.

Finally, Chapter 10, "Parting Words," gives us an opportunity for a brief reflection on the scope and limitations of this volume.

Throughout the book we'll show you how to get the most out of Together, whatever formal process (or lack of it) you may have adopted. For example, we'll be exploiting Together's open API – an extensive Java-based API that constitutes a comprehensive plug-in architecture for Together—to develop modules to make development and documentation easier. We hope it will encourage you to explore this powerful and flexible facility in Together ControlCenter. Together is, after all, a development platform rather than a development tool. As teams discover specific tools, patterns, audits, or integrations they need, but which are not yet delivered out of the box, the open API is the obvious place to turn.

And that's it. We're enthusiastic about Together, and we hope it comes across. If you're as enthusiastic by the time you finish the book and have explored its accompanying software, then we'll be happy. If it gives you a different perspective on how to build software in an efficient and quality-focused manner, we will have achieved our goal.

The version of Together referenced in this book is Together ControlCenter, Version 6. In some cases pre-release versions of the software were used, and so the functionality or user interface may differ somewhat in the version that you may be using. Each version of Together ControlCenter sees improvements and enhancements to its user interface, so we have avoided making instructions to navigating its interface too specific, lest those instructions become out of date in a future version of the product.

Together Versions

acknowledgments

A book like this is never just the work of those whose names appear on the cover. We are immensely grateful for all those who have encouraged us, advised us, argued with us and worked with us over the years, and whose ideas and insights have inspired and honed our own. Our special thanks go out to Alex Aptus, Bruce Anderson, Dave Elton, Dave Astels, Dietrich Charisius, Eric Lefebvre, Gareth Oliver, Jo Perry, John Nicholls, Jon Kern, Karl Frank, Ken Ritchie, Laurence Wilson, Mike Swainston-Rainford, Miroslav Novak, Nick Dalgliesh, Paul Field, Paul Kuzan, Peter Coad, Randy Miller, Richard Pitt, Robert Palomo, Ron Norman, Steve Palmer, Tim Shelley and Tom Lee.

We'd especially like to thank Robert Palomo, Bruce Anderson, Richard Pitt and other reviewers for their helpful comments and their improvements to the manuscript and case study software; also our thanks to Paul Petralia and Mary Sudul for their editing and page layout work respectively. We'd like to thank Peter Coad for commissioning us to write this work, and for the inspiration his own writing has provided. Pete has the courage to simplify, which is why his work is so valuable. It is something we have striven, not always successfully, to emulate.

Finally we would like to thank our families: Sarah, Amy, Laura and Olivia Carmichael; Sue and Phoebe Haywood. Thank you for your understanding when our minds and diaries are filled with such trivia as improving software development. But thank you most of all for what makes working for living worthwhile—your love.

Andy Carmichael
Southampton, England.

Dan Haywood
Maidenhead, England

chapter 1

Together–
The Difference It Makes

The power of one...
Ladysmith Black Mombaso

Too little process—it takes extraordinary people to do ordinary things. Too much process—extraordinary people can't do extraordinary things.
Jim Lee, Hewlett-Packard

There can be no single software development process.
Ivar Jacobson

The impossible we do today—miracles take a little longer.
Anonymous

What can development teams do when faced with impossible demands for more functionality in ever-shorter timescales? This chapter opens with a consideration of the dilemma that many project managers face. We then introduce the model-build-deploy platform, Together ControlCenter, and consider how the new way of thinking about software development processes that Together encourages can provide a framework for dealing with such impossible demands and delivering quality software in short timescales.

"I'm sorry David. The TV advertising campaign has been booked for weeks now, and we can't afford to delay launch of the new services by even a day. It must go live in three months time!"

We Need It Now!

As the marketing manager sat down after his presentation, David, who had been the leader of a small team developing the bank's Internet project for a little under a year, decided not to ask the string of what-if questions that were stacking up in his mind. Like, *What if we can't deliver the new architecture, let alone the new functionality, in these timescales?* and *What if your advertising* *campaign actually **succeeds**, and we triple the number of registered users within two weeks of the first screening?*

David was proud of his team's achievements. Without much of the hype and hyperbole of other Net banks with stranger names but far fewer users, they had built a service that was gaining week by week in terms of the number of registered users and frequency of use. At the current geometric rate of growth, they would outgrow their hardware and software architecture in about 9 months. If the new TV campaign was successful, that window would reduce to little more than 3 months. Meanwhile, they already had a backlog of desirable features that would have kept the team very busy for all of that time, without all these new must-haves from marketing. What were his options now?

In today's speed-driven markets this scenario is all too common. It has probably always been true that time to market and meeting schedule targets are the key drivers determining the success or failure of major investment projects, but software projects in the current decade are likely to find those two drivers override most other considerations. Jennings and Haughton (2001) put it most aptly in the title of their study of the influence of "speed" in the competitive business environment: "It's Not the Big that Eat the Small...It's the Fast that Eat the Slow."

So, if team leaders accept that timescales for delivery of the system are paramount, how can they deal with the fact that what has been asked for is actually impossible? Brooks' Law (Brooks 1974) tells us that putting more software developers onto a late project will make it even later! If David just recruits more staff, he won't solve the problem.

He could say "never mind the quality—just release it." He could, but it is an obvious recipe for disaster, and even in the short term, it will cost his company far more in lost business and tattered reputation than could be compensated by early entry to the market. In banking and many other industries, it could also compromise security, reliability, and safety. Or it might simply be illegal or negligent. Software teams must ensure all software is "fit for purpose," which implies defining measures and standards of quality and then ensuring each release reaches this mark.

One option—one we are primarily concerned with in this book—is transform the processes and the development environment of the software development team to make it radically more productive. We have at this point to declare an interest in the Together platform, which is the principal subject of the book. We both consult and train teams using Together, and one of us (Andy) is an employee of the company that develops and markets it. Whatever our prejudices, our experience does show that Together genuinely accelerates software development projects, so we would certainly recommend that David adopt Together on his project.[1]

However, even with significantly enhanced productivity, David's team will not be able to do everything the marketing department has asked for in the timescales. David's final option must be to reduce the scope of the

---

1. As you will have guessed, "David" is a fictitious name for a real client who faced a similar situation. David did adopt Together for his project, a decision he now feels contributed to its success.

project. By discovering what the business imperatives are, the team can deliver enhancements to the current capabilities within the specified period while also preparing for longer term requirements. If the team follows this route, it will need a flexible and lightweight development process with rapid feedback loops to report holdups and roadblocks—and it will need to plan contingencies accordingly. The other implication of this choice is that there will need to be many deliveries of the software, each adding incrementally to the desired functionality. The development team's question to the business team is not so much "Which of these requirements do you not want delivered?" but "Which ones will contribute most to the business now, and therefore, which ones should be delivered first?"

The users and business planners always want all the new functionality delivered yesterday. The financial controllers would like to spread the expenditure of very small amounts of money over very long periods of time. It is the role of the development team to push back against both these pressures to deliver the highest priority features in the shortest possible timescales. Month by month (or timebox by timebox), the team needs to focus on the functionality that is of highest priority and deliver "frequent, tangible, working results."

This iterative and evolutionary approach to software development is the process that runs through the whole of this book. It is a process of which Together is a central part, since it allows us the flexibility to build on existing software and to add new functionality piece by piece. The aim of this first chapter is to introduce: the principles which underlie our approach (regardless of development platform); the essential elements of the Together development platform; and the essential elements of a simple yet generic development process.

There are four foundational ideas that we return to several times in the following chapters and which we believe are essential to an efficient and quality-focused development process – whatever tools are chosen to support that process. They are:

The Principles Behind This Book

1. Maintaining just one single-source model
2. Conforming to a minimum meta-model
3. Evolving through a perturbation change model
4. Continuously measuring of quality

A single-source model is one which, however many different editing tools are used, keeps its information in one place. This means when the information is changed in one view it is immediately transformed in every other view. Of course Together is famous for its treatment of source code files in this way, and we discuss this aspect of the environment in the next section. But there are many other tools, albeit less comprehensive than Together that take a similar approach. We expect there to be more in the future because this is too powerful an idea not to be adopted by competitors. Not only should the model be single-source, this first principle states that we should maintain just one such model. It is tempting to simply continue practices such as the use of separate logical and physical (or analysis and implementation) models that were introduced when single-source technology was not available. We believe this is missing an immense opportunity. Now we can support analysis-level and implementation-level views of the same one model and as a consequence introduce changes more quickly and much more reliably. We also discuss this aspect in more detail in the next section.

A metamodel is simply the structure of the language used for modeling. As we are using the Unified Modeling Language (UML), its metamodel is our starting point. But UML is a very comprehensive and complex language. In order to work efficiently we need to focus primarily on the bare essentials—the minimum metamodel—that can provide the basis for coherent and consistent development. The elements that we emphasize in this minimum metamodel are requirements, tests, design, and implementation. Simply stated: Each requirement accepted into a build must have a fair set of tests that pass and a design; the design should specify how objects in the system interact with messages to fulfill the requirement, and these objects and messages should be instantiations of implemented classes and operations; each class and operation (whether referenced by a design or not) should have a fair set of tests that pass. The minimum metamodel is explained in more detail later in this chapter.

At one time the prevailing view of how to develop large software systems was the waterfall model with its separate phases, each containing very different types of activities from requirement specification to deployment. The perturbation change model is different, in that its starting point is not a blank canvas but a complete and consistent system. The equilibrium of this consistency is disturbed by the desire for improvement (introducing a new requirement, say) and then the system must be brought back to the complete and consistent state by undertaking some development. Taking small steps—perturbations as we refer to them—results in a process that is evolutionary (moving from one stable state to the next) and iterative (repeating similar types of activity timebox by timebox).

Finally to make iterative evolutionary lifecycles work we must move the measurement of quality from specific points in the lifecycle such as critical design reviews and integration test phases to be an almost continuous activity from the earliest stages of the project onwards. The mechanisms for continuously measuring quality that we discuss in this book are tests, metrics, audits, document generation, and inspection.

Why Is Together Exciting Technology?

Better
Software
Faster

Together is exciting for software development teams for a simple reason—it takes multiple steps out of your job while increasing rather than reducing the quality of the end result. It automates the "nausea" (those jobs you know you ought to do but hate doing because they are repetitive and error-prone) while leaving you maximum freedom to work creatively at the "hard" part of the job—thinking, inventing, modeling, and producing excellent software. As a result, you are much more likely to get "in the flow" and stay there, where you are more productive, less error-prone, and more satisfied with your job.

There are several aspects of Together that enable this to take place, we discuss these in this section:

- Maintaining a single source (LiveSource)

- Controlled collaboration through configuration control
- Automation of the mundane (document generation, deploy, audit, code layout)
- Disseminating expertise through patterns
- Continuous monitoring (and feedback) of quality

Maintaining a Single Source (LiveSource)

There may be over 28 patents pending for Together technology, but even so, the secret of its success is not rocket science. If you look at what software development teams produce, it is not just software. There are many other related artifacts from statements of the requirements and how to test them, to documentation of the design and how to build, maintain, and evolve the system. In many cases information is duplicated in many documents and other artifacts surrounding the system software. What Together provides are multiple, editable views of the information—all related to just one underlying set of files where the information is stored and versioned.

The classic situation to see this in Together is the set of class diagrams that show the static structure of the software (its basic design) and the source code implementing this structure. Before Together, tools had for some time been able to generate code skeletons from design diagrams. A few had even been able to "reverse-engineer" from code back to design diagrams. The revolutionary step taken in Together was to choose only *one* storage format for these artifacts (in this case the source code).

Figure 1-1 shows a class diagram generated by Together showing three classes, `Person`, `Employee`, and `Company`. The diagram gives information about the attributes, operations, and associations of the classes, and about constraints on objects of the classes. For example, according to this model, an object that is an instance of `Person` may (or may not) be an employee and therefore associated with one or more `Employee` objects. This is shown by the `0..*` multiplicity on the association. Every `Employee` is *part of* (aggregation being shown in UML by the open diamond) exactly one `Company`. The role of the company in this relationship is `employer`; the 1 multiplicity on the aggregation link shows that the `Employee` object must be associated with exactly one `Company`.

The Java code associated with this class diagram contains all the information shown here—as well as quite a lot more, of course, if the design has been implemented. Some information, such as the multiplicity and role names on associations, is stored as javadoc[2] tags. Together uses these tags to store design information in the source code files. For example, if you delete those tags, then the adornments on the diagram will disappear. So, we don't think of those tags as just comments; they are the actual source for multiple views of this information. Other information on the diagram comes directly from the compilable Java code—the names of attributes, operations, and so on. When changes are made, whether using Together or any

---

2.   javadoc™ is a standard for self-documenting comments in Java code. Together displays such comments in generated documentation, as well as using the same style of comments for storing design information in source code files.

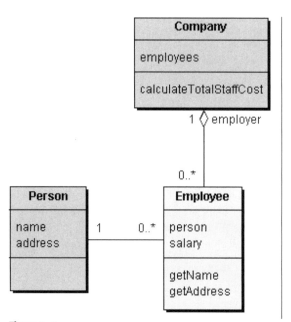

Figure 1–1
A simple UML class diagram.

other tool, Together keeps the diagrams continuously up to date.

Let's look at some of the source code for these classes. Here's an extract from `Employee` and `Company`.

```
 1  public class Employee {
 2
 3      /**
 4       * @supplierCardinality 1
 5       * @clientCardinality 0..*
 6       */
 7      private Person person;
 8
 9      private BigDecimal salary;
10
11      public String getName(){
12          return this.person.getName();
13      }
14      public String getAddress(){
15          return this.person.getAddress();
16      }
17      //other operations...
18  }
```

The comments on lines 3 through 6 store the multiplicity (or cardinality) of the association between this class and the class of the data member following the comments, in this case `Person`.

```
 1  public class Company {
 2      /**
 3       * @link aggregation
```

```
4      *    @associates <{Employee}>
5      * @supplierCardinality 0..*
6      * @clientRole employer
7      * @clientCardinality 1
8      */
9     private java.util.List employees =
10      new java.util.ArrayList();
11
12    public BigDecimal calculateTotalStaffCost(
13                     java.util.Date from,
14                     java.util.Date to) {
15      //implementation code here...
16    }
17    //other operations...
18  }
```

Similarly with the comments on lines 20 through 26: Here the comments additionally store the class of the objects (`Employee`) that will be held in the collection class, `java.util.ArrayList`. Operations such as those defined on line 30 are automatically kept in step with the diagram.

The diagram in Figure 1–1 is at a fairly high level, as in this instance we selected a view management level of *Analysis* in Together. If we wanted what Martin Fowler calls an *implementation class diagram* (Fowler 2000a), with the types and parameters of attributes and operations shown and the navigability indicators on the associations, we would not change the model at all, but merely select a different set of view management options for this diagram in Together.[3]

Alternatively, we might create a new class diagram with different options, providing a different view of the same classes. This means that multiple diagrams can be produced at different levels of detail, appropriate to their readership, and all of them can be kept up to date simultaneously.

A Single Source for All Information—One Model

Behind this simple explanation of where Together stores model information is a "big idea," one that TogetherSoft refers to as LiveSource technology, or "simultaneous roundtrip." If all it meant was that Together could easily do forward and reverse engineering, then we wouldn't really have gained that much. Other tools are competing with Together by speeding up their roundtrip capabilities, but in many ways this misses the point. What makes Together special is that there is no reverse or forward engineering. If you change the diagram, the code changes instantaneously because they both come from the *same source*. On the other hand, if you are clear on the implementation and just want to blast some code in, that's fine too—the diagram will be updated immediately when you next look at it, again because both diagram and text are merely different projections of the same source information.

Together allows you to model using all the other UML diagram types, as well as several additional diagrams such as entity-relationship diagrams

---

3. Several diagrams in this book show such additional detail. See, for example, Figure 7–29 on page 198.

and Enterprise JavaBeans (EJB) assembly diagrams, and wherever appropriate, the same approach is applied. With some diagrams, of course, there is no corresponding code view (for example, a use case diagram), and here the diagram itself is its own single source. Overall, the source code and related artifacts are all stored as simple, modular files, which can all be stored and versioned in one place.

Why One Model Works

Some development processes are designed to result in a succession of documents and models. For example, Figure 1-2 shows a UML activity diagram[4] of a waterfall-style development process. The succession of documents, or models, produced phase by phase in the process, is shown as a series of rectangles on the diagram, here named:

- Domain Analysis Document,
- Requirements Specification,
- Design Documentation, and
- Executable System.

Regardless of the names of the models—different versions of the waterfall have different names for the artifacts—the common characteristic is that there is a set of models, produced in sequence, with any work on one model or artifact potentially discovering and necessitating rework of any or all of the earlier stages.

People often assert that the waterfall is not iterative, and that is where the problem with the process lies. This is not true—even in its earliest forms (Royce W.W. 1970, Royce W. 1998) a flow back to previous stages was included. The main point about such back flows is that they require reissue and sign-off of previous phases' outputs. It is this requirement that makes iterations very costly, especially those involving changes to the models of early phases.

It should be no surprise that a requirements change is always expensive when a waterfall-style process is strictly applied—and strictly applying it is the only way to ensure the models are kept in step with each other.

By contrast, we have already seen how Together uses LiveSource to keep design documentation and the source code for the executable system always in step. We have also seen how it can maintain multiple diagrams that display different levels of detail of the same elements. Together therefore makes it very straightforward to update multiple views simultaneously—in fact, to treat both the design and the implementation as a single model. Instead of viewing the development process as moving from one phase to another with different models (probably in different formats and notations being produced in each phase), Together allows us to see the set of all the artifacts that make up one integrated and interrelated model. When we make a change, Together will help us to update all the views

4. If you're not familiar with UML activity diagrams, the rounded boxes show activities in the process and the rectangles show the products of these processes. Diamonds show decision points, with the conditions for the alternative routes shown in square brackets on the lines showing activity flow.

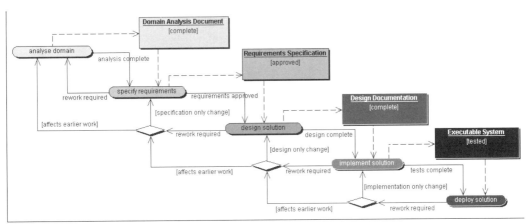

Figure 1-2

Activity diagram of a waterfall-style process.

together. Where this is not possible, we can nevertheless access all the diagrams and model elements of the single model from within Together, and it can report on outstanding issues of consistency or completeness.

The single model approach does not mean there are not separate parts of the model, which are not synchronized with other parts. For example, updating a use case diagram (discussed in Chapter 4, "The Stakeholder Step: Specify Requirements") or a features list (discussed in Chapter 5, "The Controlling Step: Feature-Centric Management") does not immediately result in generation of the implementing code—now that would be impressive code generation! What it does mean, however, is that information is as far as possible stored only once, viewed, and most importantly, updated through multiple views.

A single model is also a significant change in team organization. In the past it was not unusual for teams to be organized by phases of a waterfall lifecycle. A single model, on the other hand, encourages a much more holistic view of the system's artifacts: the domain model, requirements, architecture, detailed design, and code. The goal of the team is to continually present a consistent set of these artifacts as the conclusion of one iteration and the starting point for the next.

Corollary: Why Maintaining Two Models Doesn't Work

Some methodologies make a virtue of the need to concurrently maintain different models of the system. Sometimes, these multiple models are maintained by different workers who focus on different stages of a phased lifecycle (analysis models, logical data models, physical models, etc.). While this gives freedom to the workers to modify the models without immediate reference to others, it results in the need for either a costly synchronization process to harmonize the models or an acceptance of different models that conflict with the reality of the delivered system. We prefer the simpler and more effective route of maintaining only one model.

We have been on many projects where the analysis and design/code repositories have been managed as completely separate entities. After the first phase of the project has been delivered (and for some reason, it always seems to be a little late—we don't think it's just us), the project manager is under pressure to catch up on the schedule. Any requests to go back to the analysis repository to make those updates and modifications that came out while implementation was underway are usually given short thrift. As the project continues, the analysis and implementation views get further and further apart, and ultimately no one trusts the information in the analysis view at all.

It is also a reason why software maintenance documentation is so rarely read, even though it is produced at very great expense. The code is *always* likely to be different from what was documented. Since the maintainer of the code has to read the code—after all, it's the code that is compiled and executed in the computer, not the analysis and design documents—he or she will very often read *only* the code.

The "No Change" Directive
Andy Carmichael

On a famous, but to protect the innocent, nameless project to which I was assigned as a methods consultant a few years back, the project manager made a bold decision. He gathered the several hundred members of the project in the largest room on the site and placed his single slide on the overhead projector. It had two words on it: "No Change!"

The project, like nearly all large projects, was running late, and the deadline that was looming was not one that could be moved. The national and European law that affected this industry was being changed, and the businesses that required the new system would not be able to cope with the new legal framework with their existing systems. However, at this stage of the project, with software being delivered to system test, a phenomenon that worried the project manager immensely was observed. Modules that he thought had been finished and signed off were being checked out and changed again. Instead of the nice steady progress through the set of modules to be delivered, for every two modules getting through testing, at least one of them was being checked out again and changed. The project manager felt that something had to be done. As well as issuing this directive to the whole team, he decided to intensify the review process for what were considered essential changes to signed-off modules. His intention was that, first, his team would not try to change modules at all, and second, if they really felt it was essential to change them, the decision would be confirmed by several levels of review before the requirement for change was passed to an engineer for implementation.

I don't think you need to be a prophet to foresee what was likely to happen on this project. The directive did have the immediately desired effect in that signed-off modules were changed far less frequently. However, the changes that were needed (why else would they have been requested?) had to be made in other places—in modules that had not yet been signed off. This meant that the architecture and design of the system was being continuously compromised by "Band-Aid" modifications being made where they simply didn't belong. The code base became larger than it needed to be, and the design more complex. Changes that would have been relatively easy to make in the "right" place became harder, error-prone, and repetitive when applied in the "wrong" place. The true goal of the project manager—to deliver the system on time—was being threatened by a well-meaning but totally misinformed idea.

What is the moral of this tale?

First, rather than create an environment in which change of any kind is difficult and resisted, we should look to remove barriers to making change, enabling changes to be made as fast and as simply as possible. Protection against ill-advised change is one of the essential elements of such an environment—version control is a foundation of any development process. But developers should be faced with the minimum amount of technical and managerial constraints to carrying out even experimental changes.

Second, we should beware of thinking of the development lifecycle as a simple sequence of phases and a sequence of tasks to be completed within those phases. The analogy with evolution is more useful than the analogy of an assembly process. In manufacturing one follows a precisely defined set of steps only at the end of which is the completed article. In evolution, however, every step in the process must be an organism that will survive and provide the basis for the next generation. The project manager in this story felt that his problem arose because of poor discipline—developers changing things that were already "good enough." In fact, the problem was more likely to be related to the slow rate of change of certain parts of the software that were difficult for other developers to build on, or that were incomplete.

Controlled Collaboration Through Configuration Management

Another key reason that Together speeds development is that it is built on top of version-controlled files where all the information of the project is stored. Many modeling tools have their own proprietary databases or model file formats, and thus require different mechanisms for controlling collaboration than that used for source code and other documents, namely the configuration management or version control system.

In contrast, Together uses the same mechanism for models, documents, and code. There is therefore one place where all aspects of collaboration are defined and a much clearer mechanism for updating all artifacts. Together can be used with just about any commercially available configuration management system. This includes PVCS, SourceSafe, StarTeam, Continuus, ClearCase, and indeed any system that is SCC-compliant[5] or controllable from a command-line interface. If there is no configuration management standard for your organization, then you can install the widely used open source system CVS, which is distributed with Together. The access to the version control system from within Together will look similar, whichever version control system you use. For example Figure 1-3 shows the use of the speed menu on a class diagram for checking in a Java file.

Since all artifacts are held in the configuration management repository and are under version control, there is a single way to manage multiple developers and business analysts updating the evolving system and its requirements. While configuration control does require commitment and discipline from the team at the start of the project, once installed it

---

5. SCC is a Microsoft's Common Source Code Control (SCC) Specification, an API for SCC providers to provide standardized access to their product.

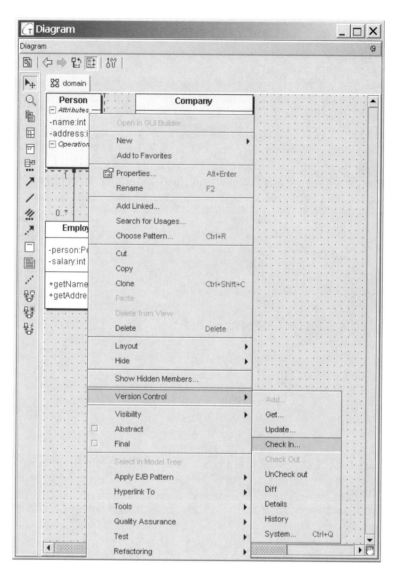

Figure 1–3
Accessing Version Control from a Together Diagram.

becomes the core storage mechanism of the project, keeping current and historic versions of artifacts and allowing the team to make changes rapidly without losing track of previously tested and working versions. Configuration management systems are the best way for intellect workers to collaborate, since individuals or pairs can work on aspects of the requirements, design, or code without affecting other workers. When their work is ready to be shared, others can be updated very rapidly.

Automation of the Mundane

Imagination, invention, creativity, innovation, and lateral thinking: These are all characteristics that we value and nurture in software designers and developers. But how much of their time is spent in such creative work?

The answer is a disappointingly small proportion. Developers and designers instead will spend a lot of their time carrying out tasks that are repetitive, boring, error-prone, and time-consuming. These are the types of tasks that computers are good at. For creativity, we need humans; for most other tasks, there's software!

As far as possible, we want to use Together for the mundane tasks like documentation generation, regression testing, and EJB deployment.[6] Throughout this book we'll show you examples of how Together supports this out-of-the-box, primarily through its J2EE deployment diagrams and wizards, its GenDoc (Document Generation) functionality, and its support for patterns and templates for quickly developing standard code. Furthermore, we'll be showing you just a few of the things you can do with Together's open API (the Java interface for customizing and extending Together). When you find that your team is doing repetitive tasks and these tasks are not already automated within Together, you can readily write a plug-in module to automate the job.

Disseminating Expertise through Patterns

Patterns have been a hot topic in software engineering for some time, with the first papers on software patterns being published around 1992 (Coad 1992; Coplien 1992; Johnson 1992; Booch 1993; Anderson 1994) and books like the Gang of Four's bible of patterns (Gamma, et al. 1995) emerging a few years later. In fact, patterns have been part of the universal experience of human learning for untold centuries. A pattern is an example to follow, an encapsulation of how to solve a class of problem that others can easily apply.

Together was one of the first tools to provide automated support for both the definition of software patterns and their application. It is a major building block in its success.

If you can capture the major patterns that are used in a particular architecture, you make the use of that architecture almost trivially easy to use compared to trying to give developers all the rules in documents or Web pages. A good example of this is the J2EE patterns that are automated in Together, and through the related scripts, plug-ins, and features for particular application servers.

There are three ways to define patterns in Together, ranging from code snippets and parameterized templates, which can be set up in seconds using menu options and cut-and-paste, to the Patterns API, which give a Java programmer full access to the source code he or she wants set up by the

---

6. Enterprise JavaBeans (EJBs) are server-side Java components that encapsulate domain-specific functionality. Once written, they must be deployed to an EJB container. They are discussed in more detail in Chapter 9.

pattern. We give some examples of using parameterized templates in Appendix D. The patterns API is out of the scope of this book, but we do discuss some possible example patterns that could be implemented. You can also find patterns, including the source for one or two of the shipped patterns, at *www.togethercommunity.com*.

Continuous Monitoring (and Feedback) of Quality

Together's LiveSource technology builds up a complete internal object model of the code. Every feature of the code, be it an operation, the types and names of that operation's parameters, or even the test expression within an `if` statement, is modeled internally as an object.

With such detailed information in its internal repository, it should be no surprise that Together is able to provide such sophisticated audits and metrics.

Audits

Audits check for conformance with standards. The out-of-the-box audits fall into the following categories:

- Coding Style
- Critical Errors
- Declaration Style
- Documentation
- Naming Style
- Performance
- Possible Errors
- Superfluous Content

An example of a critical error is "AHIA: Avoid Hiding Inherited Attributes," which according to this audit (and most would agree), is bad practice, since it makes the code more difficult to understand and modify. An example of a performance audit is "ADVIL: Avoid Declaring Variables Inside Loops"—a very bad idea if the loop is iterated through a large number of cycles.

It's not expected that all audits would be applied, so instead, custom sets of audits can be defined to be applied to your code. A good time to apply them is every night as part of an overnight build; at a minimum, it should be done before integration or system testing.

If for some reason you have a code-based standard not already provided out-of-the-box, then Together's open API also allows for the definition of new audits. We show you how to do this in Chapter 6, "The Continuous Step: Measure the Quality."

There is also a key "automation of the mundane" feature with audits. Some of the audits now have an "auto-fix" feature, which optionally refactors the code automatically so that it passes the audit. It's not realistic for all audits to be able to sport this feature, but we can hope that a growing number will.

Metrics

Metrics are packaged in Together alongside the audit functionality, though here the main user is likely to be a project manager, whereas with audits it might be the chief developer or anyone about to start a system test cycle. Metrics allow quantitative analysis of the code base, again in a number of categories:

- Basic
- Cohesion
- Complexity
- Coupling
- Encapsulation
- Halstead
- Inheritance
- Maximum
- Polymorphism
- Ratio

An example of a basic metric is "LOC: Lines of Code." An example of an inheritance metric is "DOIH: Depth of Inheritance Hierarchy." Again, if not all of these metrics are deemed necessary for your project, you can define the set of metrics to be taken daily or perhaps weekly. Together's open API allows custom metrics to be created in a similar manner to the creation of custom audits.

We heard of one project manager who used the metrics facility in Together to publish a "Metric of the Week" on the project intranet, with a league table of software packages. This was not done with a "name-and-shame" attitude, but in order to bring a focus of different aspects of quality that were being sought in the project. It's an interesting idea.

Document Generation

Sometimes, there is no substitute for a paper-based version of a project's documentation as part of the review process. Together allows an RTF format (compatible with Microsoft Word and other word processors) or plain text document to be generated, using a template that can be edited and customized for your project.

Our preference for most purposes is to generate an HTML web site version of the project documentation, which Together can also produce, giving up-to-date online access to the software design and other artifacts. Many projects generate this each night, alongside the nightly build, so that all team members can always access the most current documentation set, even accessing it from within the Context Help menu from selections in Together's editor, if you set up the appropriate paths for the Help system.

Other Possibilities

Together's open API allows for the inspection of not just the code, but indeed any artifact of the repository. For example, if you set a standard that every sequence diagram should be hyperlinked to the use case that it realizes (both of which are accessible as objects in Together's repository, even though neither are code artifacts), then this can be enforced by iterating over the repository and checking for conformance.

This feature by itself means that virtually any quality standard can be monitored, taking the QA features far beyond mere coding standards. We give examples of this in Chapter 6.

So, Together is exciting technology because of its LiveSource technology, its controlled collaboration support, its automation of the mundane, and its continuous monitoring of quality. We now consider the impact all this has on our development process.

Together ControlCenter doesn't constrain you to work in a particular way, but if you want to change the way you work, then you can. We have a similar aim for this book. We don't want to constrain teams to a particular process; rather, we want to introduce the philosophy and ideas that have inspired us regarding modern development processes and to help you to evolve the appropriate development processes for your own organizations and projects. So, let us lay out some of our goals.

Building Only What Is Needed

We asked in the preface to the book, What's the least that a team needs to do to deliver excellent software? There's a related question: Is it a bad thing to do more than this? We think it is.

This is a variant of what might be termed the "girls' boarding school rule," which goes along the lines of, If it's not compulsory, then it's forbidden! While this is probably a slur on modern girls' boarding schools, it is quite useful when considering the standards you want to apply to an agile software development processes. We are looking for the minimum set of artifacts that must be produced and maintained to be consistent with the actual software. At the same time, we want to remove the need to maintain all other artifacts.

To say that additional documents are forbidden is definitely an overstatement. Team members and others should feel free to produce documents that are not in the minimum set if they will be useful. The key point is that such documents will not be maintained unless they are subsequently recognized as being additions to the minimum essential set. At that point, the must be reviewed for completeness and consistency, and updated build by build.

Team members often gather around a whiteboard to figure out how to implement some feature or functionality. The diagram on the whiteboard is not considered a deliverable of the project; once it has done its job, it is erased. Only if the content of the diagram becomes the adopted design does the diagram become a delivered artifact. Of course, when you are using Together, you can get the design from the implemented source code or you can enter the diagram and use the resulting code as the starting point for the implementation. Either way, it is these elements that form the essential maintainable artifacts.

Occasionally, a document will be found to be so useful that it will become a formal part of the minimal deliverables. But when this is done, the attendant costs of maintaining that document must be balanced against its usefulness.

A Big Sheet of Paper
Dan Haywood

While contracting at one of the investment banks, I found myself assigned to keep track of hardware and system software (databases and operating systems) for the global credit and market risk department. This was at the end of the last century(!), and the bank had three major projects upcoming: merging with another investment bank, upgrading systems to support the new euro currency, and Y2K.

There was a fair degree of reconciliation required for these projects in terms of decommissioning old hardware,upgrading system software, and rationalizing system and application software onto fewer faster machines. The contingency hardware also was either nonexistent or pitifully underpowered, so this also had to be brought into consideration as part of disaster recovery planning, part and parcel of the Y2K program.

Initial efforts to come to grips with the production, test, and development environments using spreadsheets and such proved ineffective. Then I decided to use a drawing tool, invent a few symbols for elements of the configuration, and print on really big sheets of paper. Suddenly, it all became easy. The managers could immediately see which boxes were to be decommissioned, what system and application software ran on what boxes, what software would be migrating to new hardware, and which system software required upgrade.

I left that contract a while ago, though occasionally still visit the folks at the bank. I note that even now they keep a big sheet of paper up on the wall, even though those three projects are long finished. Though this particular artifact was discovered almost by accident, its value was proved, and so now the effort to keep it up to date is accepted.

Essential Elements

If we are seeking to build only what is needed, what are the essential elements of the system and its documentation? Every development process seems to involve the following essential elements:

- Requirements (use case, user story, feature, requirements paragraph)
- Design Statements (interaction diagrams—sequence or collaboration)
- Implementation Elements (class, operation)
- Tests (functional test, unit test or level-of-service test)

These are the four basic elements that we must maintain and keep in step and up to date. These elements have a natural relationship with each other, as Figure 1-4 shows.

Each *requirement* is tested by a *functional test*, and its design is shown by *interactions*, for example one or more sequence diagram. These interactions reference a set of *operations*, each belonging to some *class*, and in turn tested by at least one *unit test*.

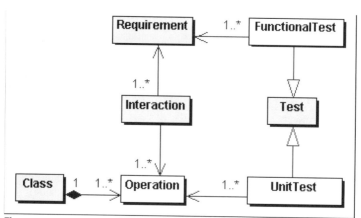

Figure 1–4

The essential elements of Requirements, Design, Implementation, and Test.

The relationships between these elements of requirements, design, implementation and test are important, and we need to capture the links in the model we store in Together. The relationships are

- *Design* (interaction diagrams) fulfills *Requirement*(s) (use cases, say)
- *Design* is implemented by *Implementation Elements* (classes and operations)
- *Functional Test* tests (*Functional*) *Requirement*(s)
- *Unit Test* tests *Implementation Element*(s)

The directionality of these relationships in Figure 1-4 shows the dependency between the elements,which is also important as it shows what needs to be checked and updated when things change. The design fulfills the requirements and so is dependent on it. The design refers to implementation elements, which are used to implement the feature, and so is dependent on them. The implementation elements, however, are not necessarily dependent on the requirements of this project. Many classes and operations, for example, may be reusable elements developed independently from the specific functional requirements.

When a requirement is added, deleted, or changed, the design and its tests must be reviewed to ensure they are still consistent and applicable. Dependency has a well-known effect in source code where it controls, for example, the order of compilation and recompilation. In an iterative lifecycle this effect extends as well to the other elements of the single model and will drive the consequential actions resulting from a change.

We'll revisit the essential elements shortly, looking at how they might be represented within the Together model. Let us consider for a moment the process of change that surrounds them.

Nonlinear Lifecycles Are Always in the Middle

Most software development processes get defined in terms of what you do in sequence from the start point, say the award of the contract for the project to customer sign-off of the finished software. Like our waterfall model in Figure 1-2, they are defined from end to end with feedback loops. However, as soon as the process has started and some of the feedback loops have been followed, we are "in the middle" with activities from multiple phases actually happening concurrently. We therefore have to address concurrent updating of all the essential artifacts.

From the point of view of the technical tasks of defining the requirements, the tests, the design, and the implementation, it is perhaps more useful to think of the development process in this way: when a reasonably complete set of artifacts exists (from end to end of a traditional lifecycle), what do you need to do to *change* the model, rather than define it from scratch? You are never at the start here, or for that matter at the end; you are always in the middle of the lifecycle, addressing the four essential elements of requirements, design, implementation and tests in all the phases of the project.

Linear lifecycles are an oversimplification. It is useful to stress that comprehension (the goal of analysis) must precede invention (the goal of design), and invention must precede implementation. But the actual activities cannot be divided into phases of the project lasting some number of weeks or months. D. L. Parnas and P. C. Clements expressed this well in the title of a paper they published in 1986, "A Rational Design Process: How and Why to Fake It." They emphasized that the usefulness of the linear lifecycle was not that it told team members what activity to do next—many different activities from the different phases of the lifecycle in fact have to be addressed simultaneously. The real value of such a rational design process was that it defined a scheme for organizing the artifacts produced in the process in such a way that designers, reviewers, new members of the project, and maintainers could find the necessary information easily.

When developing a software system, there will be some features that are being specified—the requirements are being gathered and tests for them being defined. Meanwhile, the design is being worked out for other features. Yet other features are being implemented, and there could be a unit, integration, or system test being carried out on yet other features. At different times in the project, a different emphasis and differing amounts of time will need to be spent on each of the four elements. The important point here is that to some extent *all of these things are happening at the same time*.

We talk more about this style of development and how well it works in Chapter 5, "The Controlling Step: Feature-Centric Management."

The Minimum Metamodel

Let us combine the two ideas presented above: the four essential elements and being always in the middle. We like to refer to the essential elements of the process as the *minimum metamodel*, constituting the minimum set of deliverables needed for the system.

A Model of Completeness

A metamodel defines the basis of the modeling system (Carmichael 1994a), and this minimum metamodel provides the basis (as simply as possible) for defining the model's completeness. Figure 1-5 shows a metaclass

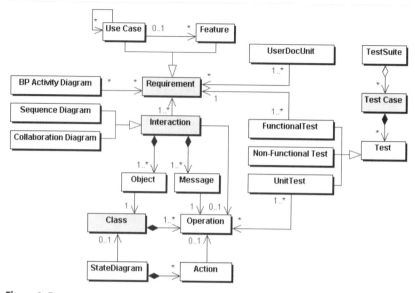

Figure 1–5

The minimum metamodel.

diagram for the concepts concerned. Effectively, this figure views the same metamodel as Figure 1-4 but displays more details. It also shows some optional features, such as business process activity diagrams that describe the process behind a given requirement, and *state diagrams*, which give more detailed definition to the behavior of a *Class*.

The minimum metamodel builds upon the four essential elements introduced earlier, making concrete the artifacts and required relationships that realize these elements within a Together project. Let's walk through this diagram observing how Together can make the relationships concrete.

- Requirements are realized as use cases, features, or both.
  - Use cases are catalogued in use case diagrams.
  - Features can be recorded using feature lists.
  - Together allows use cases to be hyperlinked to lower level use cases or features that implement a higher level use case.
- Business process activity diagrams also have a relationship with requirements; usually, such a diagram specifies the human activity or business process associated with the requirement.
  - In Together, activity diagrams can hyperlink to the use cases (or features) that realize the requirements.
  - Units of user documentation can also be hyperlinked to their related requirements.
- Interactions are realized as either sequence or collaboration diagrams.
- Interactions fulfill requirements.
  - In Together, interaction diagrams can be linked to their requirements.

- Interaction diagrams contain references to objects and messages, where an object is instantiated from a class and a message is an instance of a call to an operation provided by the class of the object to which the message is sent.
  - These links are contained within a Together interaction diagram. If an object's class is identified in a sequence diagram, then the message can be associated directly with the operations of that class.
- Classes have operations.
  - This relationship is explicit in the source for the class. In Together, this relationship is obtained directly by the Live-Source engine parsing the code.
- Some classes may also have a state chart diagram.
  - The state chart diagram should reference the class directly in Together.
- State chart diagrams identify a number of actions that can occur.
  - When the target class for the state chart diagram is identified, the actions within the state chart diagram can be associated with the operations of the target class.
- Test suites consist of test cases, which in turn consist of tests. Tests are functional tests, nonfunctional tests, or simple unit tests.
  - Functional tests link to functional requirements.
  - Unit tests link to operations of classes.
  - Together's test facilities can be used to implement the tests and link them to the tested elements.

When following the minimum metamodel in Together, some links between artifacts are implicit and some are explicit. Explicit links can be defined using Together's hyperlinks or by references in the Properties Inspector. We discuss in more detail which are appropriate links to add in Chapter 6. We also discuss how we can customize the audit facilities to report on the completeness of our models.

Perturbations Cause Iterations

The point of this metamodel is to define the set of artifacts (within a single model) that should be created by specifiers, designers, and implementers, and the cross-references between them. When a stable build is produced, its requirements will have corresponding designs, and these designs will reference its implementation, and the requirements and implementation will have valid tests that run and pass. This is our destination, but it is also our starting point—a starting point that unfortunately does not last! Accepting another requirement into the build (or indeed a fault report, which is a kind of requirement) disturbs the equilibrium and will result in the model becoming inconsistent, incomplete, or both.[7] This triggers the development process to return the build to equilibrium.

7. No inconsistent model can possibly be complete, but that is probably a point for mathematicians to argue about rather than engineers!

In fact, not all of the requirements that have been defined at any point in time need have valid tests and fully implemented designs available. Requirements can be considered to be in one of two states relative to a given build:

- *on* (i.e., implemented in this build), or
- *off* (i.e. not implemented in this build, but planned for a later build)

If a requirement is on, then (according to the meta-model)

- There should be at least one valid *functional test*.
- That test should pass (this is verified by running the test).
- There should be a design for the requirement.
- The *design* should reference (be implemented by) *implementation elements* (that is, classes and operations).
- All implementation elements should be tested by a valid *unit test*.
- That unit test should pass (verified by running the test).

Conversely, if a requirement is off, then the constraints in the meta-model (for example, that there is at least one test) do not apply.

Suppose you have a valid build of your application, and now you wish to start work on a new feature. First, you must ensure that your current build represents a stable system; we are wasting our time if we attempt to make a change to an unstable system. So, accepting the feature into a build triggers the change.

Let's run through some sample iterations:

- We start off by running the full set of tests on our build. These pass and confirm we have a stable starting point.
- We then change the state of a particular new requirement from off to on.
- We retest the existing code with the full set of tests that now include those for our new requirement. Unsurprisingly, the tests fails[8] (say, with 20 errors).
- We consider how to design a solution for this feature and express that as one or more sequence diagrams.
- We make some changes to the code. We compile, and get compilation errors. We refine our code some more and get a clean compile.
- We test our code, and it fails, say with 15 errors. We figure out where the problem is (it's either in the implemented code or in the test) and make the correction. We test again, and we now get fewer errors.
- We continue to refine our code or our tests, all the time learning more about both the problem and the solution.
- We update our design diagrams to ensure the references to objects and messages link directly to real classes and operations.

8. Why test the unmodified code? Well, first, there's always the chance that we over engineered our code previously and it already supports the required functionality! Second, it checks that the test does indeed fail, as it should, if the functionality is missing.

- Maybe we find an error in the specification, so we clarify that and update the tests before continuing.
- Eventually, all the tests pass; the feature is implemented.
- We have code that can be integrated with the team's current build. This may be different by now from the build we started from if other team members have integrated changes in parallel, so we book in our changes and rerun the tests.
- Sadly, an interaction between our change and the parallel changes arises. We go about fixing the problem.
- Eventually. all the tests pass, and the feature is now implemented and integrated with the team's latest build. We are back to the equilibrium state.

Figure 1-6 shows a simplified view of this sequence of activities.
There are a few observations that we need to make on this process:

- In order to start enhancing a system, you need to deliver a system; you need a stable state to begin with. This means that delivering a system—even a very small one—is critical to future development.
- The system you are trying to change must be stable.

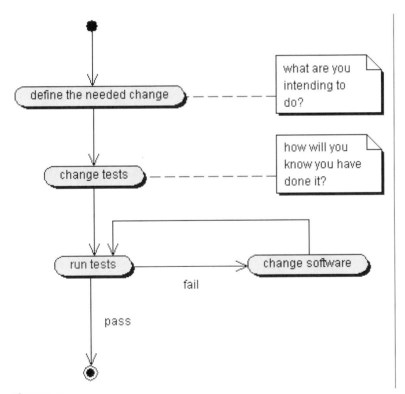

Figure 1–6
Perturbations cause iterations.

- Testing (and measuring) is the activity that "closes the loop"—it tells us when we no longer need to iterate.
- Small perturbations will require fewer iterations than larger perturbations.
- If the perturbation introduced is too large, then there's the chance that no number of iterations will get back to the stable state.

There is another interesting change that this approach to development. The whole team may be involved in evolving all the different artifacts and the different aspects of the application. This is in contrast to more rigid team environments that consist of business analysts, designers, coders, and testers organized into separate teams, possibly even using different tools and languages. Here, everyone is involved in all the aspects of software development lifecycle concurrently, sometimes collaborating with other team members and sometimes working by themselves, in order to deliver a particular feature. One model, one team. We believe this a very positive aspect of the approach and is good for both morale and the effectiveness of development.

What's Next?

In this chapter we've discussed how the minimum metamodel provides the basis for ensuring we have a complete and consistent set of deliverables. Together does not automate the minimum metamodel directly, but does provide a significant range of audits, and its open API allows for the construction of customized audits to validate the model.

We shall return to the topic of planning the incremental release of features of a system in Chapter 5 and to the topic of quality audits in Chapter 6. But now it's time to move on to the last step—deploying and running the software!

chapter 2

The Last Step—
Deploy and Run!

Stand and Deliver!
Adam and the Ants

Keep your car regularly serviced.
The Highway Code

The last shall be first.
St. Matthew

Make it run, make it right, make it fast.
Jeff Langr

In this chapter we introduce our case study example and use Together to build, deploy, and run the application in a reasonably complete state. We show how the application can be tested from Together, and how to change, rebuild, and redeploy the application. The chapter provides a fairly extensive walkthrough of the capabilities of the case study application and of our development environment.

Our starting point in considering how to improve the development process for small teams is what many people would consider the destination—deploying and using the software. But the process we are discussing is iterative and evolutionary which means that when compared to a linear process we are *always* in the middle. There's always a configuration of the software that works (as far as it goes) and there's always more that we would like to add in terms of functionality and/or quality. If the software we have developed so far will not run, we need to fix the problems before adding any new functionality. This is why what appears to be the last step is actually the logical place to start.

First of all, we'll introduce you to our case study's software.

If you own a car, you probably get it serviced now and again. Perhaps it's a new car and there's a regular service schedule that you follow, or maybe it's an older car and you just take it in whenever you hear a rattle or start feeling a bit guilty at the lack of attention you've given it. When you do take your car in, the garage has to do a number of things, like booking the time, booking the mechanic, recording the work and the parts, and billing the customer. An automated system can help with this task, and that's where our *CarServ* system comes in. It's a familiar and hopefully easy-to-understand domain that we'll be using as the main example throughout the book.

The purpose of the system is to allow the staff of a service department to keep track of cars and car owners, to take bookings for regular or ad hoc services, and to track time and materials spent on the servicing so that information can be passed to the billing/accounts system and the performance of the garage tracked over time.

The software that has been developed for this case study is available for download from the Web site at *www.bettersoftwarefaster.com*. We recommend that, if possible, you read this chapter with the software running on your computer so you can see it in action as you read. Details of installing the case study software are given in Appendix A and on the Web site.

On the other hand, you might be reading this on the train or subway; we certainly get a lot of our technical reading done that way. Or perhaps you haven't the inclination to follow a load of installation instructions. We sympathize. So, we've tried to provide enough information in this chapter for you to understand the key features that we discuss without running the software itself.

As well as the source code for the case study and links to the Together download, which provides the development and test environment, you will need the database management system, Cloudscape, which we have used in the case study as the persistent data store.

Cloudscape

Cloudscape is a pure Java relational database management system (RDBMS) written by Informix Corporation (now part of IBM). We have used Cloudscape for the database, since it is bundled with the J2EE Reference Implementation, which in turn is bundled with Together.

Install

Run through the installation instructions in Appendix A to install Together and the case study software, and to set up the database. In order to configure Cloudscape, you'll also need to make one small free download from *www.cloudscape.com*.

Compile

If not already running, start up Together and load the case study project using *File* → *Open Project*. You need to navigate to the project file, `carserv.tpr`, and open it.

First, check that the project properties are consistent with the directories you are using. Go to *Project* → *Properties* and inspect the *Search/Classpath* tab to ensure all the libraries referenced are in the same place on your system. If they are not, add the appropriate paths, removing the ones that are wrong.

Next, compile the project using *Project* → *Make Project* (or Shift+F7). Because of the way we've configured the project, the Java source will be compiled into a subdirectory `carserv\classes`.

Run

We're now set to run the application. First, check that the correct run configuration is selected. A configuration is simply a mechanism to invoke some main class, along with arguments if needed.

Choose *Run* → *Run/Debug Run Configurations* (or Shift+F10). You'll be presented with a dialog box, something like that shown in Figure 2-1.

Select the `CarServAppUI` configuration (if it doesn't appear use the *Add* button), and if necessary, hit *Set Default*. Then hit OK.

Now hit the *Run* icon on the toolbar (or CTRL+F5). Together will compile any changed files, so if you hadn't already compiled the whole project, it would do so now.

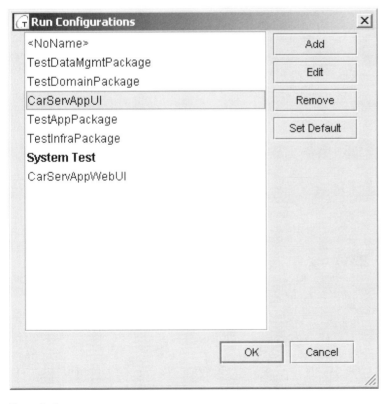

Figure 2–1
Run configurations allow different applications to be run from a single project.

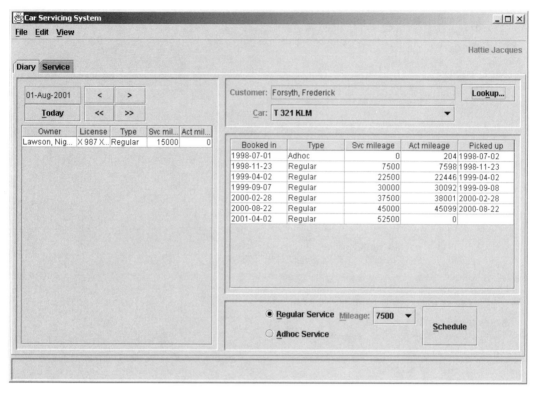

Figure 2-2
Diary tab of the CarServ GUI application.

When the *CarServ* application starts, you'll need to sign on (*File* → *Sign On*). You need to enter a valid employee name to sign on (e.g., Hattie Jacques). You'll then be presented with a screen similar to that shown in Figure 2-2.

This is the main GUI front end for use by the service manager. On the left is a diary of cars booked in for a certain date, and on the right are services past and present for a specific customer.

Try the following tasks to get familiar with the *CarServ* GUI application:

- Change the diary date forwards and backwards. Scroll to a date when there are cars booked in or have been serviced (e.g., 1 Apr 2001 or 1 Aug 2001). Note that changing the date is an undoable/redoable operation (*Edit* → *Undo* and *Edit* → *Redo*).
- Book in a car for servicing—that is check it in when the car actually arrives (e.g., 1 Aug 2001). Note that this is undoable.
- Cancel a service. Again, this is undoable.
- Look up a customer. You'll need to enter the start of the customer's name or address in correct case (e.g., there are two customers named Smith). When you select a customer, her cars are shown (e.g., the customer named Forsyth has two cars).

- Schedule a regular service for a customer. Note that the mileage depends upon the car type. Note again that this is an undoable operation.
- Schedule an ad hoc service for a customer. Again, undoable.
- Log out (*File* → *Logout*).

As you play around, you'll note that the most recent completed service is dated 1 March 2001, and the earliest scheduled (but not started) service is dated 1 April 2001. In other words, the test data corresponds to a "now" date of mid March 2001. We decided that a "now" date in the past was in general preferable to one that in the future.

You'll also notice that there is a second Service tab (*View* → *Services*). This tab is to view the detail of a particular service, for use by mechanics actually performing the service. The service tab is shown in Figure 2-3.

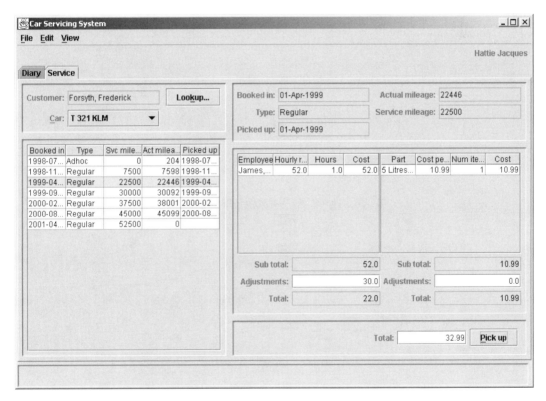

Figure 2–3
Service tab of the CarServ GUI application.

You may find some of the functionality implied by the user interface is not yet implemented. This should not surprise you, as this system is not yet complete, even to the minimum level required for an initial release to the users. We have developed the application to the level of a fairly early internal project milestone, as we decided that this gives us more than enough

The Last Step—
Deploy and Run!

material to illustrate the development process and the model artifacts.[9] Still, there is plenty of functionality for you to play with. Try the following tasks (you'll need to sign on if you previously logged out):

- Look up a customer. This works in the same way as the Diary tab.
- View the details of a service.

Evolving the System

We have achieved this "last step" of running and using the software. In fact, this step is also the starting point for further evolution of the system, and as we have seen, there is still plenty of work to do.

Evolution can work only if there is a system (or an organism) that is stable enough to survive and spawn further generations. In software terms, we need a starting point that is of proven quality for further development. The main test we use for this is that all the unit tests that are developed along with the code for the system run and pass. This practice is one of the most important ideas in the eXtreme Programming (XP) process (Beck 2000), but it is applicable to whatever development process you are using.

Our case study system has a reasonably complete set of unit tests, one test suite for each package. These have been combined into a single system test suite. To run the system test, ensure you have activated the Test Framework module (select *Tools* → *Activate/Deactivate Features* to check). Then select the *Test Plan* tab in the Explorer and open *Test Plan/Build Test Suites/Daily Build Suite*. Right-click on *Daily Build Suite* and select *Run Suite*. This will launch the test server and, if we have a stable starting point, all tests will pass, as shown in Figure 2-4.

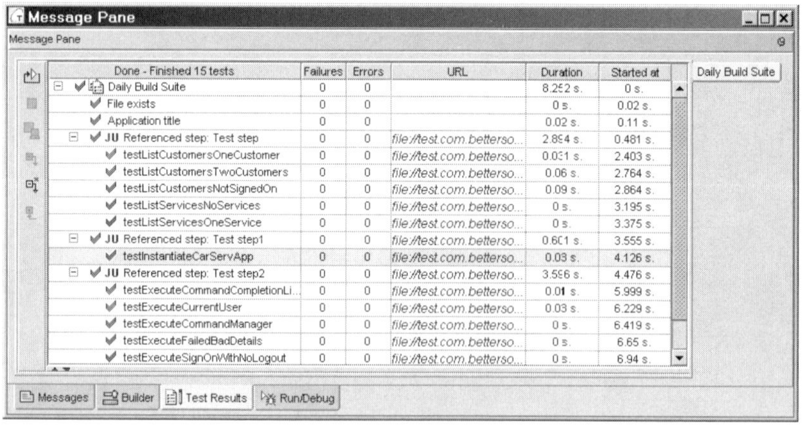

Figure 2–4
The case study passes its "Daily Build" test suite.

9. In fact, the domain and datamgmt packages—the second and third tiers of the *CarServ* architecture—are fully functional and tested. It's just the UI that's a little anemic.

If some of the tests fail, then there's something in the setup, the data, the environment, or the software that needs to be fixed before we start thinking about new functionality. In this case one possible cause is that the data has been changed in the database. If this is the case, re-create the database using the steps described in Appendix A and retry the tests.

We'll return to the subject of unit testing in later chapters.

To learn a little more about the case study, let's use Together to inspect the model. The project is organized into a number of packages:

- `requirements` – use case diagrams, activity diagrams, overview of domain classes
- `architecture` – component diagrams, deployment diagrams
- `ui` – user interface classes for a Swing client
- `webui` – user interface classes for a (minimal) Web application client (used only in Chapter 9, "The J2EE Architecture")
- `app` – classes that represent the logical actions supported by the application (a direct software equivalent of the use cases)
- `domain` – classes to represent the domain, plus supporting implementation classes
- `datamgmt` – classes to persist domain objects to a relational database
- `infra` – infrastructure classes for all of above
- `patterns` – defines patterns that are used to document the design

The project is probably best viewed from the directory `com.bettersoftwarefaster.carserv,` one of the root packages of the project (*Project* → *Properties*). There are also test packages under `test.com.bettersoftwarefaster.carserv`, the other root package of the project.

The package class diagram for `com.bettersoftwarefaster.carserv` shows each of the packages, as well as the diagrams within those packages, and a number of implementation diagrams that involve classes from several packages. We've hidden class names within the package icons (*Tools* → *Options* → *Diagram Level*; then select *View Management* and filter out all classes and interfaces from the diagram), so the package class diagram in Figure 2-5 just shows the packages and diagrams within each package, which makes it act as a useful table of contents to the project. Two sets of dependency arrows are shown on the diagram: the dependencies specified by the designer and the actual dependencies discovered by the parser in the code.

Have a look at the use case diagrams within the `requirements` package. You can do this either via the Explorer in Together (generally on the left of the screen) or by right-clicking on the diagram name on the package diagram and selecting *Open*. You'll see that there are two use case diagrams: the higher level business use case diagram and a lower level system use case diagram. The system use case diagram is shown in Figure 2-6. The system use case diagram shows a number of different subsystems, though as yet we've implemented use cases from the car servicing subsystem only.

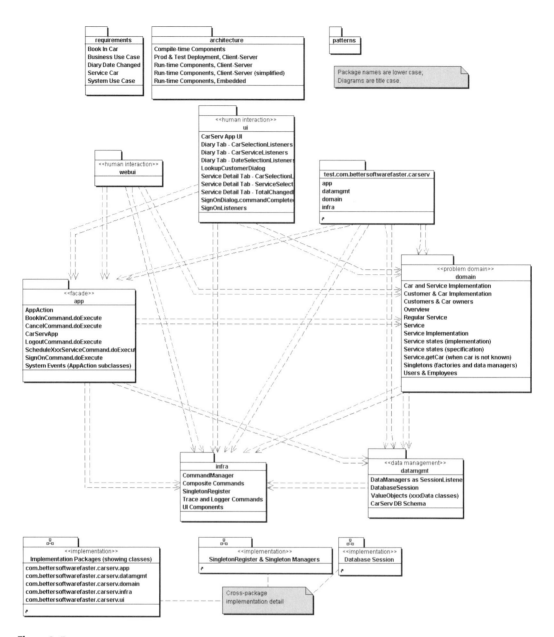

Figure 2–5

Root package diagram, acting as a table of contents to the rest of the project.

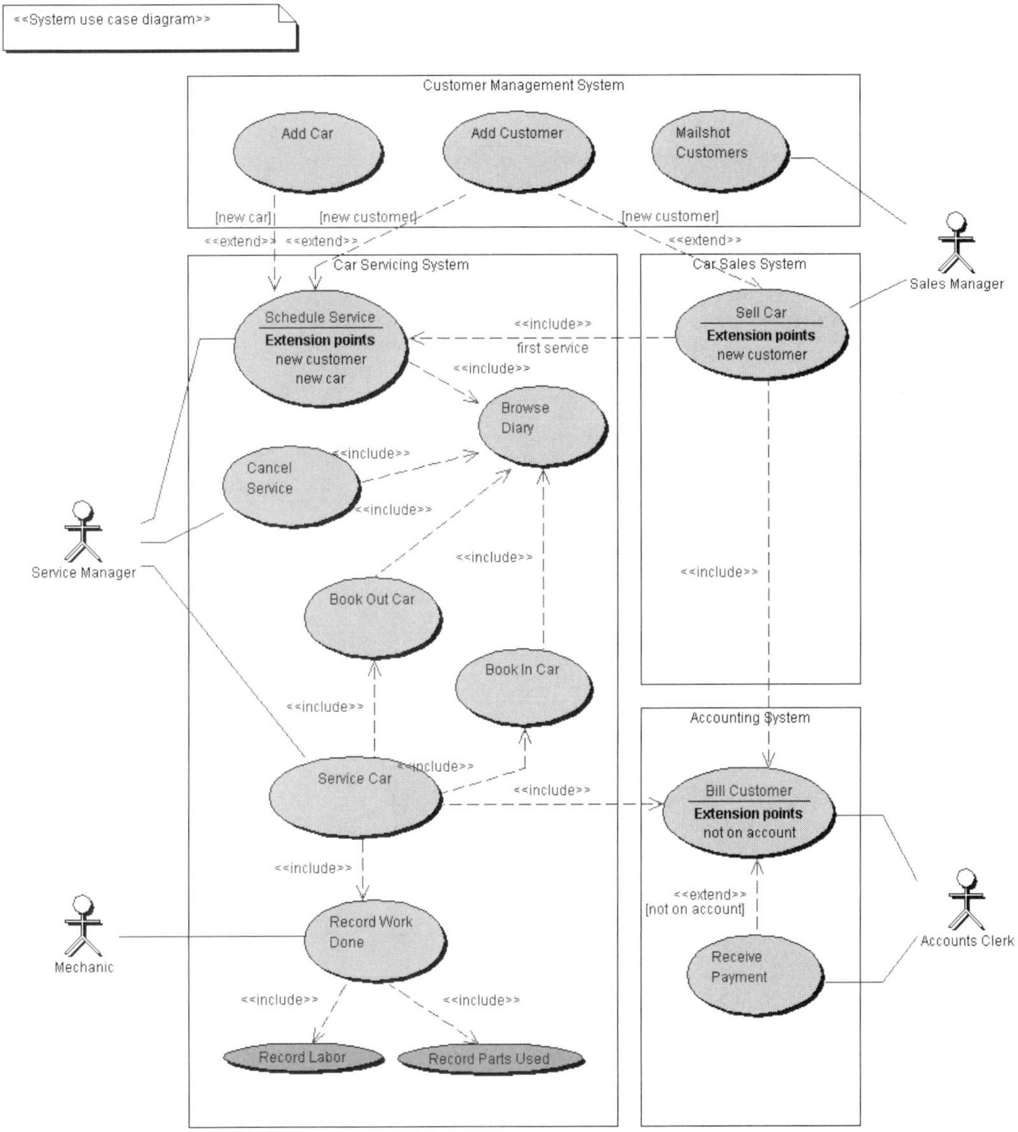

Figure 2–6
The Car Servicing application is just one of a number of interrelated systems.

While you are within the `requirements` package, look also at the `Service Car` activity diagram (shown in Figure 4-2 if you are not running Together as you read this). This diagram ties together several of the use cases to show the order in which they occur and which actor initiates them.

Try following the hyperlinks from the `Book In Car` use case to the activity diagram, and also to the sequence diagram of `BookInCommand` that implements the use case.

The `architecture` package has several component diagrams showing the major software components of the system, some key interfaces and their dependencies. Since the system is designed to run in one of two modes: embedded (single user) or client/server (multi-user), there are separate diagrams for each. There's also a deployment diagram in this package, showing the deployment of the client/server alternative. A simplified client/server component diagram is shown in Figure 2-7.

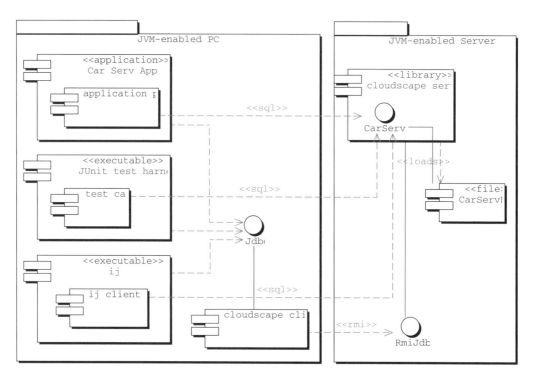

Figure 2–7
The CarServ application can be run in a client/server configuration.

Try following the hyperlinks from the component diagrams to the deployment diagrams, and also to the implementation packages (`ui`, `app`, `domain`, and `datamgmt`).

Let's now have a look at some of the domain classes. Open up the `domain` package, and you'll see shortcuts to several class, sequence, and state chart diagrams. You'll also see all the classes in the `domain` package; however, members (operations and attributes) and dependencies have been hidden because to show it all would be too much detail (*Tools* → *Options* → *Diagram Level*; then select *View Management* and filter out *All Members*). To have a look at some detail, open up the `Overview` class diagram and acquaint yourself with the main domain classes. The `Overview` class diagram is shown in Appendix G.

To learn about the domain in a little more detail, find and open the `Car and Service Implementation` class diagram (there should be a shortcut from the `domain` package), and have a look at some of the underlying implementation classes. (This diagram is also in Appendix G).

Now, let's look at how some of the application works. In the `app` package, find and open the `BookInCommand.doExecute` sequence diagram (also in Appendix G). With the code editor up (*View* → *Editor*), click on the objects to see the corresponding class. Click on the message links (from object to object) to see the operation that is being invoked.

Finally, let's have a look one more time at the packages that constitute the application. Go back to the root package diagram and note the packages and dependencies. At the bottom of the root package diagram are a number of class diagrams; one is called `Implementation Packages` (showing `classes`). Open this up, and you'll again see the `ui`, `app`, `domain`, `data-mgmt`, and `infra` packages, along with the package dependencies (in Appendix G). This time, however, you'll also see the classes within each package. Most of these class's names are in blue, indicating that they have hyperlinks to other parts of the model. In all such cases, at least one of those hyperlinks will be to a class diagram that shows additional detail about the class and the other classes with which it collaborates.

One of the quality requirements applied to the *CarServ* system was that—wherever possible—every action should be undoable. In order to support this, the application has full support for undo/redo as part of the `infra` package. `Commands` are passed to the `CommandManager` to be executed, and then are saved in an undo stack. Undone `Commands` may also be redone.

`Commands` indicate whether they can be undone or redone by their return code. The return code is an instance of an enumerated type—specifically, the nested static class `Command.ExecReturn`. This class is shown below:

Change and Redeploy

```
 1  public final static class ExecReturn {
 2    public final static ExecReturn UNDOABLE =
 3      new ExecReturn("Undoable", 1);
 4    public final static ExecReturn NOT_UNDOABLE =
 5      new ExecReturn("Not undoable", 2);
 6    public final static ExecReturn IGNORE =
 7      new ExecReturn("Ignore", 3);
 8    public final static ExecReturn CLEAR =
 9      new ExecReturn("Clear", 4);
10    private ExecReturn(String name, int value) {
11      this.name = name;
12      this.value = value;
13    }
14    public boolean equals(Object other) {
15      if (!(other instanceof ExecReturn)) return false;
16      return (value == ((ExecReturn)other).value);
17    }
18    public int hashCode() { return value; }
19    public String toString() { return name; }
20    private String name;
21    private int value;
22  }
```

The Last Step—
Deploy and Run!

There is a similar nested static class `Command.UndoReturn`. This enumerates the possible return values allowed when a command that can be undone *is* undone. The idea here is that some commands, once undone, can be redone; others cannot. This class is shown below:

```
1   public final static class UndoReturn {
2     public final static UndoReturn REDOABLE =
3       new UndoReturn("Redoable", 1);
4     public final static UndoReturn NOT_REDOABLE =
5       new UndoReturn("Not redoable", 2);
6     public final static UndoReturn CLEAR =
7       new UndoReturn("Clear", 4);
8     private UndoReturn(String name, int value) {
9       this.name = name;
10      this.value = value;
11    }
12    public boolean equals(Object other) {
13      if (!(other instanceof UndoReturn)) return false;
14      return (value == ((UndoReturn)other).value);
15    }
16    public int hashCode() { return value; }
17    public String toString() { return name; }
18    private String name;
19    private int value;
20  }
```

If a `Command` indicates that it is undoable, then it is saved on the undo stack. A `Command` that is not undoable causes the undo stack to be cleared, since that would be a break in the chain. `Commands` that are not undoable but that would not break any chain can indicate that they should be ignored. Such `Commands` cannot be undone, but the undo stack is not affected either, so previously undoable `Commands` can still be executed. Similarly, if an undone `Command` indicates that it is redoable, then it is saved on the redo stack.

The principle of being able to undo every action has even been extended to the `SignOnCommand`. If an employee signs on and then immediately changes his mind, he can simply hit *Edit* → *Undo*.

Let us now do some role-play and imagine that we have shipped the application to the end-users. In general, they are happy with it; however, they have noticed that when a user undoes a Sign-On, it is also possible for that command to be redone. In other words, user A could sign on, undo his sign on, and then—perhaps several hours later—user B could redo user A's original sign on: a possible security breach.[10]

So, at this point a change request or bug report would be raised. Let us check the unit tests to see what's going on. The unit test we need is

`test.com.bettersoftwarefaster.carserv.app.TestSignOnCommand.`

10. You must indulge us here a little; we have no passwords for our users yet, so in fact all that our fictitious user B really knows to effect a security breach is user A's name! But you appreciate the principle, we're sure.

Looking at the method `testUndo()`, we see the following (original) code:

```
assertEquals("redo list", 1,
    commandManager.getSizeOfRedoList());
```

In other words, the writer of the unit test expected that the `SignOn-Command` would be redoable. Our change request means that these expected results need to change. So, go back to the `testUndo()` method and change it:

```
assertEquals("redo list",
    0, commandManager.getSizeOfRedoList());
```

Our expected results for `testRedo()` are also different. Here is the test of the original requirement:

```
1   commandManager.redo();
2   signOnLanceCommand.getThread().join();
3
4   assertEquals("undo list", 1,
5     commandManager.getSizeOfUndoList());
6   assertEquals("redo list", 0,
7     commandManager.getSizeOfRedoList());
8
9   assertNotNull("app", getCarServApp());
10  assertNotNull("current user",
11    getCarServApp().getCurrentUser());
12
13  assertEquals("current user last name", "Percival",
14    getCarServApp().getCurrentUser().getLastName());
```

And here it is updated for the new requirement:

```
1   try {
2     commandManager.redo();
3     fail("redo should fail.");
4   } catch(CommandException ex) {
5     // expected
6   } catch(Exception ex) {
7     fail("Expected to catch CommandException");
8   }
```

Make these changes to update the tests, and let's run them. Use the Test Plan tab in the Explorer and open *Test Plan/Unit Tests/test/com/bettersoft-warefaster/carserv/app*. Right-click on *app Suite* and select *Run Suite*. Unsurprisingly (since we haven't yet implemented the new requirement), the tests now fail; see Figure 2-8.

So, now it's time to make the change to the code itself. Open up `SignonCommand` (in the app package). The change we need to make is in `doUndo()`, and it's quite straightforward. All we need to do is change the return code, from

```
return Command.UndoReturn.REDOABLE;
```

to:

```
return Command.UndoReturn.NOT_REDOABLE;
```

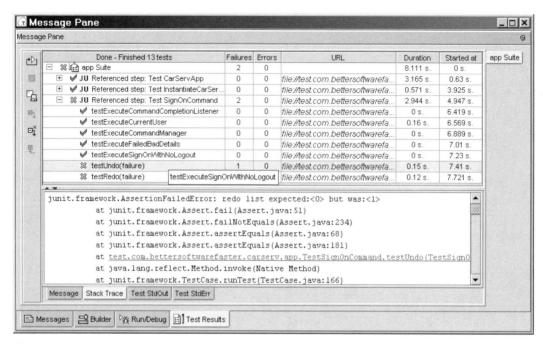

Figure 2–8
Tests fail when the expected results are changed.

Now, rerun the tests. With a bit of luck and a following wind, they should run through successfully. As a sanity check, change the *Run Configuration* back to `CarServAppUI`, and run the application itself. Check that after signing on and then undoing, it is not possible to redo. All being well, we can close the change request and ship the new version of the code.

Documentation Generation

We've already seen how we can explore the *CarServ* project using Together, but what if you want to make project documentation available to someone who does not have Together? In such a case we can use Together's documentation generation functionality.

Together can generate documentation either as an HTML Web site or as a Rich Text Format (RTF) document (i.e., loadable into Microsoft Word or equivalent).

To generate the HTML documentation, use *Project* → *Generate* → *Documentation*. In the resulting dialog box, select HTML and specify options such as the output folder. We used a subdirectory of `my\projects\carserv\html` but you can direct the output to any directory.

Depending upon the speed of your PC and memory available, you may need to wait a little while for Together to generate all the documentation. The case study, after all, is reasonably substantial. When Together has finished generating the documentation, it will launch your browser against the generated index file, `index.html`. This index page is split into three regions. The top is very similar to the `com.bettersoftware faster.carserv` package class diagram that we used in our explorations earlier; bottom left is an explorer similar to Together's Explorer, and bottom right is the *javadoc* documentation. You can see a screenshot of the HTML output in Figure 2-9.

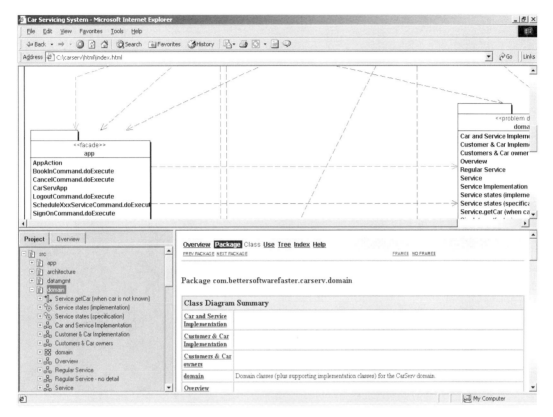

Figure 2–9
DocGen creates HTML Web sites.

To generate the RTF documentation, again use *Project* → *Generate* → *Documentation*, this time selecting an RTF template instead of HTML. You can generate to the suggested output folder or specify a different one. Figure 2-10 shows a screenshot of the index page of the RTF output, displayed in Microsoft Word.

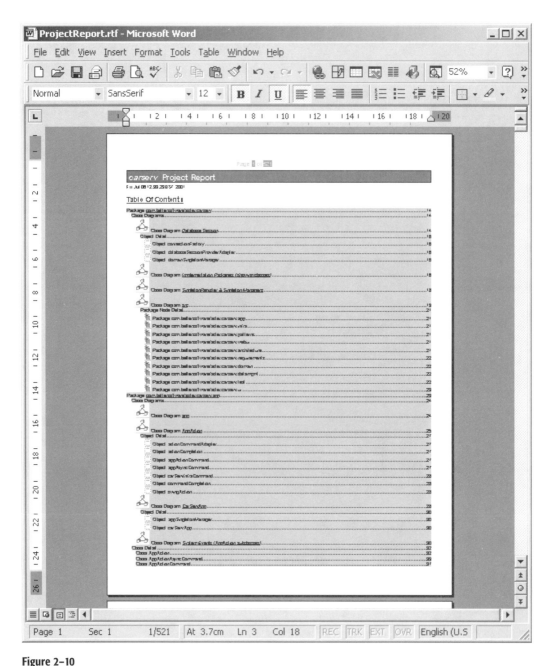

Figure 2–10
DocGen creates RTF documents.

Hopefully this chapter has given you an overview of the current state of our project and our software system. Continue to explore the project through these generated documents and Together, or if you are just working from the book, look at the diagrams in Appendix G to get a feel for the scope of the application.

Reverse Engineering

Together provides very effective support for reverse engineering. To demonstrate this, try reverse engineering the Java source code for the Car Servicing example as you might need to if you received undocumented source code from another project.

Reverse Engineering CarServ

First, let's get another copy of CarServ on our disk. Create a new directory `carserv2`, and under it create an `src` directory:

```
c:\
  carserv2\
    src\
```

Also, create an empty diagram subdirectory within `carserv2`:

```
c:\
  carserv2\
    diag\
      com\
        bettersoftwarefaster\
          carserv                 // empty
```

Then, from your hard disk, copy the `com` directory in `carserv\src` (and all its contents) to your `carserv2\src` directory.

Now, let's create a new Together project

1. **File** → **New Project Expert**; location is the `carserv2\com\bettersoftwarefaster\carserv` directory, project name = `carserv2`, and select creation scenario = existing source files; then choose **Next**.

2. Specify directory with source files = `carserv2\src\com\bettersoftwarefaster\carserv`, and specify the package prefix as `com.bettersoftwarefaster.carserv` (Together should have already detected this prefix if your directory structure is correct); then choose **Next**.

3. When asked if diagram files should be in same folder or separate, indicate that they should be separate; choose **Next**.

4. Specify folder for diagram files = `carserv2\diag\com\bettersoftwarefaster\carserv`. All other options in the expert should be correct, so click Next through the remaining pages or choose **Finish**.

5. Together now parses the Java source code and builds up its in-memory representation of every feature of that code. When this is finished, Together will display the packages in a package class diagram, as shown in Figure 2–11.

Depending on the version of Together you are using and your set-up, dependencies between packages may not be shown on this diagram. Dependencies are usually suppressed for new projects. To get Together to draw up the dependencies between the packages if they are missing select **Tools** ◊ **Options** ◊ **Project Level**. Then set the **View Management** options to show dependencies. Use **Layout All** from the diagram's speed menu to get Together to lay out the packages automatically.

The Last Step—
Deploy and Run!

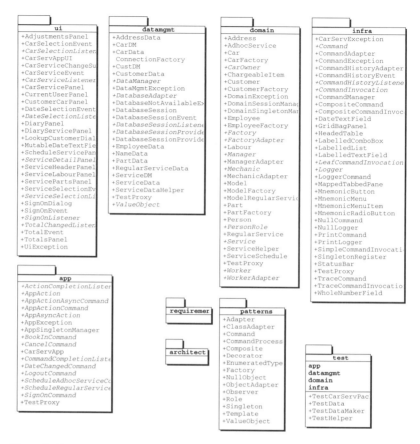

Figure 2–11

Reverse-engineered package diagram.

From this root package diagram, open up the `domain` package (double-clicking the icon on the diagram is one way to do this). You should see a package class diagram similar to the `Overview` class diagram in the original CarServ project (see Appendix G); the main difference will be that all classes (specification and implementation) will be shown, not just the specification classes. You might wish to choose rectilinear links (**Tools** → **Options** → **Diagram Level** then set **Diagram/Links** to rectilinear) and auto-layout (right-click on the diagram background and select **Layout** → **All**) to tidy up the diagram a little.

Like the root package diagram, this diagram of the domain package has also been created out of the information in the source code. However, this isn't a one-off reverse engineered snapshot; subsequent changes to the source code will be reflected immediately in the diagram.

To illustrate this, bring up the text editor (**View** → **Editor**) and select the `Service` class. The Search facility is a useful way to find classes in large diagrams like this one (**Search** → **Search on Diagrams**). At the end of the file, make the following changes:

```
private String bookInNotes;
public String getBookInNotes() { return bookInNotes; }
/**
 * @supplierRole bookInNotesMadeBy
 */
private Employee bookInNotesMadeBy;
```

The idea behind this change is that when a customer brings in her car, the employee (the manager or mechanic) can put in additional notes—for example, "There's a funny noise coming from the glove compartment."

Okay, now click on the diagram pane. Together parses the new version of the Service *class and shows the new attribute, method, and relationship. Do another* **Layout** → **All** *to see if Together may be able to come up with a better layout (you can always undo the command if not).*

So in a sense, Together doesn't do reverse engineering to class diagrams. At least, it's not an activity that you need consciously invoke—the diagram and the code are always held in sync by LiveSource technology.

Reverse Engineering of Sequence Diagrams

You might recall from earlier that we looked at the BookInCommand.doExecute *sequence diagram. In fact, this sequence diagram was generated by Together and was then edited a little to simplify it.*

Let's recreate our own version of this sequence diagram in the carserv2 *project. First, locate the* BookInCommand *class in the* app *package and select its* doExecute() *method, either in the package class diagram or in the Explorer pane. Now, right-click to bring up the speed menu, and choose* **Generate Sequence Diagram***.*

You'll be presented with the **Generate Sequence Diagram Expert** *dialog box, as shown below.*

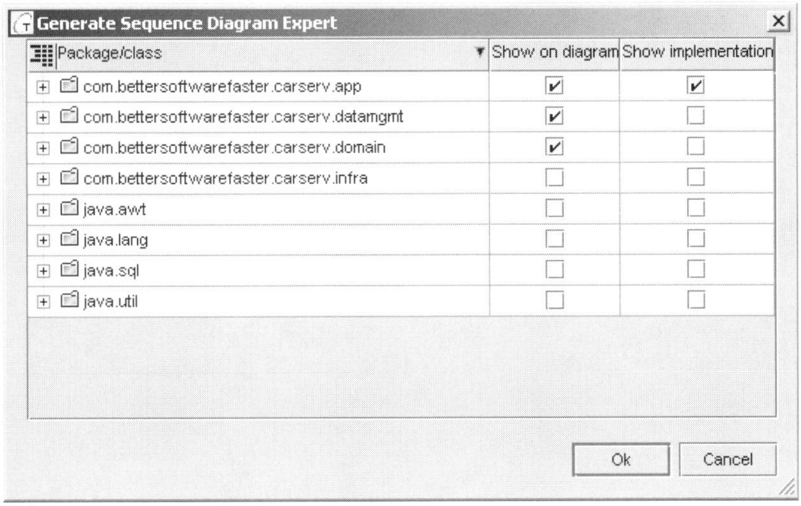

Package/class	Show on diagram	Show implementation
⊞ 🗂 com.bettersoftwarefaster.carserv.app	✔	✔
⊞ 🗂 com.bettersoftwarefaster.carserv.datamgmt	✔	☐
⊞ 🗂 com.bettersoftwarefaster.carserv.domain	✔	☐
⊞ 🗂 com.bettersoftwarefaster.carserv.infra	☐	☐
⊞ 🗂 java.awt	☐	☐
⊞ 🗂 java.lang	☐	☐
⊞ 🗂 java.sql	☐	☐
⊞ 🗂 java.util	☐	☐

Figure 2–12
The Generate Sequence Diagram Expert.

This allows you to filter out which packages/classes to show on the diagram, and of those, which implementation to show. If a class (or the package that it belongs to) is not shown on the diagram, then any messages to instances of that class will not be shown. If the implementation of methods is suppressed for an object, then Together will show only messages to that object, not messages from that object.

For our little demo, try creating the sequence diagram a few times, with different choices. For all of the following, do not show classes from java.awt, java.lang, java.sql, java.util, *or the* infra *package, but, do show classes for the* app, domain, *and* datamgmt *packages.*

Then, try the following variations:

- *Show implementation only for* app, *not for* domain *or* datamgmt.

- *Show implementation for* app *and* domain, *not for* datamgmt.

- *Show implementation for* app *and for the* domain.Service *class; deselect implementation for all other* domain *classes; do not show implementation for* datamgmt.

It doesn't take long to come up with a sequence diagram that shows enough detail to be useful, but not so much as to be overwhelming. Delete the sequence diagrams that have too much or too little detail.

What's Next

In this chapter we've shown how Together supports the last step—developing, testing, and running code. You've also seen how Together automatically maintains package and class diagrams whenever the code is changed, and how non-code-based information, such as specifications, can be captured as other UML diagrams and linked back to the code.

We've introduced you to the *CarServ* case study, which we will be using throughout the book, and you've also seen its unit tests working at first hand. Now we look back to the foundation of the system, the domain model, and see how to build this with Together.

chapter 3

The First Step:
Model the Domain

One potato, two potato, three potato, four...
—Nursery rhyme

Conceptual integrity is the most important
consideration in system design.
—F. P. Brooks, Jr.

We never wish to return to the monotonous flatland
of monochrome modeling.
—Peter Coad

The domain model stands at the interface between business stakeholders defining and prioritizing requirements and the development team implementing the functionality of the system. It should be small enough to encourage this dialogue, and yet detailed enough to capture the essence of the domain addressed by the system. This chapter discusses how such models are produced.

In previous chapters we have emphasized that we are always in the middle of the software development lifecycle. We have some software, but we want to improve its functionality or its quality, or both, and so we move from one stable realization to another. But, of course, it is also true that there are genuine starting out points in projects, usually corresponding to the allocation of funds to the project or the award of a contract. Sometimes, there is more than one such starting point, which gives rise to the very reasonable question: What do you do first at such points?

What *we* do is build a domain model, using object modeling in color. If one already exists, we seek to review, understand, and improve the model. This is the subject of this chapter.

Elements of Specification

A domain model is a set of UML diagrams and definitions, particularly the definitions of classes, which constitute the main business level objects and types in the application we are building. Why are we considering the domain model first, before even the requirements activity? (We will look at the requirements activity in Chapter 4, "The Stakeholder Step: Specify Requirement.") Both these activities are necessary to complete a specification:

- Understand the domain—what *things* we are dealing with and how they interact.
- Understand the stakeholders' goals—what they want the system to *do*.

It's a simplification, but the domain model is first concerned with the *nouns*. These concepts in a problem domain are generally less changeable than the functionality required of the system, and that is why it is both a good starting point and a good basis for considering the structure of the software. On the other hand, the procurers of a new system are primarily concerned with the *verbs*—the actions, what the system will do. As we will see in the next chapter, the domain model is helpful in specifying these verb phrases that define use cases and features. If we have established the common vocabulary of the domain early on, there will be a consistency of language that is immensely helpful and may even provide a measure of traceability from requirements to the classes that implement them.

Just as a sentence is not complete unless it has both verbs and nouns, so our initial specification work will not have reached first base until we have the first iteration of both domain model and requirements specification. We will not be able to scope particularly the operations of classes in the domain model unless we understand the likely functionality of the system. Therefore, whichever step we start with, we should move swiftly to the other and continue to iterate and compare.

The domain model tells us what the application is all about, independent from the architecture or contractual boundaries (between vendors as well as between user and supplier). It is a basis for building a coherent application. Figure 3-1 shows the influences of the domain model on other aspects of the specification, design, and implementation of the system. The domain model will indicate objects that we expect to see rendered in some way in the user interface (so, for example, we can see the state of a car being serviced or the payment history of a customer). We expect the domain model to indicate the names of classes that will be implemented (in our case, in Java), and so provide structure to the software and definitions of how data associated with the objects are held in memory. It is also reasonable to expect that many of the objects discovered in the domain model will be held in persistent storage, probably in a database management system. The domain model will therefore also inform the modeling of persistent data. And, as we have already observed, the domain model provides the fundamental vocabulary that can be used in the specification of the requirements.

By placing this emphasis on the domain model throughout the development of the system, we could say our approach is domain-model-centric. Consistently, in consulting with clients on projects of all sizes, it is the domain model that we rely on initially and throughout the project, to improve the understanding of the system, its functionality, and its design.

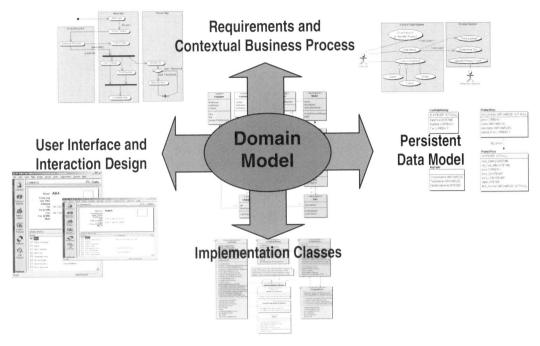

Figure 3–1
The domain model provides crucial understanding to many other aspects of the system specification, including the requirements, the user interface, the persistent data model, and the implementation classes.

Domain models are so useful that they should be preserved through to implementation. This can be tricky. For now, we'll just note this aim. In Chapter 7, "The Micro Step: Design and Implement," we'll show you how this can be accomplished in Together using views that filter implementation detail from the final form of the classes. This means that compact and straightforward models, which nevertheless are held consistent with the underlying implementation via LiveSource, can be maintained throughout the development of a system.

In this section, we introduce some key techniques for developing the domain model.

Modeling in Color

Over the years, we have built many domain models together with colleagues and co-workers. The patterns that emerge from comparison of these models were catalogued by Peter Coad and others in the mid-1990s (Coad, North, & Mayfield 1997). In a later book, Coad defined a very effective mechanism for color coding the patterns and accelerating the modeling process with color archetypes (Coad, Lefebvre, & De Luca 1999). This is the color modeling scheme that we use here.

Color Archetypes

Archetypes are a way of classifying the classes in domain models to forms that they "more or less" follow. Using color archetypes accelerates the process of domain modeling considerably, since you are building continuously on work from previous models. The patterns provide a wealth of detail, which if appropriate can be adopted in the current model or, if not, simply discarded. The color archetypes are

- Moment-Interval (pink)
- Role (yellow)
- Party, Place, or Thing (green)
- Description (blue)

The colors are based on the primary colors, with a dash of white added to make them easy to read on a class diagram. It's no coincidence that they happen to match the common colors of Post-It Notes; domain models are often brainstormed using Post-It Notes on whiteboards.

Figure 3-2 shows a typical configuration of the four archetypes. Let us run through these in turn.

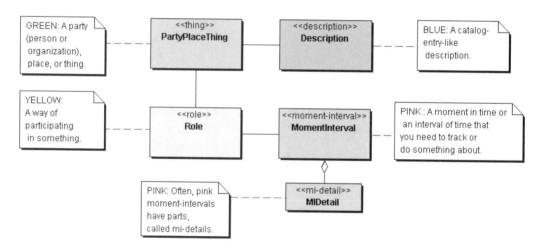

Figure 3–2

The color archetypes: Green things, described by blue descriptions, adopt yellow roles in order to participate in pink moment-intervals.

The most active color—the color of fire engines and warning lights—is red, so with a dash of white, our first archetype is pink. This is the color that the eye will be drawn to first when inspecting a class diagram for the first time, and so it is used as the color for the most dynamic classes: those that represent objects concerned with a moment or interval of time. They are referred to simply as moment-intervals. Examples of moment-intervals are objects like sales, invoices, trades, loans, reservations, bookings, flight plans, rentals, and payments. All these classes will have an attribute representing a date-time moment or a date-time interval. They also are interesting because in business systems, they represent the things that drive the business. In real-time or industrial control applications moment-interval classes also turn out to be most significant, representing things like events, radar tracks, condition violations, and timed sensor readings.

Moment-intervals sometimes have component parts that contain detail. These classes are also colored pink and have the MI-detail archetype. Examples of MI-details are line item (for sale, loan, reservation, etc.), payment installment (for a payment) and flight leg (for a flight plan).

In the *CarServ* case study, the `Service` class (representing a car being serviced) is a pink moment-interval. `ChargeableItem`, a class of object representing items of the service, particularly like the labor elements, might be an example of an MI-detail class.

One of the useful aspects of using the archetypes with Together is that you can ask for typical attributes and operations of the archetypes to be added to your class. This is done by right-clicking on your class and selecting *Choose Pattern* from the popup menu. Then, in the dialogue that is opened, expand the `Coad Components` folder and select the relevant archetype. Figure 3-3 shows how the resulting classes might look immediately after this operation.

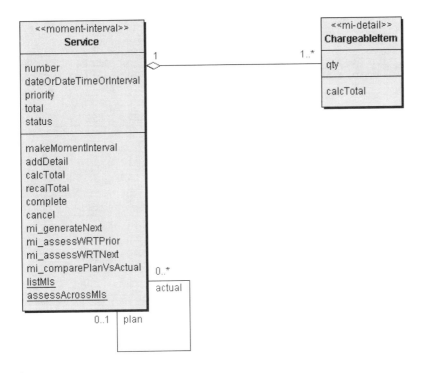

Figure 3–3
Typical attributes and operations of the moment-interval archetype.

Let's consider the typical attributes in turn:

- `number` is a unique identifying number used by external entities to reference a specific instance of the class. We might rename this `bookingNumber`, for example.
- `dateOrDateTimeOrInterval` is for the time of moment or duration of interval. In this case we could simply rename to `serviceDate`.
- `priority` can be set, for example, to high, normal, or low. For our use, it is probably not relevant, so we'll delete it.
- `total` is the cached result from a `calcTotal` method (for performance, to prevent necessary iteration across MIs). Again, this is probably not relevant.
- `status` for a `LoanApplication`, for example, might be new, submitted, approved, or rejected. We could use an attribute like this in our `Service` class to indicate whether a service is not started, in progress, or finished.
- `actual`, `plan` is a recursive association pattern that can be used if the same structure is used to record both a plan and the actual event so that a comparison can be made. In this case we will simply update the one object, so this will not be needed for our system and we can remove it from the model. If we had wanted to keep track of the differences between planned services and their actual performance, though, this pattern could have been retained.

Consider next the typical methods or operations:

- `makeMomentInterval` supports the business process for making a moment-interval. If we want to use this, we'll need to make it static and return a `Service` object.
- `addDetail` adds details (parts). We'd use this for adding a `ChargeableItem`, so we'll rename it, say to `addLaborAndParts` or `addChargeableItem`.
- `calcTotal` interacts with its parts to calculate its total. We'll need this, though we could rename it.
- `recalcTotal` recalculates its total (forcing a recalculation, regardless of any internally buffered value). This one could be safely ignored for now (or deleted).
- `complete` completes the moment-interval. It is used to record the change in state, and could be used when the `Service` is completed.
- `cancel` cancels the moment-interval. Unfortunately, `Services` in our garage are sometime canceled—we'll probably need this.
- `mi_generateNext` generates the next (subsequent) moment-interval. Moment-intervals often appear in sequence in a business process. Would this be applicable here? Possibly—there are MIs that occur after the service, like `Payments` and `QualityChecks`. If this was relevant to our system, we could use them—or else delete them. The next few methods are also relevant only when there is a sequence of "pinks", so we won't use them, at least initially.
- `mi_assessWRTPrior` assesses with respect to prior moment-intervals.
- `mi_assessWRTSubsequent` assesses with respect to subsequent moment-intervals.

- `mi_comparePlanVsActual` compares MIs representing the planned action with moment-intervals representing the actual action.
- `listMomentIntervals` class/static method: list all of the moment-interval objects.
- `calcAvgMomentInterval` is a class/static method used to calculate the average moment-interval (usually average amount, although it could be something like average weight or average fulfillment time).

Similar sets of attributes and operations apply to the other archetypes, and they can be explored using Together in the same way. We will not discuss them further here.

Returning to our list of archetypes, the next most active of the primary colors after pink is yellow, and that is used to color the roles that objects adopt when involved in performing a pink moment-interval. For example, a `Trader` (role) is an employee that makes a `Trade` (moment-interval). A `Loanable` thing (role) can be lent, resulting in a `Loan` (moment-interval). A `Serviceable` thing (role) has `Services` (moment-interval). Roles are generally played by persons and sometimes by places or things. For example, we are likely to need models in our system of mechanics and customers and possibly some other roles.

One of the reasons this is a helpful archetype when modeling is that people are sometimes tempted to model the roles that people or things play using inheritance. This is nearly always a mistake, especially if the role changes over time (and you need to continue to track the person over these changes) or if the person can play multiple roles. Rather than use inheritance, the person-role structure (see Figure 3-4) is a classic delegation pattern, where an object of one class delegates some aspect of its functionality—in this case the functionality relating to the role of the person—to an object of another class.

As an aside, notice that the link is shown as a "composition" in this diagram (filled diamond) rather than simply as an aggregation (open diamond). This is because we wish to imply existence dependency—the role object cannot exist in this case without the party object.

There are two remaining archetypes left, and two remaining colors, green and blue. Since blue is the restful color (the one that you painted your bathroom in?), we use this most passive color for the most passive objects. These are objects that describe types of things. For example, in an employment system we might have `JobCategory` or `EmployeeGrade`; in a library system we might have `BookType` (with instances like `Fiction`, `Reference`, and `Biography`); in a car sales system we might have a class `Model` to describe types of `Car`.

Green classes, more active than blue (because they are instantiated more often), are used for the parties, places or things that adopt the (yellow) roles to be involved in (pink) moment-intervals and are described by the (blue) descriptions. "Thing" is a very general word (like entity and concept), so we try to fit classes into the other three archetypes before trying green. If you end up with an all-green domain model the exercise has not been very useful!

For example, an `Employee` (green party) might have a `Trader` object (yellow role) to make a `Trade` (pink moment-interval). A `Book` (green thing)

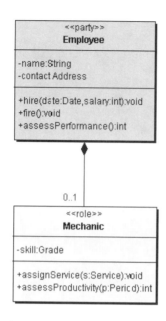

Figure 3–4
Example of person-role structure.

may have a `Loanable` (yellow role) if it can to be borrowed (as opposed to a reference book that perhaps cannot be borrowed). And a `Car` (green thing) may have a `Serviceable` (yellow role) and so can be serviced.

You'll note that blue classes often represent catalogue-like items, whereas green classes are often stock-like items. You might also think of blue classes as reference or static data; the instances of such classes are often fixed or only change relatively slowly over time. Often value objects (Fowler 00a) are colored blue.

Choo Choo Chanooga
Dan Haywood

I first realized just how well the modeling in color idea worked when doing a little modeling exercise on an object orientation course I was teaching. Although the course didn't discuss modeling in color, I thought it would be worth introducing to one of the exercises to see how it played out.

The exercise I chose was one whereby the students had to model a train. This train would have one or two locomotives and be either a freight train consisting of just freight cars or a passenger train consisting of just passenger cars. Maybe you can visualize the solution now: subclasses both for train and for car, some associations between train and locomotive with a 1..2 multiplicity, and an interesting discussion about how to constrain passenger trains to have only passenger cars and freight trains to have freight cars.

Then we did the colors. We determined that locomotives and cars were green—things. We decided that there was probably an implicit role or two missing; a locomotive performed the role of being the automotive force, and a freight car performed the role of some carrier of cargo.

However, it was the color of the train class that made me sit up. It's a pink moment-interval, and that isn't necessarily all that obvious. But then, think about how trains are described when they are announced by the train conductor: "This is the 6:57 from Cardiff arriving at London Paddington at 9:03." So, clearly, the domain expert (the station announcer) thinks of trains in these terms—an assemblage of locomotives and cars coming together for an interval of time to form a train traveling from place A to place B.

As you may have surmised, classes that conform to these archetypes often have predictable relationships with classes of other archetypes, as was shown in Figure 3-2. This means the archetypes actually prompt you to consider common aspects that are often present in models and reapply the patterns if they are applicable.

Note that it is allowable for the archetypes to have different relationships to those shown; one that is quite common is directly from a pink moment-interval to a blue description. For example, in the *CarServ* case study, the `RegularService` class—representing a car being booked in for some regular service—has a link to the `ModelRegularService`—representing the mileages at which a `Car` of that `Model` is meant to be serviced. This is shown in Figure 3-5, which uses the simplest icon for a class in UML—the plain rectangle[11]—as here we are considering just the associations between the classes and their archetypes.

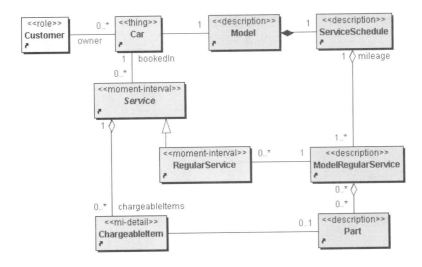

Figure 3–5
CarServ classes showing archetypes.

---

11. Contrast this with Figure 3–7, where most of the classes are shown with the more common icon, with additional compartments for its attributes and operations.

In Figure 3-5 you'll also note that there is no yellow role class between the green `Car` and the pink `Service`. This is quite common; there is no particular information that needs to be captured about the role of being serviceable, so it does not exist. The mere fact that there is a relationship between `Car` and `Service` tells us that `Car` is adopting the role of being serviceable.

Maybe if we were to broaden the domain and allow trucks as well as cars to be serviced by our garage, however, then the `Service` class would probably refer to a `Serviceable` thing rather than to a `Car`. This leads to one of two implementation choices: We can either use the role pattern (similar in structure to Figure 3-4) such that the `Car` has a reference to a `Serviceable` role object or we can make the `Car` implement a `Serviceable` interface.

The former solution allows a `Car` to adopt the `Serviceable` role for a period of time, and then drop it. The latter makes the `Car` `Serviceable` for all time. The correct model will depend upon the domain, of course. For the *CarServ* domain, it seems unlikely that we would have `Cars` (or `Trucks`) that are not `Serviceable`, so introducing an interface makes sense. But if we were a manufacturer of cars, some of which we have in a car fleet and need to service and some of which we just resell, then the role pattern might be a better choice.

Domain-Neutral Component

The archetypes can be taken a stage further by considering what Coad calls the domain-neutral component (DNC). This is actually applying the three other archetypes three times around one moment-interval:

1. For Party (considering the people or organizational groups and their roles relative to the moment-interval)
2. For Place (considering where the moment-interval takes place)
3. For Thing (considering what things the moment-interval or the MI-detail classes are dealing with)

The pattern for the DNC, which is also accessible in Together—it's shipped in Together's \modules\components directory—is shown in Figure 3-6.

In our car servicing example, the key pink class (our starting point in applying the DNC) is the service. The "place" might relate to the garage, the "thing" to the car or possibly parts, and the "party" to the mechanic and the customer. This helps us to discover a number of classes not shown in Figure 3-5. After some consideration of the DNC and of what are actually relevant classes in our system (omitting those that we may not need at this stage), we obtain a reasonable first-cut model for our system (Figure 3-7). We've also included attributes and some operations in this model.

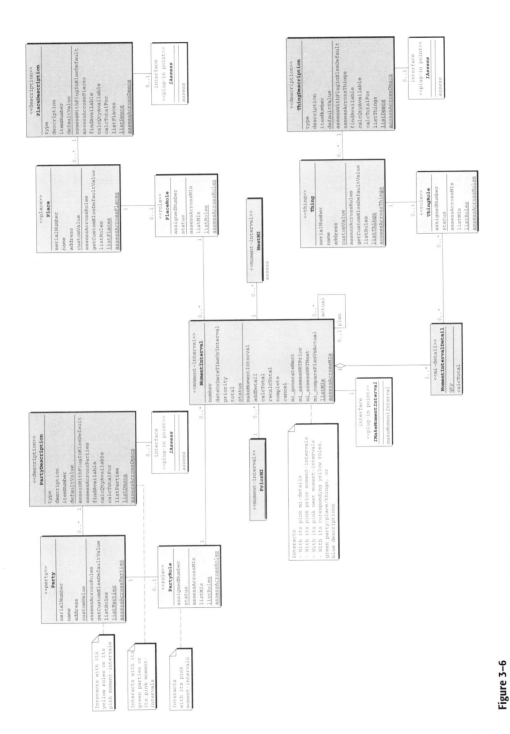

Figure 3-6

The domain-neutral component for object modeling in color.

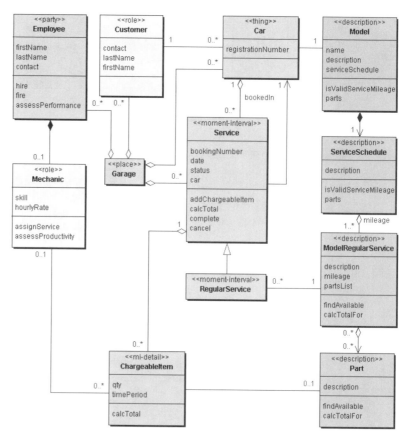

Figure 3–7

An initial domain model for CarServ.

We've stated that the domain model is made up of classes, but we feel we ought perhaps to be a little more precise, because some would argue that to model at a high level of abstraction, as we have been doing, it is types and interfaces rather than classes that are relevant.

First, we should answer the question of what is the distinction drawn between classes, types, and interfaces in object-oriented methods generally and in UML in particular. A type defines the functionality of objects in terms of how the objects can be accessed or interacted with, but the definition is entirely independent of the storage and procedural implementation for the objects. So, for example, we might define the functionality of a `Complex-Number` type or an `Employee` type in terms of the effect of the operations defined on the types (like `squareRoot` or `giveRaise`). This can be done without specifying anything about the actual data members of the objects or the algorithms of the operations. In this respect, types in UML are like interfaces in Java and UML, with the exception that unlike interfaces, types can have their own attributes and associations. In the case of types though, attributes and associations define only that certain information is accessible and not how the information is stored, or indeed whether it is stored rather than calculated.

A type needs a corresponding class to actually work, because a class has an *implementation* of the specified behavior. There are always many options for how the functionality of the system is delegated to the different classes and how the functionality of each class is implemented, so there is much more information in the class definitions than is needed initially for specification and high-level design. Thus, although generally we refer to classes in the domain model, in many ways they are more like type definitions. Indeed when implemented in Java, some of the classes may actually end up implemented as interfaces or even, in some cases, as a group of related classes and interfaces.

The overlap in the concepts type, interface, and class is shown in Figure 3-8.

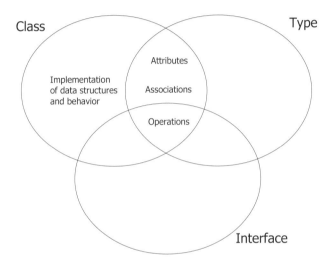

Figure 3–8
Types, interfaces and classes are related—but different.

Given that our domain model is a high-level view of a problem domain and quite far removed from the actual implementation, it is a reasonable question to ask why we are using classes on these diagrams rather than the more abstract model element, type. The answer is twofold. First, it is simpler to use classes, since we are not restricted in the elements that can be included. Second, when the system has been implemented, it will be easier to reflect back, from the actual implementation, a diagram that has the same level of detail as our original domain model and therefore compare the implemented system with that envisaged at the domain modeling stage. We are then able to continue to develop and evolve the domain model in step with implemented system.

We are, in effect, using the classes at this stage as if they were types and therefore avoiding considerations of "how" and focusing on the "what." There are three aspects that we want to consider here:

- Modeling attributes
- Modeling associations with navigability not yet defined
- Modeling operations

In Chapter 7 we'll discuss how to preserve the specification detail as the design is elaborated into implementation. For now, though, let us go through the above points in turn.

Modeling Attributes

In modeling a type, we are primarily looking for attributes and associations, and so are considering the things that objects of this type need to *know* about, and which other objects they need to know. We may also identify some operations that we think the type should support, particularly those that its color archetype might suggest, so that even this high-level model captures some aspects of the dynamic behavior of the system.

While we are interested in what objects of the type know and do, we are not interested at this level in how they do it or how they store what they know. So, when modeling a type as a class, attributes may not be the best option, since they do imply a storage mechanism (an internal data member). If the developer changes this subsequently, an unnecessary discussion might ensue concerning whether the object still "knows about" that aspect. It is quite legitimate for an attribute of a type to be calculated on-the-fly; in UML to say that a type has an attribute merely means that instances of that type can furnish that information. It does not mean that they hold that information internally. On a class, though, attributes imply data members. Another issue is that,even if we were to use an instance variable, we would then need to decide upon its visibility. This is clearly an implementation decision that we shouldn't have to make this early.

There is an alternative to showing attributes on domain model classes, however. To explain it we need a mild digression. Figure 3-9 shows three representations of a `Mechanic` domain class, similar to the one in our *CarServ* model. The leftmost representation is conventional—it shows the `Mechanic` class with three instance variables, providing accessors and mutators ("getters" and "setters") for each. While this is accurate, it is much too verbose for a domain model. The only operations we are interested in showing at this level are operations related to the required behavior of the objects in our system. Getters and setters are much too boring to warrant the space!

However, since the class conforms to the JavaBean naming convention (or the JavaBean design pattern, as Sun Microsystems calls it), we can infer the existence of three JavaBean "properties": `lastName`, `firstName`, and `hourlyRate`. The representation of the class in the middle of Figure 3-9 just shows these properties in a separate "properties" compartment. This is the form that Together displays by default. It indicates to us that it has recognized the pattern of attributes with getters and setters, a pattern referred

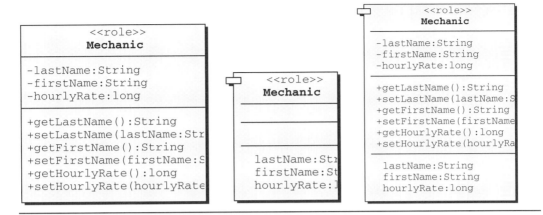

Figure 3–9
Three equivalent way to show properties of a class.

to as a *property* or *JavaBean property* by displaying the small rectangular icon on the top left-hand side of the class symbol.[12] In fact, only one operation—either a getter or setter—is required for a property to be recognized and displayed in this way; the other operation or attribute, or both, may be absent from the class. This then is a very convenient way to display what our domain types "know," since it is not dependent on the "how" of either storage or calculation.

This JavaBean recognition has other advantages too. If you rename either the name or the data type of the property in the diagram, all the corresponding code is updated for you, including inside the body of the getter and setter operations. If you want to see the class features in class UML form, then use *Tools* → *Options* → *Project Level* and in the *View Managment* → *JavaBeans/C++ properties* section uncheck the *Recognize JavaBeans* option. If you want to see the rightmost representation of Figure 3-9 (both inferred properties and the underlying members), check the *Show beans* and *Show attributes and accessors* options in the same section.

So, JavaBean properties provide an attractive way of modeling attributes. On domain types, Together will indicate the presence of the property, provided the setter and/or the getter methods are present. In particular, no underlying instance variable is needed; it would be quite legitimate for a property to be calculated at runtime, just like an attribute.

---

12. UML introduced the idea of stereotypes so that the notation could be extended in domain-specific ways. Stereotypes are usually recognized as text labels within guillemots for example, «property»—but they can be iconic, such as the stickman in use case diagrams. So, effectively, that rectangle is an iconic stereotype for a Java-Bean pattern. As long as you are "in the know" about Together's domain-specific stereotype, the interpretation of the diagram is straightforward.

How to Show the Visibility of Properties

JavaBean properties may have both a getter and a setter (read/write) or may have only one of them (read-only or write-only). This important information is not generally available on the class unless you turn on the visibility of getters and setters, something we don't want to do because of the clutter it introduces to the diagrams. Here's one way to get around the problem.

Suppose we wanted to make the `hourlyRate` *property read-only. You'll find that if you simply remove the* `setHourlyRate()` *method in the code, the properties representation (as shown in the middle icon of Figure 3-9) will not change—there's no way to see that the property is read-only. However, if you make the setter* `private`, *then it is clear that the property cannot be changed—all JavaBean properties require public accessors and mutators, so Together shows this private setter in the operations compartment. This is shown in Figure 3–10.*

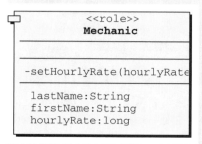

Figure 3–10
A Private setter operation indicating a read-only property.

This works reasonably well, although visually the inaccessible setter operation is emphasized rather than de-emphasized. There's a technical objection too in that read-only properties often have a `final` *instance variable, and the rules of Java dictate that such variables must be initialized in the constructor or in their declaration. Calling a setter (even a private setter) in a constructor is not allowed, so this operation would be redundant.*

So, perhaps a simpler solution is to configure Together to display "r" for read only, "rw" for read-write, and (for completeness, though it's hard to think of an example where this would be a sensible thing to do) "w" for write only. We have developed a simple .config file that does precisely this. From the www.bettersoftwarefaster.com web site, download `zzzBSwF.beanProperties.config` *and copy into* `$TGH$/config`. *Also, in the options dialog, disable the show beans ◊ show attributes and accessors, since it is no longer needed. With this configuration installed, the Mechanic bean is rendered as shown in Figure 3–11.*

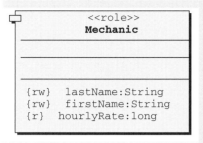

Figure 3–11
Using a special Together config shows the visibility of properties more clearly.

There are more configurations like this throughout the book, and Appendix C summarizes all of them and provides more information about installation.

Associations with No Navigability

When we draw an association in Together from class A to class B, an attribute and JavaDoc comments are created in class A to hold the semantics (multiplicity, role names, etc.) for that association.

On the other hand, if we are doing analysis, then we won't have determined the navigability. Navigability in UML indicates the dependencies in an association between two classes—which class knows about the other. The final implementation could be one of the following four possibilities:

- Class A may need to know about class B, but not vice versa.
- Class B may need to know about class A, but not vice versa.
- Class A and class B may have a bidirectional relationship with each knowing about the other.
- Class A and class B may have an association class that links the two classes, but neither class A nor B knows about the other.

Only in the first option does the code that was generated during analysis match the required implementation. Does this mean that Together has prematurely forced us into a design decision?

The answer is that although Together has recorded a provisional design decision (based on the way the association was drawn by the designer), it doesn't actually force us to consider design too early. You'll notice when you draw an association with Together that the link does not have any navigability arrows. Indeed, if you ignore the code (we usually do when domain modeling), the associations are exactly how we want them—completely ambiguous with regards to navigability.

Looking at other figures in this book, though, you'll see that many of the associations *do* have navigability arrows. This isn't usually because we asked Together to draw the arrows—indeed, although you can do that, we usually counsel against it. The reason that the previous figures did not have arrows is because the names of the corresponding attributes in the classes conformed to Together's naming convention for graphically inserted associations—their names began with the prefix `lnk`.

How does Together use this prefix `lnk`? Well, it has the effect of suppressing the display of both the navigability arrowhead and the corresponding attribute name in the class. You can see this behavior explained if you go to *Tools* → *Options* → *Default (or Project, or Diagram) Level* then look at the diagram options for associations *Draw Directed*, and also *Show as Attributes*.

So, here's how we use this feature of Together: If we see an attribute in a class that begins lnk, then we consider it indicates merely the presence of an association with some other class—and, moreover, the navigability of that association has not yet been decided upon. It indicates that we have not yet considered this aspect of its implementation.

When you move from specification into implementation, then you should go through those unadorned associations and determine navigability. In our experience most designers tend to instinctively draw the link in a reasonable direction anyway (or perhaps the design merely reinforces unspoken previous prejudices?). In any case, in these situations, all the implementer need do is remove the lnk prefix from the attribute.

In the cases where the navigability needs to be reversed, then simply right-click on the association and select *Reverse Link Direction*, again renaming the data member to remove the lnk.

In those cases where the designer wants a genuinely bidirectional association, she can select the link and apply the bidirectional pattern to it (right-click and *Choose Pattern*). This adds the necessary implementation to both classes so that the association can be navigated directly in either direction, and referential integrity is maintained when any change is made from either end.

Modeling Operations

We've discussed modeling attributes and associations; let's now consider modeling operations. Defining a color archetype suggests some possible operations, and the identification of operations of the model is important even at this early stage. The value of the system to the business comes from what the objects *do*, not just what they know.

However, there is a danger in spending too much time on searching out operations too early. First, it is essential we have genuine input from the stakeholders (users and business analysts) in order that the functionality described is actually as required. We encourage stakeholders to get involved in domain modeling, especially early in the project, but the requirements specification is more fully expressed through use cases or features, as discussed in the next chapter. Another danger is that you are assigning responsibilities to classes without yet having a good feel for the design. You should expect operations found during early domain modeling to move to other classes or even to disappear. Don't let them become a stumbling block by being reluctant to move them to some other class.

In some cases you can take the definitions of the operations even further and define sequence diagrams. However, we are going to leave this step to Chapter 7 (specifically, the section "Choosing Between Designs"), where we discuss how sequence diagrams can be used to discover operations as well as to document how they work.

Taking into account all that we've discussed in this chapter leads us to Figure 3-12 which shows a typical level of detail for a domain model at this early stage of the project, and uses properties rather than attributes to indicate the data held or calculated by objects.

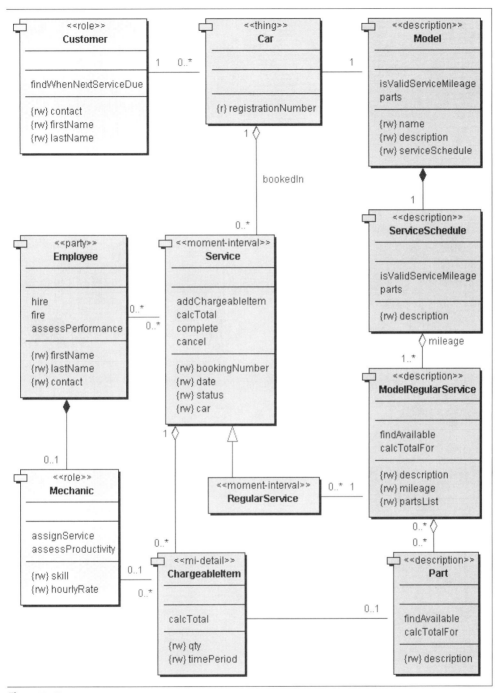

Figure 3–12
The Domain Model for CarServ after the initial modeling exercise.

What's Next

We've looked at modeling the domain, a significant first step in specifying the system. We have identified the types of objects in the problem domain (represented as classes), their attributes (represented as JavaBean properties), their associations, and to a limited degree their behavior (represented as operations on key classes). However, as yet we have a far from complete view of the functionality of the system. In Chapter 4 we consider how UML can be used to capture a more complete view of system behavior.

The Stakeholder Step: Specify Requirements

*If you don't say what you want, you've no right to
complain when you don't get it!*
Anon

*Those of you who think you know everything are very
annoying to those of us who do.*
Oscar Wilde

Whatcha gonna do?
Bob Dylan

Systems are wanted by their users and procurers because they do something for them. It's the verbs that are their priority. The functionality of
the system and the priority of which feature is needed before another must be
specified as clearly, succinctly, and unambiguously as possible—at least to the
extent allowed by our knowledge of the business drivers and how they will
change in the future. There are several options for doing this, including plain
text documents, but the approach we explain here is that of use cases, supple-
mented with activity diagrams and optionally state charts. It is vital that small
teams have an accessible, lightweight, and readily understandable expression
of the business context and the system functionality. That is our goal for this
chapter.

Ultimately, we write business software to automate business processes. It's
unlikely that we'll automate every portion—humans will always provide key
activities in most business processes—but we certainly must understand
the process before we start writing software to support it.

**Business
Process**

In some cases the business process will be profoundly changed by the
new system, as the existing process often reflects previous levels of technology. Within investment banks, for example, the front-office (trading) and
back-office (reporting, settlement) processes date from the days when
paper-based ledgers were used to record deals and the paper tickets were

reconciled by back-office clerks. These processes have changed dramatically with technology. Only comparatively recently has this business process been redefined and straight-through processing been implemented. The change in technology made this feasible and changed many people's jobs as a result.

So, when capturing the business process, we should always be aware that it is likely to be transformed (simplified, we hope) by introducing the new system.[13] The business processes provide the context for the functionality of the system that we are specifying, and so it is important to gain an understanding of what the process will be, and then communicate that process alongside the specification of functionality.

UML Diagrams

Which UML diagrams are available for capturing information about the contextual business processes for our system and its functionality? There are two standard diagrams[14] that are particularly useful:

- Activity diagrams
- Use case diagrams

One other diagram type occasionally adds important information to the specification (albeit from a different standpoint)—the state chart. In this chapter we'll look at all three diagram types as we examine ways to capture and express the required functionality of our system.

Activity diagrams and use cases are closely related, so much so that you could almost say they are two sides of the same coin.

- *Use cases* are used to specify types of business or system usage, which support various actors' goals. Actors define the roles the people or other systems play from the modeled system's viewpoint.
- *Activity diagrams* can be used to show how the use cases occur in sequence within a business process, and also how the process within a given use case triggers other business processes or use cases.

It is useful to break down some use cases into smaller use cases using the «include» relationships. The reasons for this are to limit the size of use cases to simple sequences and to specify in only one place sequences that are used more than once. The meaning of the «include» relationship is similar to a procedure call in a programming language, and it indicates that somewhere in the sequence of the including use case, a reference is made to the included use case, and at this point its sequence should be inserted.

---

13. Michael Hammer immortalized this message in the phrase "Don't automate—obliterate!" (Hammer, 1990).

14. Together supports another diagram type, business process diagrams, as defined by Jacobson, Ericsson, & Jacobson (1994), but this is not an official UML diagram. Furthermore, we find activity diagrams and use case diagrams cover the principal functionality we require in a slightly simpler format.

Functionality can also be split between multiple use cases by applying the «extend» relationship, but here we recommend you exercise caution. The effect of «extend» is very similar to «include» in that part of the functionality is placed in a different use case. However, the direction of dependency is reversed such that it is the extending use case that inserts a sequence of steps at an extension point in the extended use case, optionally controlled by a condition. Because of the reversed dependency, the relationship can be useful when adding functionality after the completion of a set of use cases (for example, when implementing a subsequent version or accommodating a late change request). However, the «extend» relationship gets used in all sorts of other circumstances and in some of these it is simply confusing. Cockburn, for example, recommends avoiding the use of «extend» completely (Cockburn 2000) and Armour recommends its use only with extreme caution (Armour & Miller 2000).

In the models in this chapter, we use «extend» to show optional use cases, where part of the functionality depends on a condition. This is so that additional information—the condition, for example—is visible in the diagram. You might wish to follow this practice in your project. However, always remember the priority is to keep your models simple, understandable, and maintainable. Sometimes this is best achieved by reducing or even eliminating the use of «extend».

Use Include or Extend—It's Up to You
Andy Carmichael

On more than one consulting assignment, I've seen confusion arising, and sometimes confusing models produced, because of overuse or incorrect use of the «extend» relationship. Here's a simple example to show you that you do have a free choice when modeling between the two use case relationships, but you should exercise caution over which one you use to ensure the readers of the model get the message clearly.

Say we have a pizza restaurant that generally serves only one kind of pizza (cheese and tomato). It now introduces the concept of "Pizza-Plus," a pizza that has a fixed set of additional toppings. No doubt we would refuse to model the use cases for this business on the grounds that it's unlikely to be able to pay our fees if it sells only two types of pizza. Nevertheless, let's try! The diagram that follows shows the use case diagram using the simpler «include» relationship.

The use cases in this case are defined as

```
Use Case: make pizza
Normal Flow:
1. Make base
2. Add tomato sauce
3. Add cheese
4. If [pizza-plus ordered] then
        <<include>> add extra topping
5. Cook
6. Serve
```

and (somewhat trivially),

```
Use Case: add extra topping
Normal Flow:
1. Sprinkle pizza-plus topping
```

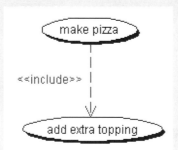

Figure 4–1
Using <<include>>.

The model is suitably simple, although the diagram gives us no clue as to when the included use case will be used.

On the other hand, here's the same situation using «extend».

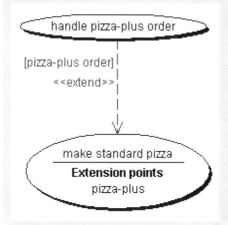

Figure 4–2
Using <<extend>>.

The use cases here are defined as

```
Use Case: make standard pizza
Normal Flow:
1. Make base
2. Add tomato sauce
3. Add cheese
Extension point: pizza-plus
4. Cook
5. Serve
```

and

```
Use Case: handle pizza-plus order
Extends: make standard pizza
Condition: [pizza-plus order]
Extension Point: pizza-plus
Normal Flow:
1. Sprinkle pizza-plus topping
```

Note that in this case the "make standard pizza" use case is independent of the extending behavior. Unfortunately, the extended use case does have to be changed when adding this behavior to the model—in order to add the extension point—but this does not modify the use case's behavior at all. The details of the new behavior reside solely in the extending use case.

If you use «include», you have a simpler model, and because the meaning of «include» is clear to most readers, and provided they read the definition of the use case (which they must anyway to understand the model), there should be no confusion.

If you use «extend», you have a more complex model but one which provides more information in the graphical view. Sometimes this is useful, especially if the diagrams are reasonably small. However, you do run the risk of confusion and argument arising from the use of this particular UML feature.

The use case model is enhanced by activity diagrams, which can show both the business process in which the use case occurs and the process of the use case itself. Use case diagrams and activity diagrams have a recursive relationship with each other. An activity diagram for the business process provides the context for use cases, and the process in each use case can be explained in terms of another activity diagram. This recursive relationship can raise difficulties when communicating the analysis and the modeler must make it clear at what level each diagram resides. In order to do this, it's worthwhile to distinguish and define both *business use cases* and *system use cases*.

Business Versus System Use Cases

Business and system use cases exist on different levels because they arise from the goals of different levels of user. A use case exists to accomplish a goal—that of a stakeholder of the business in the case of business use cases, and that of a user of the system in the case of system use cases. Thus,

- A *business use case* is a usage of the business or system such that a goal of a stakeholder of the business is fulfilled. The business use case may be fully or only partly automated through software. A stakeholder of the business is a sponsor of the business: a customer, owner, or manager, for example, who may or may not have direct access to the automated system.
- A *system use case* is a usage of the system such that a goal of the actor is fulfilled. It explains the interactions between an actor and the automated system itself. An actor defines the role of a person or external system that interacts directly with the modeled system.

We suggest three ways that you can make the distinction between business use cases and system use cases clear in your models:

- By *naming convention*. System use cases are named with a verb phrase of the form <verb> <object>, such as "Service Car," "Schedule Service," and "Receive Payment." Business use cases are named with a noun phrase derived from a verb, of the form <object> <verb>ing (or similar), such as "Car Servicing," "Invoice Handling," and "Customer Management."
- By *hierarchical level*. Business use cases are placed at the highest level of the requirements package, with system use cases being decompositions from them.
- By *color, stereotype, or both*. Business use cases are shown white or pale blue; system use cases are shown blue. If implementation use cases are used, they are shown indigo or dark blue.

The color convention (and the third level, implementation use cases) was defined by Cockburn (1997), who provides an analogy for explaining the choices. System use cases—the ones we will be primarily concerned with in understanding the functionality of the system—are at "sea level" and therefore blue. Above them in the pale blue sky are the business use cases. Below them in the murky indigo depths (where business analysts and users should hesitate to venture) are implementation use cases, which actually provide more information about *how* rather than *what* functionality is being provided. Kites up in the air, boats floating at sea level, and fishes swimming underneath the sea can provide optional icons for diagrams in black and white. These three levels represent the different levels that a system can be perceived:

- The stakeholders (or business sponsor) are up with the kites; they are interested in the business use cases and view the system from the context of the business process (or processes) that it supports.
- The end-users are at sea level; they are interested in the system use cases and view the system in terms of how they use it to complete their job.
- The IT, development, and support staff are swimming with the fishes; they take a low-level view of how the system works. Their requirements are expressed not only in terms of use cases, but also as other nonfunctional requirements that are likely to mold the development of the system.

Switching from the level of business use case to system use case often means that the actors change. For example, in our car servicing system, the actor for the business use case Car Servicing is likely to be the end customer whose *goal* is to service his car. When we consider the more detailed system use cases and which actors actually have access to the system, we may discover that only garage staff access the system and so will be the actors for the system use cases of Schedule Service and Service Car.

In this chapter we focus on capturing the functionality of the system. We mention nonfunctional requirements, sometimes called level of service requirements, briefly in this chapter, as they are also very important to the system's stakeholders and end-users. These are the primary means by which IT users, for example, can ensure that their requirements (for the system to be maintainable, supportable, secure, fast, scalable, and so on) are met. The nonfunctional requirements very often provide architectural guidelines and constraints ans so we'll consider such requirements again in Chapter 8, "The Macro Step: Architecture."

CarServ Business Use Cases

Let's take a look at the first level of use cases for the *CarServ* example, bearing in mind that the business we are considering initially may be broader that just the area we expect to automate. Figure 4-3 shows the business use case diagram for *CarServ*. We have stereotyped the entire diagram as a «business use case diagram» so that readers of the diagram are clear about the level. They should know, therefore, that the customer actor does not necessarily interact with the automated system and that the diagram focuses on stakeholder goals rather than on system user goals. You can see that the diagram includes Car Buying and Part-Exchanging as business use cases, as well as Car Servicing.

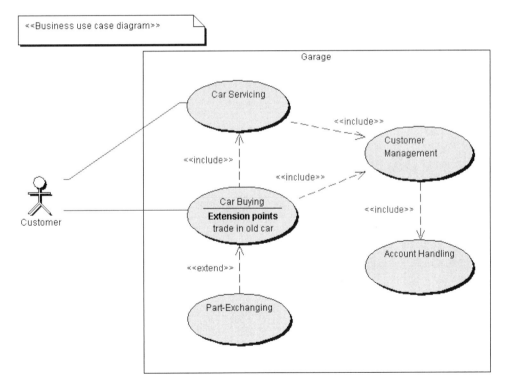

Figure 4–3
A business use case diagram for the *CarServ* garage.

At present, this business is not considering automating the car buying area, but following the hyperlinks from the other business use cases in the diagram leads us into the specification of the automated system for those areas. Following the link from the *Car Servicing* business use case for example, leads to the activity diagram for its process shown in Figure 4-4.

The names of business use cases will very often correspond closely to classes discovered in the domain model, and it is helpful to keep this link. Some of the business use cases suggested by class names in the domain model shown in Figure 3-7 might have been different, though, if we had done this—Car Exchanging rather than Part-Exchanging, for example. As you can see, we haven't felt the need to follow our own naming conventions slavishly where a more natural well-understood phrase existed.

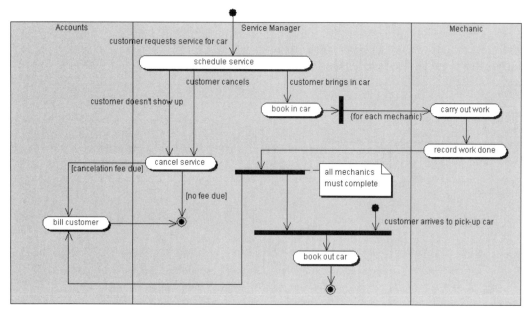

Figure 4–4

Activity diagram for the Car Servicing business use case. (Most activities have a link to system use cases.)

The business process shown in Figure 4-4 shows a number of aspects of both human and automated activity. The "swim lanes"—the three vertical compartments on the diagram labeled Accounts, Service Manager, and Mechanic—divide the activities between the individuals, departments, and subsystems responsible. Some of the activities involve interaction with the automated system, and it is these activities that we can hyperlink directly to system use cases. We'll see how these same names are used for use cases in the system use case diagram later.

There is also a certain amount of parallelism in the process, as indicated by multiple start states on the diagram (the filled circles) and synchronization bars showing where parallel activities split or join. We'll use this example to explain a number of aspects of activity diagram modeling.

- Usually, an activity takes a period of time to be carried out, and when it is completed, control passes to the next activity following an arrow. See, for example, *bill customer* or *book out car*, which have one unlabeled arrow to their next state.
- If there is more than one arrow away from the activity—see, for example, *cancel service* or *schedule service for car*—then the arrows must be labeled either with mutually exclusive conditions (in square brackets) that can be evaluated when the activity has completed or with events (plain labels) that trigger the next activity. If labeled with events, it is the first one that occurs after the activity has completed that will be followed.
- When two or more arrows enter an activity (without a synchronization bar)—such as *bill customer* or *cancel service*—either of these can trigger the activity; you don't need both.
- On the other hand, where there's a synchronization bar, all the arrows entering the bar must be present for the next activity to start.
- Arrows leaving a synchronization bar indicate parallel activities. So, the synchronization bar labeled with the note "all mechanics must complete" has several implied transitions going in (one for each mechanic), and two going out, so that billing the customer and booking out the car can occur in any order or in parallel.

Decision Points and Object Flow

Sometimes, people prefer to show decision points in activity diagrams with diamond-shaped icons. In UML these stand for activities that just evaluate the exit conditions, so the following diagram (Figure 4-5) shows entirely equivalent logic to the corresponding part of Figure 4-4, but the decision point has greater visual emphasis.

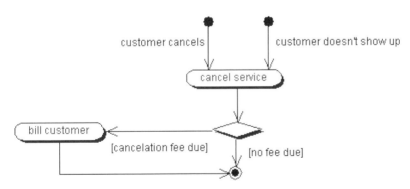

Figure 4–5
An alternative way to show decision points in activity diagrams.

Using diamonds in activity diagrams emphasizes their similarity to flow charts, an ancient and trusty notation that is familiar to so many people (from the little plastic templates they used to have in their geometry sets!). This can help make these diagrams more accessible to the users, businesspeople, and software professionals who we want to validate them—but it does take more space on the diagram.

Activity diagrams are also related to data flow diagrams,[15] although it's important to note that the arrows show control flow, *not* data flow. Object flow can be added to activity diagrams, which does add some data flow information. For example, in Chapter 1, Figure 1-2 shows an activity diagram of a waterfall-style process. This shows both activities and the flow of objects and what their state is, or how they change state, as a result of the activities.

We could show objects, say the Service object, being transferred between activities and changing state in our business process diagram, Figure 4-4. The Service object is created by the *schedule service* and its status is changed by *book in car* and *book out car*. At some point, though, you need to decide if there is already enough information on a diagram, and we think we've reached that level with this diagram. We'll come back to the changing state of the Service object later in this chapter.

When object flow is shown on an activity diagram, UML (and Together) allows the class from which the object is instantiated to be indicated as well, increasing the cohesiveness of the activity diagram with the domain model.

System Functionality

A good understanding of the business process and the business use cases that we want to support will lead to a good understanding of the essential system functionality we need to implement. As we move on to discuss the system use cases, it's worth pausing to consider how we actually gain this understanding. Our two main allies are, first, good people who are currently active in the business or are users of the current or similar systems, and second, good questions.

What, How, Why?

Discussion with stakeholders such as users, business owners, managers, procurers, customers, and IT staff is the key strategy for developing models of system requirements. We've already talked about business versus system use cases. Recognizing these different levels is one thing, but it's also necessary to move conversations and workshop discussions between these levels. We've found that all it requires is three little words: *what*, *how*, and *why*.

For example, you ask your business stakeholder, maybe even a C-level executive, "*What* is this new system going to do?" He might say something like "It will deliver business benefit to our customers." This is accurate (you hope), but you need a bit more information. So the question to ask is: "*How?*"

He will now be able to tell you, or he could be out of his depth immediately! If the latter, he will hopefully point you at someone who can answer the question, who might say, "Well, customers will be able to book in a car for services, and pay when they pick up the car or on account." This is more like it. Note that what's been described here is a selection of *business* use cases.

---

15. In fact, in the UML metamodel, activity diagrams share nearly all their semantics with state charts rather than any other sort of diagram. An activity is merely a kind of state, transition from which is generally triggered by the completion of the activity.

Let's go the other way. You ask, "What is this new system going to do?" This time, you're talking to one of the IT support staff who maintains the current system. She says, "Well, it needs to send our file feed to System X, and listen on this port for information from System Y." So the question to ask is "Why?" Hopefully, our IT staffer will tell you—but if no one knows why that file is sent over to System X, then it's probably an implementation detail of the current system that we can ignore. Note that here you've heard described some implementation-level use cases rather than *system* use cases.

This "why" question is also useful for business use cases. Let's go back to our business use case: "Customers will be able to book in their car for regular services." So, ask *why* customers would want to book in cars for a service. The answers will vary:

- One answer might be that customer wants to keep her car running. Her car could be important to her work, with a missed appointment due to car trouble potentially proving expensive. This customer recognizes that her car needs regular servicing to remain reliable.
- Another answer could be that the customer wants to keep within the law. If he has a broken taillight, then he doesn't want to be pulled over. This customer's requirement is for *ad hoc* servicing. This requirement would also apply to the customer who might be hearing mysterious squeaking from behind the glove box.

So, perhaps the garage could instead address these more fundamental user goals. For example, for regular maintenance, the garage could approximate the mileage that each customer is likely to be covering and send out a reminder when it estimates that the car must be due for a service. If the garage sold the car in the first place, then the first service could be automatically scheduled for some time in the future. For ad hoc services (for customers with old cars, perhaps), the company might proactively send out reminders for routine maintenance. And so on.

What we're specifying here is still a car servicing system, but it offers more "value-add" because it addresses a more fundamental user goal: making sure that the car is kept in good running order. It's an interesting exercise to do; try it on some systems you are or have been involved with, and see if you can come up with business generating features.

CarServ System Use Cases

Our activity diagram for the Car Servicing process led us to a number of system use cases, like *book in car, schedule service,* and *bill customer*. We might also look at the goals of actors we've identified to discover more use cases and at the domain model where system functionality has also been discussed. We need to bring together all this information in a set of use case diagrams that provides a view of the key functionality to be implemented.

Figure 4-6 shows our system use case diagram. We might have several use case diagrams, possibly even several per business use case. Here we are just using one, showing four separate systems, each representing a separate logical subsystem of the functionality. The *Customer Management System* deals with the contact management functionality and acts as the backbone to both the *Car Servicing System* and *Car Sales System*. There is also a separate *Accounting System* that deals with functionality related to invoicing and payments. We are using this functional decomposition, corresponding roughly to the business use cases, as a mechanism for organizing the functional requirements. It does not necessarily follow that the system design will follow the same decomposition, though of course it may to some extent.

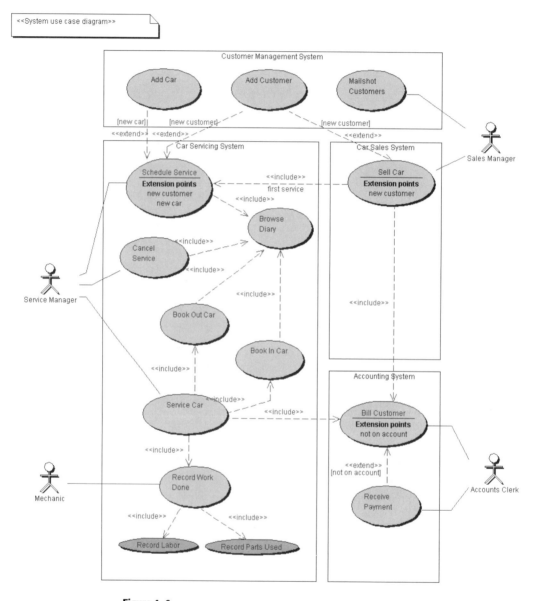

Figure 4–6
CarServ system use case diagram.

Note that the *Customer* actor from the business use case diagram is no longer an actor in the system use case diagram, because the customer does not interact directly with the automated system. Instead, it is the employee roles in the garage that are the actors: *Service Manager, Sales Manager, Mechanic,* and *Accounts Clerk.*

The *Car Buying* business use case in Figure 4-3 maps over to the *Sell Car* system use case in Figure 4-6, and the two are hyperlinked to show that one is the realization of the other. Similarly, the *Car Servicing* business use case has multiple equivalent system use cases, which are also hyperlinked, in some cases via the activity diagram.

Not all the analysis for the system use cases is completed at this stage, but the normal flows for the main use cases do need to be completed. Here are the normal flows for those involving servicing to give you a flavor.

Schedule Service

1. The service manager asks for the customer's name and zip code, and enters this information into the system.
2. The system verifies that the customer is known and displays the cars that are known to be owned by the customer.

Extension Point: *new customer*

3. The service manager confirms that the car details are correct, being sure to ask the customer which car is to be serviced if the customer owns more than one.

Extension Point: *new car*

4. Include *Browse Diary.*
5. The service manager selects a possible date to perform the service (note: The system does not automate this directly), and verifies that this date is good with the customer. When a suitable date has been chosen, the service manager schedules the service for the car and assigns mechanics to the job.
6. The system records this scheduled service and indicates that it has been recorded successfully.

Service Car

1. When a customer arrives at the service desk with the keys of the car to be serviced, the service manager enters the customer's name and car details onto the system.
2. The system lists the services outstanding for the car; there should be one for the current day.
3. Include *Book In Car.*
4. For every mechanic involved in performing the service, include *Record Work Done.*
5. When all work done has been recorded, then include *Bill Customer.*
6. When customer arrives to pick up car, then include *Book Out Car.*

Add Customer

Extends:	Schedule Service
Condition:	[new customer]
Extension Point:	new customer
Extends:	Sell Car
Condition:	[new customer]
Extension Point:	new customer

1. The service manager records details of the new customer.
2. The system verifies the data and associates the customer with the current service.

Add Car

Extends:	Schedule Service
Condition:	[new car]
Extension Point:	new car

1. The service manager records details of the new car.
2. The system verifies the data and associates the car with the current service.

Browse Diary

1. The service manager specifies a date, searching forward or back, day by day or month by month. The service manager can also reset the current date.
2. The system indicates which services are already booked for the specified date.

Book In Car

1. Include *Browse Diary*.
2. The service manager checks that the car is due to be booked in and marks the car as booked in. The actual mileage is noted.
3. The system updates the service with the mileage and marks the car as having been booked in.

Record Work Done

1. The mechanic enters the details of the car he is working on. Optionally, the mechanic can specify a date, but if not specified, then today's date is assumed.
2. The system verifies that there is a service for that car on that date.
3. Provided that the car has been booked in and has not yet been booked out, the mechanic may enter details of the work that he has done on the service.
4. Include *Record Labor*.

5. Include *Record Parts Used*.
6. If the mechanic has finished his work on the car, he may indicate that all his work has been recorded.
7. The system records the details of the work done whether or not the mechanic has finished recording his work.

Bill Customer

1. Include *Browse Diary*.
2. The accounts clerk selects the relevant service and requests bill.
3. The system calculates and displays bill.
4. The accounts clerk checks and requests printout of the bill for confirmation by the customer.
5. The system prints the bill.
6. If necessary, the accounts clerk can enter adjustments for the labor costs and the charges made for parts.
7. The system records these adjustments against the service.
8. System confirms customer is "on account" and sends the invoice to the invoice address.

Extension point: *not on account*

Book Out Car

1. Include *Browse Diary*.
2. The service manager selects the service and checks the status of the service and the bill. If ready, she indicates that the car is being picked up.
3. The service is marked as completed, and the car as picked up.

Receive Payment

Extends:	*Bill Customer*
Condition:	[not on account]
Extension Point:	not on account

1. If the customer wishes to pay for the work immediately, the accounts clerk indicates immediate payment.
2. If the customer is not an account customer, the system displays immediate payment is required.
3. The accounts clerk receives payment and enters the payment details.
4. The system records the payment against the service.

When writing down the flow of system use cases, we like to think we are on a see-saw: The actor makes this *request* to the system, and then the system does this work, and gives this *response*—and so on, until the use case completes. These system response pairs are important, and they help us to discover the system events that drive the business process within the automated system.

The examples above are only the normal flows for the use cases. As you read through them, some harder cases may well have occurred to you, such as what if the customer's credit card is declined, or what if the customer doesn't show up to pick up the car! This is what the alternate flow property is for in Together, so that you can separately record all those different conditions without confusing the straightforward normal case.

Scenarios

The normal and alternate flows will give rise to a number of scenarios for each use case. Each scenario describes a concrete execution path, where the use case either succeeds or fails, based on the defined flows. We will use these scenarios when generating test cases for the requirement. There are a couple of common approaches to documenting scenarios:

- Document each scenario in its entirety.
- Document the main scenario (normal flow) and then describe the other scenarios in terms of exceptions and variations to this main scenario.

Cockburn (1997) has shown how the second alternative works well, and this is the approach we prefer. In Together, you'll find that there are two properties of a use case to describe the scenarios: the aforementioned normal flow and alternate flow. We find that these standard properties work well enough so long as you document only the variations from normal in the alternate flow section. Alternatively, you can add additional fields to the use case template using Together's open API[16] so that each alternate flow has its own field. Sometimes we simply put everything under normal flow, which is also fine for small use cases.

An alternative way of documenting scenarios is to continue our use of activity diagrams. Every step in a scenario could be considered an activity on an activity diagram. Moreover, it is then possible to bring all the different scenarios (success, failure, etc.) for a single use case onto a single activity diagram. In effect, they are represented by the different paths through the process on the diagram. Figure 4-7 shows an example.

Note that because this is a system use case, we have a swim lane for the system to show activities to be carried out by the system. Be careful to keep activities here to descriptions of *what* should be done rather than details of sequence and algorithms, which are all about *how* and properly live in the design parts of our model.

Documenting scenarios in this way seems quite appealing, but is it always a good idea? Remember that the point of use cases and scenarios is to get sign-off from the business users that the specification and scope of the system you intend to build is correct. If the business users are happy to review the scenarios as activity diagrams, then good. But there are still two further issues. The first is that it's harder to identify the request/response pairs from a scenario when it has been expressed as pathways within an activity diagram. When we start showing the design using sequence diagrams (see Chapter 7, "The Micro Step: Design and Implement"), we will

16. We show you more about how to use this in Chapter 7. Alternatively you can use the Inspector Property builder (*Tools ◊ Inspector Property Builder*) to add simple properties.

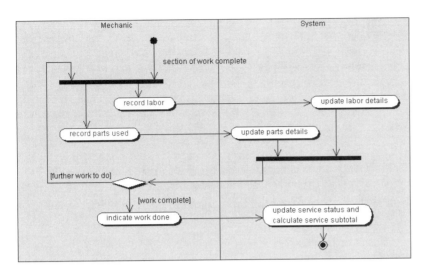

Figure 4–7
Activity diagram for the *Record Work Done* system use case.

make the system responses explicit, and this is probably the best place to keep that information. Remember, our goal as far as possible is to express each piece of information about the system in only one place. This avoids getting into detailed design, and that's the second issue—use cases are about analysis rather than design.

Actors are a key part of the use case model, and so far we have paid them scant attention. Actors represent the roles of people and systems that interact with the system being specified. We often brainstorm to discover the actors before considering use cases because it is the goals of the actors that indicate the use cases.

Looking at the actor's role in detail and examining all the ways of fulfilling the actor's goals will lead to a detailed list of required system functionality in the form of use cases. This list and the priorities we assign to them is a key tool we will use in planning the delivery of system features, release by release.

Besides forming what could be a very long list of desired features, there's another reason to consider actors in detail: to gain an understanding of the *type* of system that is needed, particularly the style of interaction with the system that will be appropriate to the users the system is likely to have. In reality, there may be thousands of users who will be adopting the actor's role, and it's likely to cause problems when the system goes live if there had been no empathy between the developer and the user/actor when the system was being developed. This is where it can be useful to use *personas*.

Actors Versus Personas

In his book *The Inmates are Running the Asylum* (Cooper 1999), Cooper observes that computer systems and consumer products such as cars, cam-

The Stakeholder
Step: Specify
Requirements

eras, and video recorders are incredibly difficult for most people to use, and that the reason for this is not the fault of the users! What is missing from so many of these systems and products is effective "interaction design": the choice of ways of interacting with the system that are natural and intuitive to the particular type of users that system has. Sometimes, long lists of use cases defining more and more functionality for the system miss the point. The few, very frequently executed use cases need much more attention to make the systems usable.

What can we do to capture requirements for the interaction design? Further lists of nonfunctional requirements, such as "the system shall be user friendly" clearly won't help. More specific goals, such as "effective staff training for the service manager shall be achievable in 2 hours," may do. They set the parameters and help inform the trade-off that must be made by the designers between providing more and more functionality and providing a system that is understandable and intuitive.

Cooper makes an interesting suggestion. He builds on the idea of actors by instantiating them as "personas," fictitious people who represent the type of people that will be using the system. He gives them not only names (Betty, Joe, Marge) but detailed personal histories, and pictures of them are created to hang on the development team's wall.

The advantage that is gained by introducing personas for the key actor roles is that the designers can make a real connection through them to the ultimate end-users of the software being developed. The developers focus their efforts on the necessary functionality (rather than the mere "nice to have") and on making the functionality accessible, intuitive, enjoyable, and natural to people who are like the particular persona that the team is designing for.

The key actors in our system that we need to understand are the service manager and the mechanic. It will be important to go and visit the garages where the system might be used and meet the people who do these jobs. Several composite personas, representing different types of people who have this role, can be built up. Some service managers are home computer users and also familiar with typical business systems. Probably the majority, though, have much more interest in automotive engineering, staff management, and customer relations, and would like to keep the amount of time using a screen, keyboard, and mouse to an absolute minimum. After defining several such contrasting personas, the team is likely to discover that one of them, more than any other, is the one who they most need to consider in the interaction design. To integrate the persona into our model, an HTML description of the persona could be linked to the relevant actors in the use case model.

Using Actors as Security Roles

The definition of actors and their links to the use cases they require turns out to have another important use—in defining security roles. Actors in UML, as we have seen, are actually definitions of roles.[17] We also encounter roles in security systems that control access to certain functionality

---

17. Ivar Jacobson's original Swedish word for actor is in fact more accurately translated as "role."

within the system. Using roles simplifies the task of security administration, since many users' permissions (all those that have some common role) can effectively be defined in one go. For example, Java's implementation of security for EJBs and for servlets provides methods such as `isCallerIn-Role()` and `isUserInRole()` so that the EJB or servlet being invoked can throw an exception if the caller does not belong to the correct role.

To determine the permissions that need be assigned to the role, we can use our use case model. The functions performed by an actor correspond to the permissions that should be assigned to the role that represents that actor in the security subsystem.

Most security implementations (the good ones) provide for a many-to-many relationship between users and roles. Please reject any system that has only a many-to-one relationship between users and roles. Administering security in this way quickly becomes unmanageable because of all the permutations of users. For example, a security system that supports many-to-many relationships might define just five roles and allow users to have any combination of those five roles. A security system that supports only many-to-one relationships would need to define up to 5! (that is, 5 factorial or 120) roles to cater for all possible combinations!

So, with a suitable security implementation, this is mostly a routine mapping from actors to roles. Each actor corresponds directly to a role. If an end-user can act as a certain actor with respect to the system, then she needs to be granted the corresponding security role to obtain permissions to actually accomplish the task.

However, there is one wrinkle of which you should be aware. UML allows the generalization/specialization relationship to be applied between actors. In other words, if actor B is a specialization of actor A, then any actor B can accomplish everything that actor A can do, as well as any additional capabilities that actor B may be granted.

If you are to use this modeling device and want to use these actors as roles in the security configuration, then the question to ask is, Does your security implementation support the idea of hierarchical roles? Some systems certainly do, but many do not. If yours does not, then you may be best advised not to specialize actors, and instead explicitly identify the use cases that each actor can perform.

Batch Processing

A question that often comes up when we're doing system use cases is where to put the work that the system does during its (typically overnight) batch. Who is the actor here?

If we stand back and look at the business use case, then it usually is possible to identify an actor who ultimately gains value from the processes performed by the batch. In our *CarServ* example, we might decide that the system should send out a mailshot to remind customers whose cars are due a service soon. Such a mailshot would likely be invoked during an end-of-week batch. Who is the actor here? Who gains value?

We suppose that ultimately it is the garage's owners who gain value, because there's more likelihood of customers booking in their car, but "owner" is not an actor, as the owner does not interact directly with the system. A simple solution is to stereotype an actor as «batch» and connect the use cases triggered by the calendar or clock to this actor.

Clarifying Requirements with State Chart Diagrams

State charts can also be used as part of the specification process, and they give a usefully different slant. Rather than look at the behavior of a whole system or business process, they describe what happens to the state of one type of object when various events occur. We discussed system events earlier in this chapter, and our models already contain many of them. Some are external events that are shown on the business process activity diagrams, such as *customer brings in car*, *customer cancels*, and *customer arrives to pick up car* on Figure 4-4. Some are system events arising on the see-saw of interaction between actors and the system, for example *accounts clerk requests printout*, *mechanic indicates all his work has been recorded*, and *accounts clerk enters the payment details*.

Let's look at the impact events like these have on a Service object. This class was discovered in our domain model (see Chapter 3, Figure 3-7) and is shown on its own in Figure 4-8.

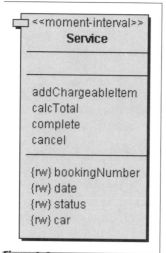

Figure 4–8

The Service class from our initial domain model.

Figure 4-9 shows a specification-level state chart diagram for this class, showing the system events that change the state of Service objects.

There is a strong correspondence (we hope) between the behavior of this object shown in the state chart diagram and the Car Servicing business process shown in the activity diagram, Figure 4-4. In the activity diagram, actions are shown in the boxes, whereas corresponding events show up on the lines (or "internal transitions") in state charts. This diagram should help us in several ways to clarify the requirements and to update the domain model to be consistent with them. Furthermore, if we then consider the operations needed on the Service class to handle the events, we can tie

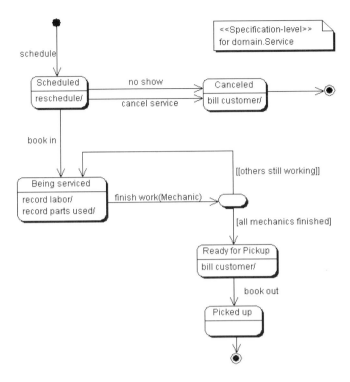

Figure 4–9

State chart for objects of the Service class showing events.

together the business process, use cases, events, state charts, and domain model classes.

Figure 4-10 shows the state chart after we have added the action expressions on the transition lines. The labels on these lines are of the form

```
[<condition>]<event>(<argument>)/<action expression>
```

each part of which is optional. So, the transition to the new state takes place when the event occurs (or after actions defined in the state have completed if there is no event), provided that the condition evaluates as true at that time. The optional argument provides further information about the event— for example, the event *finish work* in this state chart has an argument to indicate which mechanic has finished. As the transition to the new state occurs, the action specified by the action expression is carried out, where the action in this case should correspond to an operation on the target class.

By completing this information, we are able to review the correspondence between all the views and update the operations on the Service domain class. As the actions are added to state chart, we check that the domain class actually has a suitable operation and add it in if it is missing. As can be seen in Figure 4–11, several operations have been added and a number renamed or changed as a result of completing the state chart.

When we are thinking purely at the specification level, we might prefer to leave the state chart at the first stage, as in Figure 4-9, with the system

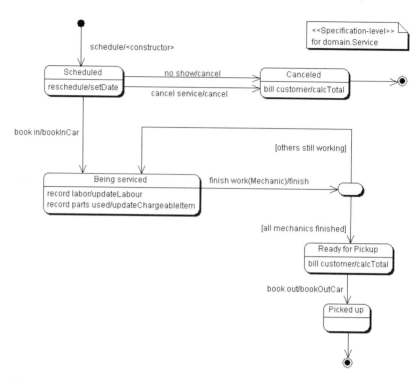

Figure 4–10

State chart for *Service* showing both events and actions.

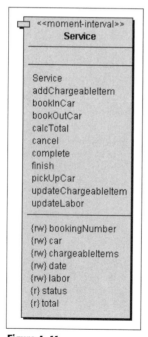

Figure 4–11

Updated Service Class showing additional and modified operations.

events identified but the corresponding operations omitted and only added later (if at all) when carrying out more detailed design (see Chapter 7 for more about this). However, if we do add operations to the class model at this stage, Together will help us to keep all the views in step—at least, it will if we use graphical editing to rename operations (or even better using *Refactoring → Rename operation*), rather than deleting them and adding new ones or using only the text editor.

UML defines a notation to capture functional requirements through use cases and activity diagrams, but it is also important to capture nonfunctional requirements. What do we mean by nonfunctional requirements? Here are some examples:

- Maximum throughput (number of users, number of concurrent users)
- Maximum response time (for the maximum throughput or for different throughput levels)
- Mean time to recover after system failure (sometimes broken out into different system failure types, such as power, hard disk, data center; this last would involve invoking full-scale disaster recovery procedures)
- Maximum acceptable loss of data in event of disk failure
- Maximum available batch window
- Maximum available window for off-line maintenance

These are perhaps sometimes overlooked because there is little standardization in how they are captured; certainly UML does not currently define any notation. However, you might capture some of these in an SLA (service-level agreement); we've certainly used these sorts of documents in the past.

There are many variations on this. Sometimes response time varies by the type of transaction, sometimes by the time of year (many businesses see seasonal variations in the amount of work to be supported), sometimes even by who is invoking the transaction (we'll make sure the response time for transactions used directly by the business stakeholder is small to keep the political tigers at bay!).

We often find that specifying required throughput is neglected; the response times tend to be stated as "less than 1 second", rather than "less than 1 second for 50 concurrent online users". But when we ask, we find that the business hardly ever insists that the system needs to support 1 million concurrent users, for example, so there must be some notional requirement—it just has not been articulated.

Also, we often find that businesses specify very high targets for nonfunctional requirements. You know what this looks like: less than 1 second response time, no data loss, 24 x 7 x 365, and so on. As technologists, we know that this is achievable, but we also know that it is very, very expensive, whereas 24 x 6.5 is often much cheaper. Will the business really generate sufficient profit in the early hours of Sunday mornings to cover the cost difference in implementing the full 24 x 7?

The user community may also have other expectations of the system being developed. For example, it probably should be

- Usable
- Reliable
- Easy to maintain (that is, enhancements should be doable within a reasonable timeframe)

The usability of the system is something that can be addressed using such techniques as personas (discussed earlier), and may be tested by user feedback and by the time required for effective training. Reliability and maintainability are ultimately going to depend upon the software architecture. Indeed, these are some of the primary motivations for defining architecture, a topic we look at in more detail in Chapter 8.

There's another type of nonfunctional requirement, this time defined not by the end-users but by the operations (production support) staff. These often involve some sort of instrumentation. Examples include

- Ability to turn on debugging or tracing, on a per-user basis.
- Ability to capture current throughput of system (for example, as the number of database calls made per second).
- Ability to dump memory in event of severe error.

These nonfunctional requirements can be used to improve the quality of the design, and indeed we sometimes refer to all of these nonfunctional requirements as quality requirements.

Another category of nonfunctional requirements is security and auditing. Often, these are nonnegotiable—they may be required for legal reasons.

In a small team environment, all of these nonfunctional requirements need to be captured; they are just as important as the functional requirements. Sometimes similar documents will have been written already for some other project from which it can be cribbed, but the information is needed to guide the implementation and particularly system testing and user acceptance.

As well as considering which non-functional requirements should be captured, the team must also give consideration to where they are stored and accessed. Some non-functional requirements may be attached to use cases in Together (such as information about response time, frequency and throughput). Others are likely to be captured in stand-alone documents which can then be hyperlinked to the requirements package. In order to assist configuration management, impact analysis and traceability the total set of these externally held requirements should be split into several files which can be separately version controlled. Composite documents can then be generated which bring all the requirements together, with information from UML diagrams, textual properties and the external documents.

In Together you'll find that use case descriptions are stored either in their own file—which allows us to version manage requirements one by one—or as a group of use cases within a use case diagram. To see this, open up the *CarServ* project and look at the `System Use Case` use case diagram. Now look at the underlying file system, and you'll see that there's a single file in the `\diag\com\bettersoftwarefaster\carserv\requirements` directory called `System Use Case.dfUseCase`. Open this file up in your favorite text editor (it's just an ASCII text file), and you'll see the information for all the uses cases in this diagram (stored in Together's internal file format). This makes it difficult for two developers to update use case requirements as part of two separate enhancements, since only one developer would be able to check out the use case file at a time.

On the other hand, by selecting the *create design elements as standalone* option in Together[18], use cases will be created in their own file and are then able to be separately version managed. With this option checked, all new design elements are created in separate files so that elements such as Objects, Actors, and States are kept in separate files in the package where the current diagram is located. The elements are assembled within a use case diagram as shortcuts.

Configuration Management

In this chapter and the previous one, we have specified a domain model—giving us an understanding of the principal types of objects in our problem domain—and seen how the functionality of the system can be specified using use cases in a contextual business process specified with activity diagrams. Finally, we have seen how for a few classes it is worth bringing all these views together with state charts that reflect how the state of objects change as the business process proceeds, requiring operations on the class to handle the system events.

When discussing the minimum metamodel, we noted that every requirement—in our case functional requirements map to the system use cases—requires a set of tests. We'll be looking at testing in Chapter 6, "The Continuous Step—Measure the Quality," but first we need to consider how to control the project, particularly in the iterative and the changeable environment that modern projects need to work in to stay competitive. So, next we look at Chapter 5, "The Controlling Step: Feature-Centric Management."

What's Next

---

18. The way to do this may vary between versions of Together, but it should be found under *Tools* → *Options* → *Project Level* (or *Default Level*). In version 6.0 the *Create design elements as standalone* is found under the *General* category.

The Controlling Step:
Feature-Centric
Management

*A plan does not predict the future. Rather it provides
the basis for responding to an unknown future.*
Anon

*I love deadlines. I like the whooshing sound
they make as they fly by.*
Douglas Adams

*The sooner you fall behind, the more time
you will have to catch up.*
Paul's Second Law

*Proposal managers tend to be optimistic; project
managers tend to be pessimistic.*
Barry Boehm

I never predict anything, and I never will.
Paul Gascoigne

How **do you manage small but fast-moving projects? One important aspect
is to specify requirements (or features) in a form that allows them to be
separately planned and implemented. Feature-centric management means
combining the units of requirements with the units of planning, and this in
turn means that changing your mind about priorities as the project develops is
both feasible and desirable. This is the focus of this chapter.**

Small teams have certain inherent advantages over large teams.
Although they may not have the large resources, back-up teams and corporate infrastructure to smooth their path, the evidence is that they can usually outperform large teams for software development in productivity,
creativity, and quality.

The reasons are not hard to imagine. Software development is a creative activity as well as an engineering discipline.[19] To work in any creative field, we need an environment that helps individuals to experiment, to change, to try out different alternatives and keep what works, to create without interruptions or distractions, and to take time to think. In their groundbreaking work *Peopleware* (DeMarco & Lister 1987), the authors refer to "being in the flow" for this state of highly efficient working, whether for intellect workers, sportsmen, or others. It happens when your brain switches into another gear, taking care of the mechanical parts of the job, leaving the brain free to focus on the purpose of the activity.

Unfortunately, it takes some time of uninterrupted working to get "in flow." So, then, the tasks and structures that we put in place to help make management, quality control, and planning easier are the very things that interrupt the creative work of intellect workers and stop them performing to their true potential. In large teams this effect can be most marked, and it is not unusual for software development teams to contain a *minority* of people who actually produce and test software. It is almost inevitable that productivity will be lower in such teams compared to those where there is very little overhead of non-development staff and where the management processes do not obstruct productive work.

This does not mean that small teams do not need management, planning, and quality control. In the next chapter we will spend some time looking at how we can make quality measurement a continuous and as far as possible subliminal part of the software development process. The hope is that we can make this so much a part of both the automated environment and the culture of the team that it is not intrusive to the point of taking people "out of flow." In this chapter we focus on making management and control processes effective but unobtrusive.

Management of a small team needs to provide the structures for planning, monitoring, and change without losing the inherent advantages of the creative small-team culture. It is a difficult balance to strike, particularly as there is fierce debate raging in the industry between the "lightweight" or agile process camp and the "heavyweight" or mature process camp. To avoid projects becoming casualties of religious wars, it is important for project managers to understand the common goals that both camps are striving for—productivity and quality being two of them—and choose the techniques that are appropriate.

Getting in Control

There are a number of planning questions that the development team and their management are primarily concerned with on the project. Here are the questions that shape the initial decision making:

- What is required?
- What benefit will it provide?
- How long will it take?
- What will it cost?

19. Actually, this statement may turn out to be controversial from two camps: those that think it is not "creative" and those that think it is not "engineering." Writing great software, however, is clearly a discipline that combines art and science.

Such questions need to be addressed in the feasibility study for projects and in the decision making that secures their funding. It is important that this analysis is taken into account as the project moves forward too. Circumstances are likely to change, which affects what is required and what the benefits will be. Knowledge of how requirements can be achieved will also be gained, which will change the estimates of schedule and budget.

Once under way though, the focus of the planning questions shift somewhat, to:

- How are we progressing (time and budget)?
- What are the priorities, and have they changed?
- What issues and risks does the project face?
- How can the issues and risks be addressed or mitigated?

These questions are the underlying drivers for our management process, along with the guiding principle for all projects—"keep it simple," or as Einstein said "as simple as possible (but no simpler)."[20]

To achieve this simplicity, the guidelines we propose are:

- The process should be *feature-centric*, by which we mean that the units of requirements (e.g., use cases) should be unified with the units of planning (e.g., tasks or activities).
- Project planning should be based around *timeboxes* (rather than phases), making the process essentially "self-similar" throughout the lifecycle of the system.
- The project plan should be *adaptive*, responsive to the changing risks and benefits of the system and business environments.

Why Feature-Centric?

Iterative lifecycles are more complex than linear ones with the same steps. The concurrency implied by the iterations and the dependencies between stages of the process make this inevitable. Given our goal is to simplify the lifecycle in order that whole teams can understand and implement it, we need to regain some simplicity. The first strategy for simplification of the lifecycle is feature-centric planning.

We use the term feature-centric to refer to development processes that combine (to differing degrees) the expression of requirements with the units of activity for planning purposes. A feature in such processes can be viewed as a unit of "plannable functionality."

Feature-Driven Development (FDD) uses features in this way (Coad, Lefebvre, & De Luca 1999; Palmer & Felsing 2002; Carmichael & Swainston-Rainford 2000), as does the development process EVO specified by Tom Gilb (Gilb 1997, 2002). Extreme Programming (XP) has "user stories" (Beck 2000) and to some extent Unified Process (UP) is feature-centric with its use cases (Jacobson, Booch, & Rumbaugh 1999; Kruchten 1998; Ambler & Constantine 2000; Hunt 2000) as is the Dynamic Systems Development Method (DSDM) with its requirements catalogue (Stapleton 1997).

---

20. In fact, for small projects, "simpler than possible" (meaning not including absolutely everything that should be there) may actually work better than overcomplication.

In describing FDD, Coad defines a feature as a "schedulable piece of user functionality, something that delivers value to the user." The emphasis on schedulable is important. We would also broaden this definition to include some "nonuser" functionality. For example, what if we want to provide runtime debugging so that production support or the technical help desk can track down a thorny bug? This is certainly going to need some development effort, but it doesn't deliver any direct user value. So, instead of talking only about users, let's talk about system stakeholders. Typically we mean end-users, but we also mean those who support the system, occasionally even other developers.

So, we use the term "feature" to refer to these units of schedulable functionality. Why introduce another term when we are already using use cases to capture and express functional requirements? The answer is that use cases are not derived primarily from the *planning* perspective and therefore may not always be suitable for scheduling. However, as the first cut ,we can take the use cases as the starting point for features, as shown in Table 5-1.

Table 5–1
Initial Features List

Req-ID	Name
10001	Schedule Service
10002	Service Car
10003	Add Customer
10004	Add Car
10005	Browse Diary
10006	Book In Car
10007	Record Work Done
10008	Bill Customer
10009	Book Out Car
10010	Record Labor
10011	Record Parts Used

To be useful for planning, the features list must also contain information about estimated cost and schedule priority. Usually, development time is the key driver on cost, so an estimate in person days is usually sufficient. Information about priority can be expressed in various ways, but ultimately it will come down to the order in which features are implemented. We return to both of these topics shortly, after we have considered timeboxes.

Features Mean Flexibility
Dan Haywood

While I was working at Sybase Professional Services, I was the project manager for a year on a 10-person project for one of the investment banks in London. The previous project manager had delivered two releases of the application over the preceding 12 months, on a fixed-cost contract. Such contracts usually generate arguments about what was or wasn't included in the requirements specification, and I was glad I hadn't been involved with that stage. But they delivered a good, working system, and that was my starting point.

When I took over the project management role, the new engagement was on a time and materials basis; the customer was starting to trust that we could deliver and that we would explain when we could not deliver. My initial plan was for a new version every 3 months, and indeed our first release was 3 months after my taking over. But it very soon became clear that the business would be pressuring us to deliver new functionality much more rapidly, even on a monthly basis.

One of the first steps I took was to persuade the customer to invest in some scalable configuration management software. The main capabilities I needed were (a) parallel checkout to allow fixing of production defects alongside new development features, (b) proper support of workspaces to allow developers to create a working environment quickly, and (c) automated build management.

Another innovation for the project was the introduction of "workpackages"— closely related to features. The three types of workpackage were (a) specification or analysis work, where the deliverable was an update to the functional specification documentation only; (b) development and implementation, where the design and the code were changed and unit-tested; and (c) system test, which involved system testing new functionality as well as regression testing existing code.

Production defects*also did not get fixed until they were wrapped up in workpackages. Generally (and as is typical), these defects were small and simple to fix, and so several would be fixed in a single workpackage.

Each week the primary business analyst, technical architect, and I would meet with the business sponsors, and we'd negotiate. We would inform the business of which workpackages were complete, which were on schedule, and which were slipping. If a workpackage had slipped, then the business was able to make a decision—hang on and defer the release or have us pull the workpackage from the release and deliver the remaining functionality. Being developers, we weren't in a position to make these decisions, but the business was and had enough information to do this sensibly.

Further, the business would inform us of new business requirements; and these would in turn give rise to new analysis workpackages. If a requirement was urgent, then work on one or more currently ongoing workpackages would be suspended; it was the business's decision.

We couldn't have offered this flexibility to the business without this feature-centric approach backed by effective configuration management software. And this flexibility brought further trust between the business and the developers.

The main problem with getting the workpackage approach (specification, development, system test) to work was in getting the requirements and design documentation up to date. Despite the best efforts of the preceding project team, it had become more and more out-of-date because—under a fixed-price contract—their focus had to be on shipping code, not documents. However, once the documentation had been updated, the workpackage model worked most effectively, following a straightforward pattern that was easily understood.

---

*. Production defect = bug, but the term "bug" sounds all cute and cuddly, something that Dan might even enjoy collecting! In contrast, the term "production defect" tells it how it is—a mistake, an error, a fault, a blunder, and something that needs to be fixed.

Why Timeboxes?

The emphasis in most formal development processes is on the *phases* a project goes through and then on the steps within the phases that may or may not be carried out iteratively. This is as true of modern processes, such as UP, as it was of early variants of the waterfall process.[21] Yes, it is clear that projects go through phases. Generally, this is related to the funding and approval processes that start and sometimes terminate them. However, for the day-to-day processes required by software development teams, timeboxes are, in our view, a much more important division than phases. Similar activities take place within every timebox. The timebox has a set period, usually a few weeks at most, and the regular review of progress and requirements makes for agile planning that can respond to problems and opportunities quickly (McConnell 1996).

While phases may be observed in most projects, they are not necessarily something to standardize—they are more the natural consequence of budgeting, team experience and knowledge, and product life-expectancy. We do acquiesce to the use of phases on large projects with multiple teams and organizations, and with multiple levels of sign-off and approval for project funding. With small teams, however, they are an unnecessary complication.

A cynic once put forward a now well-known view of the six phases of a project:

1. Unbounded enthusiasm
2. Total disillusionment
3. PANIC!
4. Frantic search for the guilty
5. Punishment of the innocent
6. Promotion of the uninvolved

You may know of projects where a very approximately mapping can be made from these phases to process phases such as initiation, elaboration, construction, and deployment!

If you do use phases for project management, we still recommend an emphasis on timeboxes within each phase. Timeboxes require frequent, tan-

---

21. Iteration in the waterfall process has always happened, but it was also undesirable. In lifecycles aiming to provide evolutionary delivery (Gilb 1989), iteration is necessary and desirable.

gible, working results and therefore provide essential views of progress at short intervals because a succession of software builds are delivered in an evolutionary manner.

Timeboxes are part of a self-similar development process. Self-similarity in the process can be seen in two ways: The process is

- Similar to itself, regardless of scale.
- Similar to itself, throughout its lifecycle.

Let's look at these in turn.

Self-Similarity by Scale

Self-similarity is a concept used in a number of fields, from chaos theory and emergence to computer graphics and psychology. Certain concepts are similar to themselves regardless of the scale at which they are examined. For example, consider the shapes of clouds, trees, or waves. When you zoom in and look at them at a higher magnification, you find the same patterns repeated at the different scale. Iterative development processes can also display this characteristic so that the general definition of the process applies to

- The activities of a single programmer (or pair of programmers) working over one afternoon,
- The activities of the team over an entire timebox, or even
- The coordination of a group of subcontracting teams between major milestones.

There are certainly differences in these scenarios, but there is also striking similarity. Consider the process shown in Figure 5-1 (you may remember a similar diagram, Figure 1-5 from Chapter 1).

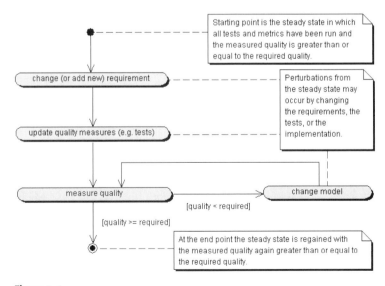

Figure 5-1
A development process that is self-similar at different scales of iteration.

This process is valid at a very large scale to describe, say, a 9 month project to add new functionality and level of service requirements to the system. First, these requirements are identified and suitable acceptance criteria defined by updating the tests and metrics, then measurement of quality and change to the system is carried out iteratively until all the tests and metrics pass. Equally, the process applies at a very fine scale where a single programmer accepts a change request, updates the tests, runs the test, and changes the code until it passes—all within the space of a few hours.

But there are differences in the application of this process at the different scales. Figure 5-2 shows a representation of three important scales in the project: the "day," the timebox, and the milestone, where the milestone will normally represent the delivery of significant new functionality of the system to end-users. The "measure quality" activity is done to different depths at the different scales. On a daily build, the criteria are that

- The developer attests that the software is ready for use by other developers.
- The unit tests for the new code are complete and pass.
- The new code has been integrated with the latest build and regression unit tests completed with no failures.

On a timebox boundary, one of the key metrics that is required for planning purposes is which features have been completed. For this, the functional tests as well as unit tests must be run. Where team size allows, we recommend a separate test team, and it is this team that runs the tests for timebox builds. So, the criteria are

- The test team attests that the tests for the identified features pass.
- The unit tests for all the delivered code are complete and pass.
- The test team attests the quality is suitable for external testing.

On milestones, even more tests and quality measurements are required to pass for the build to be suitable for a milestone build. Usually, as well as the test team there will be some form of user acceptance, beta test, or other external testing for these builds. Additional criteria, such as up-to-date user and maintenance documentation, also apply. The criteria might be

- The test team attests that the tests for the identified features pass.
- The unit tests for all the delivered code are complete and pass.
- Feedback from external testing indicates build is suitable for delivery to users.
- User documentation, user training materials, and software maintenance documentation has been reviewed and is up to date and accurate.

One final question concerning timeboxes is how long should they be. The ideal frequency for a given project depends mainly on the reporting structure of the project. With small teams working directly for empowered end-users with rapidly changing competitive pressures, timeboxes of 3 weeks or less are desirable. Users get new functionality sooner and can change the priorities of the team as situations arise. However, where more formal reporting and control is required by the business, or where there are multiple subcontractors or complex contracts, timeboxes of at least 6 weeks are preferred.

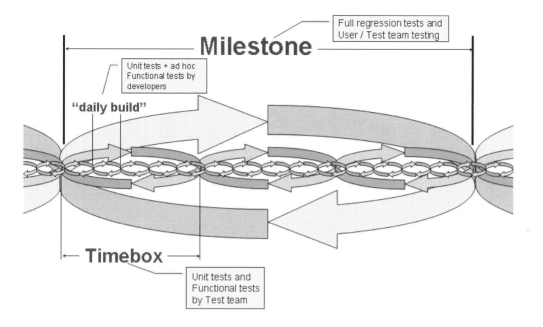

Figure 5–2
Different scales of iteration.

Self-Similarity Through the Lifecycle

As well as being self-similar at different scales, the development process should also be self-similar throughout the lifecycle of the software system. In other words, whether acting in the early stages of a feasibility study for the system or updating a system that has been in the field for many years, the defined process is not essentially different.

The process always starts from a consistent model, where all accepted requirements have tests and these tests pass. The perturbation from this state occurs when a new requirement is accepted into the model. Activity to change the model must then continue until another stable realization of the model is achieved.

We asserted that the simple-as-possible process we apply to controlling software development projects should be feature-centric, based on time-boxes, and finally adaptive. Adaptive means[22] "showing, or having a capacity for, or tendency toward, adaptation"—that is, both adaptable and adapting. Adaptive is also used to imply evolutionary change and organization through emergence. As Highsmith (1999) puts it, "The alternative idea [to deterministic, cause-and-effect driven processes] is an adaptive culture or mindset, of viewing organizations as complex adaptive systems, and of cre-

Why Adaptive?

The Controlling Step: Feature-Centric Management

22. Merriam-Webster's Collegiate Dictionary: *www.m-w.com*.

ating emergent order out of a web of interconnected individuals." While true emergent behavior such as that of ant colonies or fish shoals[23] is a far cry from the management processes of small team projects, there are lessons to draw from them. Perhaps the most important is that management must focus more on culture, communication, feedback, reward systems, pattern recognition and learning than on more traditional command and control.

Enough of philosophical musings—let's be practical about the adaptable and adapting process that development teams need.

The management process we require, like the software we produce, must be flexible enough to deal with the rapidly emerging uncertainties of our world and our business, and it must actually change with those changing priorities.

Having small teams is one key strategy for agility. They are much easier to adapt and direct in changing circumstances. Shifting the management control away from auditing activities and towards measuring the quality of the products is another. That is why much of the management control that we discuss is focused on testing and quality measurement.

We also want to capture the priorities and the changes of priority in the business throughout the development. The features list is where priorities can be recorded using what DSDM calls the MoSCoW rules. DSDM provides some very helpful guidance in ways to control and plan its requirements catalogue, to involve businesspeople and users in the projects, and provide the infrastructure of project management in the tools used by the project. DSDM is not specific to object-oriented systems, UML, or any other analysis/design notation. It must therefore be used in conjunction with methods that do specify these elements of modeling. The MoSCoW rules help with prioritizing requirements—MoSCoW stands for four priority levels: "must have," "should have," "could have," and "want but won't have (yet)." In DSDM the users or business representatives are asked to apply these categories to functional requirements.

Unfortunately, when carrying out workshops to capture these requirements, it is not unusual for nearly all the requirements to be labeled M except for a trivial few that probably would take very little time to implement anyway! If this happens, the prioritizing has gained us nothing. So, two other dimensions need to be included. The first is date of delivery of the feature, and the second is the cost of the feature.

The cost must be estimated by the development team and revised as more information about what is really required and about how it will be implemented emerges. The choice of date of delivery is down to the business representatives, within the constraint that only a fixed amount of cost can be expended each timebox. Of course, the business could assign more resources—always remembering Brook's Law that states if you add resources to a late project, it will become later. Assigning additional resources is a medium to long-term fix, not a way of getting more features completed in the next timebox.

---

23. See Johnson (2001) for a fascinating discussion of *emergence* and how it may be applicable to human organization and software development.

By way of example, let us look at our features list with some costs and MoSCoW priorities added (plus a few more features). See Table 5-2.

Table 5–2
Features List Showing Costs and Priorities by Timebox (TB) and Milestone (M)

Req-ID	Name	Cost (units)	TB1	TB2	TB3	M1	M2
10001	Schedule Service	7	M			M	M
10002	Service Car	6	W	M		M	M
10003	Add Customer	3	S	M		M	M
10004	Add Car	6	W	C	S	S	M
10005	Browse Diary	7	M			M	M
10006	Book In Car	5	W	S	M	M	M
10007	Record Work Done	10	W	W	M	M	M
10008	Bill Customer	2	S	M		M	M
10009	Book Out Car	1	S	M		M	M
10010	Record Labor	1	C	M		M	M
10011	Record Parts Used	2	C	M		M	M
10012	New feature	5	W	W	C	C	M
10013	New feature	10	W	W	W	W	M
10014	New feature	5	W	W	C	C	M
10015	New feature	16	W	W	W	W	M
	Total (M)	**86**	**14**	**15**	**15**	**44**	**86**
	Total (M+S)		**20**	**20**	**21**	**50**	**86**
	Total (M+S+C)		**23**	**26**	**31**	**60**	**86**

The costs in some arbitrary units are shown along with the priorities in each timebox (there are three: TB1, TB2, and TB3) and at the two milestones (M1 and M2). The further timeboxes that would exist between M1 and M2 are not shown, as these are not required while planning for the first milestone.

The assumption is that there are approximately 20 units of development effort available in each timebox. Around 75 percent of that is assigned to must-have features. Depending on the level of risk associated with the features, this might be reduced to 50 percent—if it goes much higher than 75 percent, it is probably only wishful thinking to call them must-haves. The should-have features absorb another 25 percent to bring the combined resources needed for both must-have and should-have features to around 100 percent of the available resources in the timebox(assuming just the must-haves from the previous timebox have been completed). In case the estimates for the must-have and should-have features are too high, a number of could-haves representing a further 25 percent of the timebox resources are also included.

One of the problems of assigning MoSCoW rules to features is keeping the must-haves below a level that they can definitely fit in the timebox. An alternative that we now prefer is to prioritize simply by *ordering* the features list. The MoSCoW attribute for a feature can be derived directly from its position in the list, the cost of the features above it, and the range of effort assigned to each category. For example, the top features in the list are automatically recognized as must-haves up to the point at which 75 percent of available effort has been allocated; in the range 75 to 100 percent of then available effort, they are should-haves, and so on.

Table 5-2 shows just the starting point of the plan, since timebox by timebox we can measure the effort spent on each feature compared to the estimates, and re-estimate the remaining features from this experience. The plan is adaptive, continually re-estimating which features will be delivered on which dates based on the changing business priorities and the actual feedback from the development costs to date.

Estimating the Costs of Features

A key input to the features list is the estimate of effort required for that feature. How does the team arrive at these estimates?

As far as possible, we try to make estimates of features independent of the order in which features are carried out. Some dependencies must be recorded, and these may constrain the plan. For example, all features may require database access and installation of the application server. However, dependency analysis adds a layer of complication to the planning process, and in many cases it is better to ignore dependencies and try to allocate sufficient effort to each feature regardless of the order in which it is carried out.

The first step in estimating the cost of features is to gather your most experienced developers, architects, managers—maybe the whole team, if it is small—with the key business representatives who can explain the purpose and nature of the features being discussed. Each item on the features list is addressed. First, it needs to be described so that there is understanding around the table of what the feature involves. Then, the group needs to put an estimate of development time against each one. It is worth getting each individual to write down his or her own estimate before discussing as a group. Often, it will then be a case of discussing how the highest and lowest figures arose and reaching some consensus on what is most likely. It must be stressed that this is only the first stage of estimating and that as work begins on the features, the estimates will change. However, we do need a starting point.

Each feature will have three workpackages associated with it:

1. Specification: use case and acceptance test specification.
2. Development: development and unit test.
3. System test: running acceptance tests, ad hoc testing and regression tests.

However, during the initial estimation, the figure we are interested in is the "ideal" development cost—that is, the number of hours or days to add this feature, including changes to the documentation and unit tests, assuming all of those hours or days are dedicated to the task.

Depending on the context of your project, you can derive an estimate of specification and system test costs as a percentage of the development cost of features. Or, you can carry out feature-by-feature costing of these work packages as well.

Three-Point Estimating

Three-point estimating is a useful system for estimating projects, and it gives a bit more detail than a single estimate (Putnam & Myers 1992).[24] The team needs to come up with three effort estimates for each feature: the best possible case, worst possible case, and most likely.

An example is shown in Table 5-3. The risk associated with the estimate is captured in the gap between best and worst cases. A very wide range shows that the group really has no idea how much effort is required for that feature!

A spreadsheet can be used to combine the three-point estimates in a number of ways. To total a best estimate for a number of features, use the following formula, which gives weight to the most likely but also takes into account the range from best to worst cases:

$$E = \sum_i \frac{(w_i + 4m_i + b_i)}{6}$$

where b is the best case estimate, w is the worst case estimate, and m is the most likely.

Assuming some sort of normal distribution for your estimates, you can go further and estimate a pseudo standard deviation, ó, for the estimates:

$$\sigma = \sqrt{\sum_i \left(\frac{w_i - b_i}{6} \right)^2}$$

This allows you to give a range and probability for the effort required for the set of features listed:

- There is a 68 percent probability the cost will be between $(E - \sigma)$ and $(E + \sigma)$.
- There is a 95 percent probability the cost will be between $(E - 2\sigma)$ and $(E + 2\sigma)$.
- There is a 99.74 percent probability the cost will be between $(E - 3\sigma)$ and $(E + 3\sigma)$.

The one caution about the three-point estimating technique is that it comes up with such authoritative estimates for what we know is a risky and uncertain business. In a world where nothing is certain, "three-sigma," or 99.74 percent, is as close to certain as you can get. However, if you can find a bookie to give you odds of 10,000 to 26 that the actual effort will be outside the range $E - 3\sigma$ to $E + 3\sigma$, take it every time!

---

24. This reference provides a detailed review of many rigorous estimating techniques of which three-point estimating is just one.

Table 5–3
Three-Point Estimate for a Features List Showing Cost Ranges

| Req-ID | Feature | Cost (units) | | |
		Best case (b)	Most likely (m)	Worst case (w)
10001	Schedule Service	5	6	10
10002	Service Car	5	7	12
10003	Add Customer	2	3	6
10004	Add Car	4	6	8
10005	Browse Diary	6	7	12
10006	Book In Car	3	5	10
10007	Record Work Done	5	10	12
10008	Bill Customer	1	2	4
10009	Book Out Car	1	1	2
10010	Record Labor	1	1	3
10011	Record Parts Used	2	2	5
10012	New feature	3	5	8
10013	New feature	4	10	15
10014	New feature	3	5	10
10015	New feature	10	16	20
		54	**86**	**137**

Most Likely Duration =	**89.1**	
Standard Deviation =	**4.0**	

	Cost will be between		
with 68% probability	**85.1**	and	**93.1**
with 95% probability	**81.1**	and	**97.1**
with 99.74% probability	**77.1**	and	**101.1**

The standard deviation will get smaller if you break workpackages down into smaller and smaller units. So, the larger the number of subtasks with separate estimates, the more accurate the estimate is—that is, the cost range will be narrower. But you must be careful when doing this that the subtasks contain everything implied in the whole task. Otherwise, you will just have a more accurate estimate of the cost of doing only part of the job!

Project Velocity

The prioritized features list with estimated costs for each feature encapsulates the project plan. We now need to ensure that we get feedback from the actual development to ensure that we can not only monitor progress against this plan but also refine its accuracy in the light of experience.

There are two factors that effect how much the actual progress will deviate from the plan:

1. Project velocity.
2. Accuracy of the estimates.

The project velocity is a factor used in XP for adjusting estimates of "ideal development effort" required to complete the feature to the actual effort expended by the project team to complete that feature. See, for example, *Planning Extreme Programming* (Beck & Fowler 2001). The advantage of using project velocity is that it can be assumed to be constant over timebox boundaries, and so, since it is simply measured for the previous timebox (from the sum of the estimated effort of completed features divided by total project effort), this factor can be used to estimate how many features will be completed in the next timebox:

$$project\_velocity = \frac{estimated\_effort\_for\_completed\_features}{actual\_project\_effort}$$

Using the project velocity alone, there is no need for detailed time recording against each feature and each activity. All that is monitored is the total effort expended by the team and how many features are actually completed (i.e., pass their respective tests).

The simplicity of this approach is wonderful, and for many small teams, it will be good enough. The payback from a more complex approach may not yield much greater accuracy, and the greater discipline required from the team—particularly in time recording—may be hard to justify.[25]

However, there are problems with using just project velocity. One problem is, when is it "fair" to update estimates for features? If you update the estimates based on the progress in the previous timebox, should you also adjust the project velocity? If you don't update the estimates, but keep them standard so that all the adjustment is handled by the project velocity factor, the estimates lose their absolute value and become only relative measures. Also, the system gives no feedback on the accuracy of individual estimates.

If your team records actual hours spent on each feature, then a more sophisticated update of the plan is possible, one that can adjust the plan almost continuously as recorded time is received week by week, or even day by day. Also, individual developers can update estimates as they are working on features so that more accurate reports of which features will be delivered on a particular date become feasible.

The timesheets for each team member should record the effective time spent on features (specification, development, or system test), as well as effective time spent on refactoring and other project activities. With this information project velocity can be measured by:

$$project\_velocity = \frac{effective\_time\_spent\_on\_features}{actual\_project\_effort}$$

If the two calculations of project velocity are significantly different, this is because the estimates were inaccurate. This information in turn can feed

---

25. Fortunately, there are tools coming on the market, including, we expect, enhancements to TogetherSoft's own products, that will make the feedback from actual effort to plan much more effective without a lot of manual manipulation of data from timesheets.

back to improve the estimates for features not yet implemented, again updating the overall plan and providing a better view of which features will be delivered when.

After the first few timeboxes, the project velocity and the accuracy of estimates will have been measured directly from time booked to features and other activities. Estimates for tasks that are not related to software delivery (for example, writing a document or reviewing design) can simply be self-fulfilling prophecies: "Because I've got two days for this document, that's how long gets spent on it." On the other hand, if the task is to deliver working functionality, with independent tests that pass, you can't fudge the finishing line. Once the project velocity has been measured, the estimated finish date for a set of features can be immediately updated. It's also better to report this week by week based on measured velocity rather than the approach many projects adopt, which is "We're behind, but I think we'll catch up later." Don't do it. Report actuals. If, God forbid, the inevitable should happen and you fail to catch up, you're more likely to be prepared!

Use Cases Versus Features

In Chapter 4, "The Stakeholder Step: Specify Requirements," we used use cases as the primary means of identifying the requirements of the system. In this chapter, we have focused mainly on features. So, what is the precise relationship between the two?

Use cases arise from considering the scenarios of use of the system from the perspective of the various actors. Use cases will generally specify the functionality without consideration of development planning.

However, as we've seen in this chapter, feature-centric planning needs requirements expressed in a form that allows them to be scheduled, and therefore implemented, within one timebox. Coad expresses this constraint in FDD as a "feature per fortnight"—that is, no feature should take a team more than 10 elapsed days to implement. In EVO a similar metric is applied—a maximum of 2 percent of the annual project budget per feature. In other words, we may need to transform our system use cases into separately plannable features.

We considered a hierarchy of use cases in Chapter 4: business use cases, system use cases, and implementation use cases. We can map implementation use cases one-to-one to features. There may be other features, though—bug fixes and enhancement requests, for example—that do not relate to use cases, and these can just be added to the features list without cross-referencing them to use cases. In the minimum metamodel that we discussed in Chapter 1, (see Figure 1-4) use cases relate to many features, while any given feature relates to, at most, a single use case.

Use Cases and Features in Together

As you saw in Chapter 4, Together directly supports use cases but does not (at least in version 6.0) have direct support for features built in to the product. However, it is relatively straightforward to implement many of the aspects of feature-centric planning in Together, and indeed some users have done this, even distributing some of the configuration files through the Together Community Web site (*www.togethercommunity.com*). Within the project distributed with this book, we have kept just to the standard Together and UML facilities though, so all requirements are stored simply as use cases.

Cost of Refactoring and Architecture

A common question asked by teams implementing a feature-centric approach is, Where do the estimates for the cost of refactoring and architecture get stored? Refactoring is defined as changing the implementation code of a program without changing its functionality. It's apparently a change with no business value. In fact, the value of refactoring comes from improving the flexibility, understandability, and performance of the system and its design. The business benefit of that can be very high. Refactoring on a small scale is something that you need to do continuously, feature by feature, as the system evolves, and such refactoring is absorbed within the time allowed for implementing features, or if it is separately recorded on timesheets, results in a slightly lower measured project velocity (Pitt 2000).

However, there is some refactoring that involves much more effort and cannot usually be tackled within budgeted time for features. It involves the architecture of the software and its "re-architecting." Together itself is a software system implemented initially by a very small team. Now there are scores, even hundreds, of developers working in parallel on different aspects of Together's functionality. Such "massively parallel development" doesn't happen by accident. It happens because architecture is taken very seriously, even to the extent of rewriting the framework or architectural software several times over the life of the product. Like refactoring on a smaller scale, such rewrites demand courage and commitment to a vision. They also require budget, which means that we do need to be able to include architectural features in our features lists. One way to view such features is that the stakeholders or users for the architectural features are actually other developers who will use the features to implement the functionality they are delivering to users more quickly.

You need to keep the desire for writing elegant architectural frameworks in perspective. Kent Beck reputedly kept the phrase "YAGNI" up on his whiteboard—it stands for "You Ain't Gonna Need It"—to discourage his teams from going too far in the direction of writing for tomorrow's requirements (which we don't know) rather than today's (which we do). Every time someone suggests writing some software that is not based on a known requirement, the response is YAGNI! The complexity and cost introduced by trying to implement general-purpose features, when the specific purpose is the only one we actually know, is sobering. If you don't need it now, it's usually better to implement the simplest thing.

However if you just pile feature upon feature into an application, its architectural underpinnings will eventually prove inadequate. The application will become more fragile and brittle, making changes increasingly difficult to implement. The "simplifying assumptions" previously made when developing the initial set of features may no longer be true. Rather than YAGNI, the point has now come when you *are* gonna need it. This is when we need to take a time-out and refactor. It's the responsibility of the architect or chief developer to keep an eye on the architecture and determine when it is becoming inadequate for the emerging requirements to be implemented.

Unfortunately, these refactorings do not deliver any new functionality. The whole point of refactoring is for the application to behave in precisely the same way as before. This can be a hard proposition to sell to the stakeholder who holds the purse strings: "You mean that you want me to sign off on two man-months work, and when we get the new release, it'll do nothing new?!" He needs to know that the business benefit comes from improved flexibility and productivity in future changes.

Suggested Refactorings for *CarServ*

If you look at CarServ, you'll see that there are some architectural refactorings just begging to be done.

1. Move listeners from UI to Domain.

This is a case of piling feature upon feature so that the architectural principles are starting to be compromised. Each UI component notifies others when there's been a change so that they can update themselves. This works fine, but really, it should be the domain objects that do this. We'd need to make this change if the stakeholders decided that CarServ needed a different user interface, such as a ruggedized handheld PC for the mechanics.

2. Combine Employee/Customer.

A simplifying assumption was made that Employees and Customers are separate entities. However, if the domain is extended and the stakeholders decide that Employees should get a 10 percent discount for the servicing of our own cars, then we would need to combine these entities.

3. Support optimistic locking.

This is a case of YAGNI. We don't need it yet, but we might do in the future, say if multiple garages were sharing the same data center.

4. Get rid of singletons to support J2EE Web architecture.

Another case of YAGNI.

Most of these refactorings can be addressed as related features are implemented and the cost absorbed within the cost of those features. If this is done continuously, the project velocity will reflect the activity, but there will be no slow down over time as there would be if the basic design was not evolving to keep a coherent and understandable structure.

Configuration Management

It is in the nature of a feature-centric approach to project management that many different features are being implemented at the same time. Inevitably, there will also be defects that have been detected in production, and these will need fixing also. So, a decent configuration management system is an essential part of the development and management framework.

Implementing any feature will cause a number of configuration items (source files and diagrams) to change. The feature identifier (from the features list) should be used as the tag for checking out these configuration items (CIs). If CIs for a feature are checked in for testing but do not pass that testing by the end of the current timebox, then they can be simply backed out from the build.

Ideally, the software configuration management (SCM) system should support multiple checkout of the same CI, though it may be necessary to set up branching. Many fixes to defects are one-liners, and it is not dangerous to make that change while the CI is being changed elsewhere to support some new feature. Some teams, especially small teams where communication between members is easier, prefer an approach to CM that allows any changes to be made in parallel—even to the same CI. Certainly in source code files, merging multiple changes is feasible provided that the integration is carried out by the developer herself as she checks in her change, and provided that unit tests are comprehensive so that the system can be tested regressively.

In this chapter we've discussed how to get in control of your projects, using features as a way of prioritizing, estimating, and monitoring progress of the work. Feature-centric planning is a simple but powerful way to manage software projects and keep on the track of delivering the highest level of benefits possible to the business while estimating and monitoring costs accurately.

Project management never stops. In the next chapter we look at another activity that must never stop—measuring the quality of the product using Together's facilities for metrics, audits, testing, and document generation.

What's Next

chapter 6

The Continuous Step:
Measure the Quality

You can't control what you can't measure...
Anything you don't measure at all is out of control.
Tom DeMarco

The only thing more expensive than writing software
is writing bad software.
Alan Cooper

A common mistake that people make when trying to
design something completely foolproof is to
underestimate the ingenuity of complete fools.
Douglas Adams

Quality is as much a function of the means of production—the process—as it is an attribute of the product itself. The generic process we describe in this book has continuous measurement of the quality of the product at its heart. We measure quality primarily by testing but also by metrics, audits, document generation, and inspection. The feedback from this measurement is the basis of controlling the process. We need the measurement of quality to be automated as much as possible, in particular by automating regression testing, metrics, audits, and document generation. We also need to tailor these measuring tools to the specifics of the project's process and the software design. This chapter shows how you can do this with Together and make continuous quality measurement part of the culture of your team.

In the previous chapter we talked about making sure we deliver what we said, when we said. But if the deliverables are defect-ridden or just don't work, that would be of little value. How do you ensure that you produce only high-quality deliverables? In this chapter we discuss how to use Together's power to continuously monitor the quality of the models and software that you and your team produce. Continuous monitoring helps to converge on high-quality outputs and also highlights major or minor crises in quality at the earliest possible stage. It should not be an interruption to address unit testing or design reviews. Rather, these traditionally separate activities of software development should be fully integrated into the way the team functions.

How to Measure Quality

Quality is notoriously difficult to measure. We recognize quality in a product that makes previously difficult or impossible tasks easy, and does it in a way that is elegant and logical. We recognize the lack of quality when products fail to behave as we expect, give us the wrong answers, or simply stop working and cause us to lose our precious work. But giving quality a numerical value—that's hard.[27]

Just because it may be difficult to measure something does not mean we should not measure it. Indeed, as many people have observed, only by measuring something can we control it. We suggest there are five main ways software development teams should measure quality, and we'll consider each of these in this chapter:

- Testing
- Automated metrics
- Automated audits
- Document generation
- Reviews and inspections

Ultimately, from all these means of measurement, we are trying to determine whether a particular configuration of the software and its related artifacts meets the criteria for a given quality level. The many individual measures contribute to the decision process to apply a quality status to individual files and components, and ultimately to complete configurations of overall systems. There are four significant levels of quality that many teams use. Here they are in ascending order:

- *Developer* quality—suitable for use by other members of the team.
- *Alpha* quality—suitable for system testing.
- *Beta* quality—suitable for testing by users in controlled conditions.
- GA (general availability) quality—suitable for release and normal use.

Every project must consider how it decides whether a given configuration merits a given quality status. For some projects, particularly small ones, the Beta status maybe unnecessary. But at the very least the project does need to decide how it bestows the quality status of "suitable for release" on a configuration. Often, projects rely on the instincts of developers, testers, or managers because no formalized criteria exist. But this is not helpful, not least because if you eventually discover that the quality of a previous release was insufficient, it is very difficult to ensure the next release will be any better. Formalizing the criteria doesn't mean you have to make quality measurement overly "heavy" or time consuming. It merely means that the way the quality level is recognized is recorded and followed.

27. Actually, thinking of the quality metric as a vector—made up of many separate measures and scores—rather than a single number is probably more useful. This is an idea we've explored previously (Carmichael 1994b).

There is a fifth quality level, which unfortunately it is the default state of all software, namely *unqualified*, undefined, or unknown. When a change is made to a configuration, the quality reverts to this level until the quality measurement can establish the higher quality levels.

Since software is continuously changing in iterative lifecycles, it follows that the quality measurement must also be continuous in order to prevent the inexorable slide into the unqualified state. For the measurement to be continuous, most of the measurement must be automated, particularly regression testing, which involves rerunning the tests that have already been carried out to ensure defects are not re-introduced and previously working features disabled by changes to other parts of the system.

Figure 6-1 is a state chart that shows the changing quality status of a software product through the five quality levels. Note that with any change, the status reverts to *unqualified*. From *Alpha* quality, the configuration may move directly to GA quality if a previous configuration with the same functionality had achieved this status.[28]

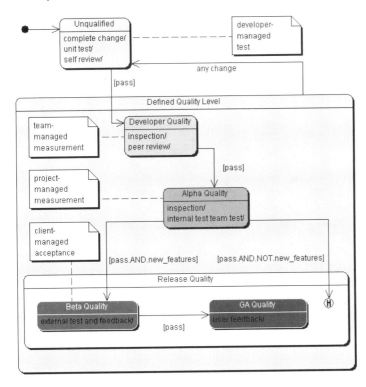

Figure 6-1
The quality status of a product may change as it is measured. However, with any change to the product itself, the status reverts to *Unqualified*.

---

28. This is shown on the diagram using the UML pseudo-state labeled **H**, which stands for the historical substate; that is, the state that the object was previously in (in this case GA or *Beta*) when it was last in the containing superstate (in this case *Release Quality*).

If we accept the rule that a changed configuration reverts to the *unqualified* quality level until remeasured; then we must look for strategies that

- minimize the scope of what must be remeasured.
- re-establish previously achieved quality status levels with minimum effort.

In fact, the principal strategy that addresses both these concerns is componentization. By dividing larger products into smaller components that can be separately certified for quality, then only those components that have themselves been changed or that are dependent on a change to another component's interface need to be recertified. The time taken to reestablish a previously achieved quality level is also minimized by having smaller components. However this must be balanced by the need to minimize the dependencies between components which is essential to make componentization successful. We consider this in more detail in the next chapter.

We can also reduce the time required for recertification by analyzing what the change is and what behavior it could possibly effect within the component. This requires detailed comparison between the two configurations, something that Together supports to some extent in version 6 through its interface to the version control system.

Black-Box Measurement and White-Box Measurement

Our mechanisms for measuring quality can be applied in one of two ways: "black box" or "white box." This is an analogy with hardware testing—where the electronic components often consists of black boxes with plugs, sockets, knobs, and dials (analogous to signal inputs and outputs, and inputs and outputs from and to the user). You can test and inspect this component without opening the box (black-box testing) or by opening and probing the internal circuits (referred to as white-box testing, or sometimes as clear-box testing). The contrast is not the color of the boxes but whether you can inspect *how* the box works as well as *what* it outputs given different inputs (see Figure 6-2).

In software development terms, white-box measurement is implemented by reviewing how the program implements the required features, including the design, documentation, and coding standards. Together provides impressive support for the white box through both its audits and metrics features and through its Open API, where project-specific checks can be defined. We sometimes refer to applying such checks as "compiling the model"—an allusion to the fact that it's not just the code that must be syntactically correct to get a clean build; the rest of the elements in the model must also be complete and consistent. Unit tests may also be white-box measurements in that the units they are testing are "internal" with respect to the externally specified functional requirements.

Meanwhile, black-box measurement is implemented by reviewing the program from the outside—knowing its specification and observing its behavior. The most important measurement in this case is testing. Together has a

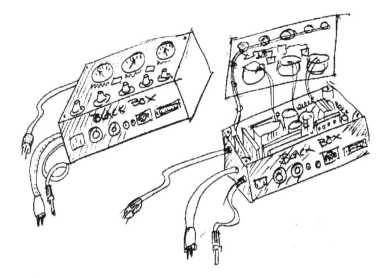

Figure 6–2
Black box, white box—a white box is actually just an *open* black box.

number of facilities built in to help both the definition and running (rerunning of tests). These facilities can substantially reduce testing overheads.

Let's now look at testing, metrics, audits, document generation, and inspection in more detail.

Our minimum metamodel identifies three different types of tests (see Figure 6-3 and also Figure 1-4 in Chapter 1):

- Functional tests
- Nonfunctional tests
- Unit tests

Functional and some nonfunctional tests are black-box tests derived from the specification of functional requirements (features) and the level-of-service constraints (or nonfunctional requirements). These tests ensure that the delivered product is fit-for-purpose and meets its specification. Unit tests are defined by the developer based on her design, and so in that sense they are white-box tests. In some senses they are also black-box tests, merely of smaller units. For example, a unit test of a class's operation should not rely on any knowledge of how the operation works, merely on its required behavior and the operation's signature. We want to ensure that every operation in the design is exercised by at least one test. At this level of granularity, a white-box test would look at internal values of objects, for example, with the debugger, rather than just test the functionality of the operation against its defined behavior.

Each of these three types of test will compare the expected results from a set of inputs and initial conditions with the actual results. We can use the features of Together to automate the setting up, running, and rerunning of the tests.

The Continuous Step:
Measure the Quality

115

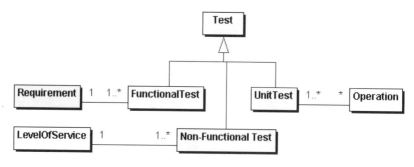

Figure 6–3
Three kinds of test: functional, nonfunctional, and unit tests.

As well as three types of test, there are three main occasions when the testing must be applied (see Figure 5-2 in Chapter 5, which shows the different scales of iteration):

- Daily build, when the tests are applied by the individual developer in order to establish *Developer* level quality status.
- Timebox build, when tests are managed by the team in order to certify which features are complete and ready for internal testing (*Alpha* level quality).
- Milestone build, when tests are managed by the internal testers—preferably separate from the developers provided the team size warrants this—in order to establish release level quality (*Beta* or GA level quality).

Let us look at each type of test in turn. Following that we'll consider how Together's testing framework can be used to define test suites that correspond to the three main occasions that testing is applied.

Functional Testing

Functional testing is all about ensuring that the application meets its specification, defined, for example, by its use cases and activity diagrams. Functional testing is applied to establish *Developer* quality at daily builds, but generally only for the features related to the change the developer is integrating. It is used at timebox boundaries to establish which features have been implemented to *Alpha* quality status so that they can be further tested internally. It is fully applied for all the features—new and existing—at milestones to attain release-level quality.

The scenarios for use cases can easily be adapted into functional test scripts. Some people like to document scenarios using actual example data, in which case this process is pretty mechanical. Others document scenarios in not quite such concrete terms. This means more work in generating the functional test scripts, but on the other hand, it is possible to create a coherent set of test data and output results.

This correlation back to the use cases (or, more likely, the features that constitute the use cases) is important. As each use case or feature is implemented, one or more system test cases should also be developed to exercise that feature from a functional standpoint. And since features are added one by one, so are the system test cases.

It is commonplace for the developers to both write and perform the functional test cases, and this makes sense with use cases and features acting as the specification of the system. An improvement on this, however, is to use separate testers for the project-managed tests that lead to *Alpha* quality status. Bringing a business stakeholder, an expert user, or an ambassador user[29] into the project team to specify the tests is also an advantage. It can help guard against misunderstandings of the problem domain or the required functionality by the developers.

All of the above presupposes that the system specification is accurate and has been correctly understood. However, you won't find out this is the case until you ship the application to the end-users, at which point the complaints may start flooding in. So, many organizations use beta testing or user acceptance testing as an additional form of functional testing. This is often quite informal in nature, whereby the users simply attempt to do their job using the application provided but in a controlled environment, understanding that the software they are using is not yet fully certified for general use. This can highlight both where the specification may have been misunderstood and (just as worrisome) where the specification is correctly implemented but doesn't address the actual requirements of the end-users. If it is the specification itself that is at fault, then you should review the development process, as it may indicate that real end-users were not involved earlier on in the cycle when the use cases were being specified or reviewed.

These styles of functional testing—developer-managed testing, development team-managed testing, project-managed testing, and beta testing—are complementary. Some organizations use end-users to perform scripted system tests, which is okay, but relies on those scripts being realistic. However, while it is possible to ship an application that has been (formally) system tested and not (informally) beta tested, it is a bad idea to ship an application that has only been informally beta tested and not formally system tested. Doing so is just planting (or ignoring) a whole bunch of defects that will come back to haunt you later.

Nonfunctional Testing

Nonfunctional tests measure the system's compliance with level-of-service constraints (or nonfunctional requirements). These may relate to a particular functional requirement (for example, the maximum response time for a

---

29. Ambassador user is a term used in the DSDM method (Stapleton 1997) to mean members of the user community that have been seconded to the development team. The analogy is appropriate. Ambassadors leave their own countries (the departments where they were "users") and go to another country (the project team) in order to represent the views of their own country. It's important ambassador users don't "go native," losing touch with the users they are supposed to represent and becoming simply ordinary developers in the project team. Equally, it is important they do actually *join* the project team and are a resource available to the project rather than being just a nominal user contact, who in practice is out of touch with the project and not available when needed.

particular use case), but often they refer to the system as whole, as in security constraints, for example.

Nonfunctional tests are often more difficult to devise because they are more open ended. Consider, for example, the tests that you could devise to show compliance with the following level-of-service constraints:

- The user shall never wait more than 10 seconds for a response to any command.
- The system shall not allow users to view other users' account details nor to view any system data.
- The mean time between failures shall be greater than 3,000 hours.
- Use of the system shall be able to be mastered by typical users after 3 hours of training.
- The performance of the system shall not degrade significantly with up to 1,000,000 accounts and 10,000 concurrent users.
- The design shall allow new types of investment product to be implemented quickly, typically with less than 5 hours of developer time.
- The system shall be implemented entirely in Java.[30]

These sorts of requirements need a completely different view of testing in many cases than the typical approach for functional and unit testing, namely, "run the software with these preconditions and these inputs and check the results are identical to this data." Some nonfunctional tests can follow this pattern—for example, specific performance tests for features— but most will require different means of validation, maybe even involving specially written audits, test harnesses, or even psychological experiments. We can perform nonfunctional testing, for example, using

- Performance tests (often based on underlying functional tests)
- Audits, metrics, and modules (compiling the model)
- User acceptance tests, pilot office schemes, beta testing
- Due diligence of the project manager and senior developers

The sorts of things we might expect the nonfunctional requirements to cover include performance, load (e.g., number of site hits per minute), volume (of data, network traffic, requests, etc.), usability, maintainability, learnability, and implementation constraints (e.g., the implementation language or compatibility with a particular vendor or system).

An SLA document makes an obvious starting point for developing nonfunctional tests. Some SLA documents explicitly name business transactions and target response times for specified throughput, so for such a document a test harness can be developed that aims to simulate this situation. The `RepeatedTest` decorator of the JUnit framework might help, for example (this is discussed in Appendix B). Other SLA documents may require certain response times for all business transactions, so here some inspection of the code to determine the most complex might be advisable.

Nonfunctional requirements also impact the operational support environment—for example, the mean time to recover following a disk crash. The

---

30. We would tend to categorize this more as an architectural constraint, something that we look at in more detail in Chapter 8.

test to ensure this requirement has been addressed will most likely rely on the existence of operational support procedures being written and some simulation of the failure. (A quote from a poster we saw once in a machine room: "The first time you test your recovery procedures had better not be when you need to recover!" We wholeheartedly agree.)

Audits, metrics, and modules (see in this chapter the section "Compiling the Model") all have a role to play in ensuring that development standards as defined by the architecture group are adhered to.

As you can see, the above sampling of nonfunctional tests is somewhat diverse; perhaps attempting to fully define a comprehensive set is a lost cause. User acceptance tests, beta testing and even pilot office schemes (where the application is rolled out to only a small proportion of the end-user population) are traditional techniques for validating functional requirements; but, they also can help show up issues with nonfunctional requirements. However, finding ways to highlight such issues earlier is definitely worthwhile, since otherwise they will incur much higher cost than if they had been identified earlier in the development process.

Unit Testing

Most programmers think that writing unit tests is boring and time consuming. Wrong! Unit testing can be easy, it can be fun, and it can speed up development itself! An increasing number, particularly of Java programmers, are realizing that writing unit tests, and writing them before they change their code, makes life easier, more effective, and more satisfying. Probably the greatest influences in this realization has been a small open source program developed originally by Kent Beck and Eric Gamma called JUnit[31] (see Kent and Gamma's online resources at *www.junit.org*)—as well as the many books and articles that support its use, such as *Refactoring* (Fowler 2000b); *Planning Extreme Programming* (Beck & Fowler 2001); "JUnit Good Practices" (Schneider 2000).

We have seen the iterative process for concurrent development and unit testing before (the perturbation change model), for example Chapter 1, Figure 1-6. Figure 6-4 is another more general variant of the process, which emphasizes that in fact it can be triggered by a change to any of the artifacts of requirements, design, implementation or test. When we want to make a change to the implementation of the system (that already works, as far as it goes), we write a new unit test for the change we are about to implement. When we run this test it will probably fail because we haven't changed any code yet. If it does pass, we've probably written an unfair test, one that doesn't really test the change we're about to introduce. Naturally, we have to change the test if this happens.

If the test does fail, we can change the implementation and then run the test again. We keep going around this loop until we pass the new test. We run the rest of the tests too, to make sure that we haven't broken any of them either. If they all complete successfully, then we're done.

---

31. …and its many variants now available for languages other than Java, like VB, C++, COBOL, and HTML.

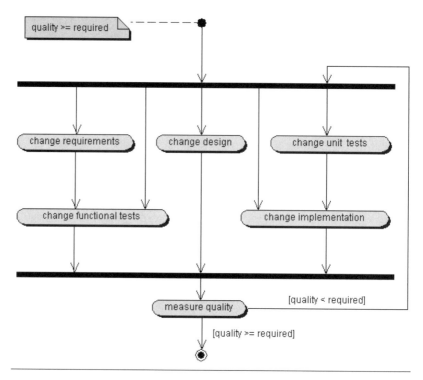

Figure 6–4
A more general view of the perturbation change model.

As you can see, writing the test is not done at the end of the cycle; it's an intrinsic and continuing part of the implementation step. Indeed, it's fun dividing up your time between writing tests and changing the implementation; you get to play good cop *and* bad cop!

Together's Testing Framework

Now let's look at how Together supports many of the types of tests that we have discussed. Together Version 6 was the first version to introduce a comprehensive testing framework into the product, and it had several aims:

- To help define unit tests quickly using design patterns
- To allow the running and rerunning of the tests partially or in full
- To record visual interactive tests for Java Swing or AWT user interfaces, replaying these scripts as regression tests
- To support the creation of a Test Plan and to store test results
- To display and edit test processes visually using activity diagrams

A key part of this framework is the JUnit program and some extensions and made by Andreas Heilwagen, called JUnitX (see *www.extreme-java.de* for more background). Together's test framework allows you to write unit tests to validate your design, and functional tests to validate that requirements (or bug reports) have been addressed. And of course, once defined these tests are always available for checking and rechecking the code base. It allows you to easily create test suites, edit them, and add specific test logic. When the source code changes, you can refactor the relevant test cases to ensure the tests are still "fair", complete and working properly. You can generate separate test suites for the different occasions testing is applied (e.g. the daily build, timebox builds, milestone builds), and extend them as necessary, so they reflect new requirements and previously discovered defects. You can reuse the same test cases in different test suites so that the suites are tailored to the different occasions when they are used, without increasing the total number of tests that need to be maintained.

Together's testing framework is enabled as an activatable module, so the first thing to do is to ensure it is checked in the list of activatable modules by selecting *Tools* → *Activate/Deactivate Features*. Various configuration options become available from the *Options* menu once the testing framework has been activated (*Tools* → *Options* → *Project Level* then select *Testing Framework*). For example the location of required JAR files and whether tests are created within the application packages or in a parallel hierarchy can be set.

Configuring and using JUnit and JUnitX (and the structure of the packages themselves) is described in more detail in Appendix B, whereas in this section we focus on the support provided by Together.

The Definition of Unit Tests by Pattern

Together's testing framework provides a number of patterns to make almost trivial the task of creating of unit tests. For example in the JUnitX testing patterns the following are included:

- `PrivateTestCase`: This is applied to an existing class that requires a test case; it creates a new class with test methods corresponding to the methods in the class under test. The generated class extends `junitx.framework.PrivateTestCase`.
- `TestPackage`: This creates a class that automatically defines a `TestSuite` consisting of all the `TestCase` classes in the package.
- `TestProxy`[32]: This is created in the package of the class under test; part of the JUnitX enhancements, it provides the ability for test cases to test package-level and protected features of the class under test.

The case study uses the parallel hierarchy approach for organizing test cases, so that the tests for classes in `com.bettersoftwarefaster.carserv.app` will be found in `test.com.bettersoftwarefaster.carserv.app`. Moreover, the case study combines this structure with Together's package prefix facility, to split up the case study source and diagrams into four root directories:

- `src\com\bettersoftwarefaster\carserv`: Java source code with package prefix `com.bettersoftwarefaster.carserv`.
- `diag\com\bettersoftwarefaster\carserv`: Corresponding diagrams for the Java source code, with same package prefix.

---

32. It generally isn't necessary to invoke the TestProxy pattern, because it is invoked automatically whenever the TestCase pattern is invoked.

- `testsrc\test\com\bettersoftwarefaster\carserv`: Java test source code with package prefix `test.com.bettersoft-ware.carserv`.
- `testdiag\test\com\bettersoftwarefaster\carserv`: Corresponding diagrams for the Java test source code with a similar package prefix.
- `tests`: the directory containing the XML files that define the Test Plan and results.

Figure 6-5 shows the parallel package hierarchies, along with the project paths.

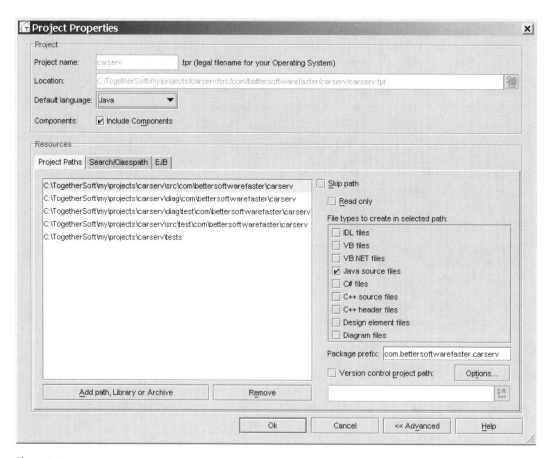

Figure 6–5
The case study uses multiple project roots to separate out the test code.

As an extra bonus, setting up these project paths means that the tests and test code are stored in completely separate areas of the version control repository, and indeed could even use a completely different version control repository if this were needed.

Applying the patterns can only give you the skeletons of the test cases; you still need to write the body of those tests. Here's the code that is generated by the JUnitX pattern for the `PickUpCar` method in the `Service` class:

```
public void testPickUpCar() throws TestAccessException {
   System.out.println("The \"testPickUpCar\" is started");
   fail("not implemented");
   System.out.println("The \"testPickUpCar\" is finished");
}
```

If you do run the tests immediately after generating them, this code ensures that they will all fail with a "not implemented" message. You need to replace line 3 above with code that calls the `PickUpCar` method and tests its effect. To write the test bodies requires some familiarity with the JUnitX and JUnit packages so if you've not seen them before, read about the use and structure of these packages in Appendix B.

Running and Rerunning the tests

In the case study the unit tests were originally designed independently from the testing framework and run from Together by defining multiple run configurations (*Run* → *Run/Debug Configurations*). You can see them in the Run Configurations shown in Figure 6-6.

Figure 6–6
Run Configurations can be used to run test suites.

However the testing framework allows a much simpler approach to defining and running tests. For example you can immediately run a test in the Test Plan from its speed menu, just by right-clicking and invoking *Run Test*. Figure 6-7 shows the Message Pane with a typical set of results (3 tests with one failure) when this is done. Clicking on the highlighted failed test will open the relevant test in the text editor. The case study tests have now been imported into the testing framework so that they can also be run from the Test Plan in this way. (To import existing tests, right-click on the appropriate collection of the Test Plan and select *Import JUnit Test*.

Let's now look at how you might create a Test Plan.

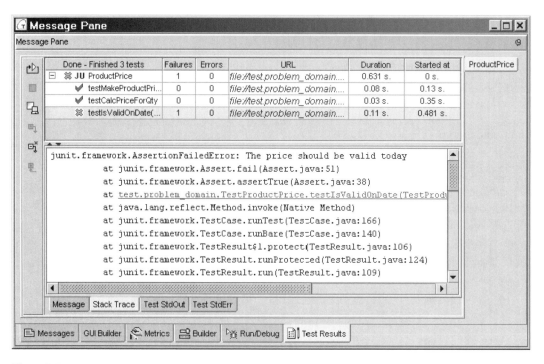

Figure 6–7

Tests results shown in the Message Pane of Together.

Creating a Test Plan and Storing Test Results

Creating a test plan in Together is done in the Explorer pane (see Figure 6-8) by first selecting the *Tests* tab (only visible if the testing framework is activated). We've created four top-level Collections for the three types of test: Functional, Nonfunctional and Unit Tests; and another for Build Test Suites which will contain different combinations of the tests for the different occasions we want to use them—particularly for the daily builds, timebox builds and the most comprehensive suites for milestone builds.

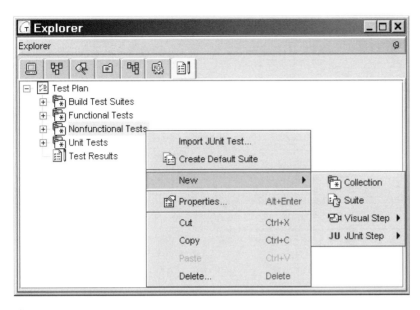

Figure 6–8
Creating a test plan in Together.

In Figure 6-9 the tests have been added to the Functional Tests and Unit Tests collections. Visual tests have been used to test each use case scenario and JUnitX tests to test the classes in the relevant packages. When generating Tests for a particular package, tests will be generated for each method of each class in the package and all its sub packages. If you select the topmost package of a large program it is therefore likely to take some time to complete! It is quite likely there are certain types of classes (like Exceptions) and certain types of method (like data accessors) that you will want to filter out of the test generation process. To do this you should select *Project Options* again and under *Testing Framework* find the particular test template that you are using. Filters can be set on packages, classes and methods to exclude or include them from test generation.

Each of these tests can be selected and *Run* to execute just that test. It is more useful though to collect them into Test Suites. Figure 6-10 shows a number of test suites that have been defined for different test purposes. The contents of the Daily Build suite is visible which contains a number of functional and unit tests as well as a number of other assertions that are tested during the running of the suite, For example certain files may be asserted to exist (or not exist), ranges for the size of the file or another file that its contents should match may optionally be specified.

The sequence in which the tests are run may be specified in an activity diagram, as shown in Figure 6-11. The diagram can be generated from a test suite defined in the Explorer Pane or alternatively the activity diagram may be drawn in the Diagram Editor and used to generate the contents of the test suite.

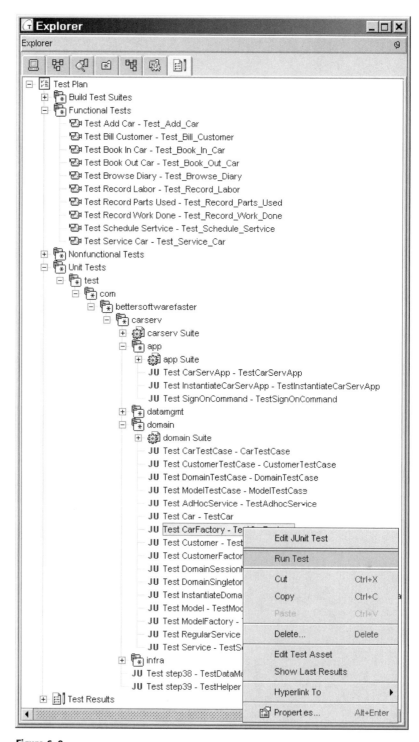

Figure 6–9

Functional Tests related to Requirements and Unit Tests to Classes.

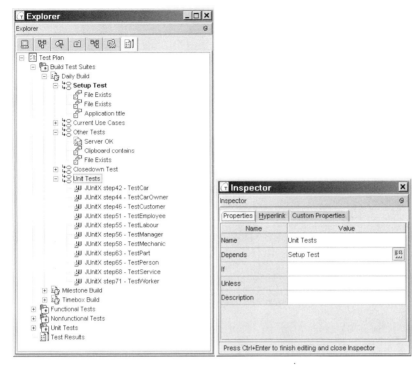

Figure 6–10
The Build Test Suites collection contains suites of tests for Daily Build, Timebox Build, and Milestone Build.

The example test suite given here is probably not comprehensive enough for the daily build tests, unless it is at a very early stage of the project. One would expect the number of tests to grow very rapidly through the life of the project, although it is important to constantly prune tests so that the daily build suite will run in a reasonable timeframe. If it takes too long to run programmers will use it less frequently and its value will diminish. It is likely that individual programmers working on a specific task will also define smaller test suites to test just the area they are working on. Once this is working they can use the Daily Build suite or possibly the Timebox Build suite to check the changes have not affected other areas.

The test results of every run, including performance timings, are stored by Together and can subsequently be viewed in either XML or via HTML in a browser. By including test results under version control the testing and release process becomes readily auditable at a later date without requiring any additional effort on the part of the developers and testers.

Recording of Interactive Tests

Sometimes we want to run functional tests from the user interface. It's very difficult to fulfill our goal of continuous measurement of quality via regression testing, if tests need to be repeated by human testers rather than being run automatically. Together provides the visual test facility for record-

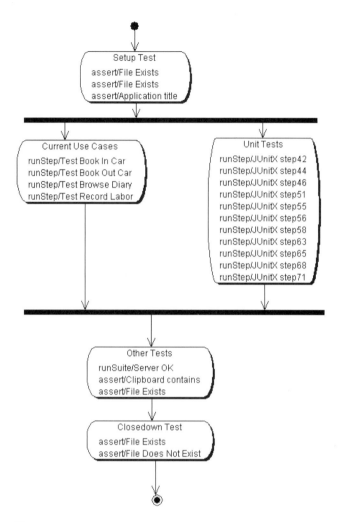

Figure 6–11

Activity Diagram for the Daily Build combines a number of different types of test.

ing the keystrokes and mouse movements of testers so that they can be replayed automatically to repeat the tests. At the end of the testing, the test results—for example, the contents of the clipboard or a specified file—can be checked against previous results to record either success or failure.

Visual tests can be created in the same manner as other tests, for example from the Test Plan in the Explorer. When they are created the relevant application is launched and the tester's mouse movements and keystrokes are recorded so that they can be replayed. In fact the storage of these user actions is done in a Java program. Here's a excerpt from a typical visual test:

```
    public class Test_step1 extends TestBase implements
AWTEventListener {
    public static final int SCRIPT_VERSION = 21102001;

    public void operation0() {
      moveMouse("VIEW", 26, 3);
      moveMouse("HELP", 11, 17);
      moveMouse("CANCEL", 49, 25);
      moveMouse("JAVAX-SWING-JTOOLBAR", 137, 30);
      moveMouse("POINT OF SALE", 107, 90);
      moveMouse("SCAN", 26, 13);
      mouseClick("SCAN", L_MBUTTON, 1);
      moveMouse("SCAN", 25, 13);
      mouseClick("SCAN", L_MBUTTON, 1);
      mouseClick("SCAN", L_MBUTTON, 1);
      mouseClick("SCAN", L_MBUTTON, 1);
      moveMouse("SCAN", 26, 19);
      ...
```

Each user action is recorded as a statement in the Java program. This makes it straightforward to edit scripts rather than having to re-record them for minor changes. It also means that any other valid Java can be included making the test facility very flexible and configurable.

How Much Is Enough Unit Testing?

Although unit testing is a great way to exercise all the code that has been written (at least once), and functional tests can check that there is at least one scenario in which the functional requirement is fulfilled, *comprehensive* testing—that is, checking the results for every possible scenario—is generally accepted to be impossible. Even just checking arithmetic operators comprehensively for reasonably sized integers and real numbers could take a length of time approaching the age of the universe! So, the question inevitably arises, How much testing is enough testing?

Since the unit tests themselves are written in Java, we can use another quality measurement facility of Together, metrics, to measure the relative size and complexity of the unit tests compared to the code under test. We might also run audits against the test code. If we choose metrics that give an indication of difficulty of maintaining code, we can show whether maintaining the test code is likely to be harder than maintaining the code itself. At this point we have probably reached a point of diminishing returns as far as testing is concerned. Choosing size metrics (for example, lines of code) for comparing test code with actual code might also be used to give an indication of how well tested some code is.

We tried this approach with the *CarServ* packages. Table 6-1 shows the results of running metrics for lines of code (LOC), Weighted Methods Per Class (WMPC2), and Halstead Effort (HEff—see the sidebar at the end of this section) on the unit tests of the *CarServ* case study.

Table 6–1

Metrics for the Application Packages and Corresponding Unit Test Packages

Package	HEff	LOC	WMPC2
app	555	978	44
datamgmt	6009	2126	47
domain	1738	1442	38
infra	1995	1456	41
ui	2683	2215	33
test.app	1402	328	13
test.datamgmt	1573	889	23
test.domain	1553	905	18
test.infra	1358	1202	24
test.ui	0	0	0

Spending a few minutes with a spreadsheet to create some pictures from these numbers can give you results like the following figures. Figure 6-12 compares the lines of code for the source and the corresponding unit tests.

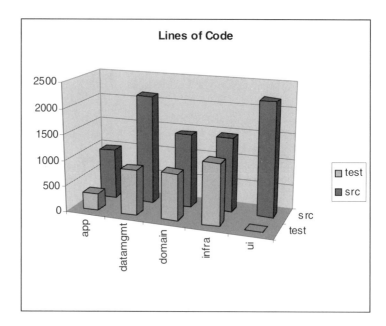

Figure 6–12

Comparative metrics of source and test can be plotted.

We can see a reasonable number of tests in all packages (except the ui package, which has no tests yet). Comparatively, the infra package has a high ratio of tests—perhaps it is overtested? The ratio of tests in app and `datamgmt` are similar, about 1:3, and for the `domain` package the ratio is about 1:2.

Figure 6-13 shows the weighted methods per class 2 metric. Together describes this metric as follows: "WMPC2 is intended to measure the complexity of a class, assuming that a class with more methods than another is more complex, and that a method with more parameters than another is also likely to be more complex. Only methods specified in a class are included; that is, any methods inherited from a parent are excluded." The ratios seem similar to those of LOC.

On the other hand, the figures for the Halstead Effort metric tell a different story. The chart is shown in Figure 6-14. Here, the figures suggest that we may have tried too hard for the `app` package to build the unit tests, because it is going to take more effort to maintain them than the actual source code under test. Perhaps, then, over time we should aim to simplify these tests.

All of this provides a simple, if crude, assessment of the amount and complexity of the test code relative to its tested code. It is a starting point for acceptance of code ready for check-in and for answering the question, Does it have enough tests?

It also leads us from testing to our next topic of continuous quality measurement—metrics.

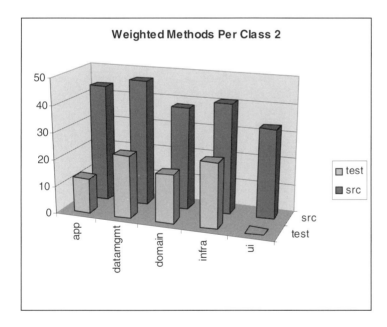

Figure 6–13
The ratios for WMPC2 are similar to LOC.

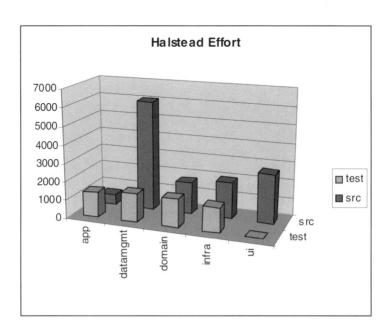

Figure 6–14
The HEff figures tell a different story.

Halstead Effort Metric

This metric (Halstead 1977) aims to measure how much effort is required to maintain some code, and is defined as:

$$H_{Eff} = \frac{t_u d_n}{2d_u}(t_n + d_n)\log_2(t_u + d_u)$$

where

t_u *= number of unique operators*

t_n *= total number of operators*

d_u *= number of unique operands*

d_n *= total number of operands*

The metric, which is one that has been used for a long time in software engineering, focuses on the textual or lexical complexity and doesn't measure complexity arising from logical branching or looping. However, it is still effective, as Edmond VanDoren observes on the SEI's Software Technology Review site (www.sei.cmu.edu/str). "The complexity of code with a high ratio of calculational logic to branch logic may be more accurately assessed by Halstead measures than by Cyclomatic Complexity, which measures structural complexity."

Empirical studies seem to show that the Halstead metrics provide a reasonable correspondence with actual module maintenance costs, even taking into account the quite different programming languages than Halstead himself was using in the 1970s.

The metrics are an important way for software teams to monitor the quality of their product (Kan 1995). The metrics featured in Together are a key way for the project manager, and indeed the architect, to keep an eye both on progress and on the evolution of the application.

Metrics are one part of the Quality Assurance features of Together, the other being audits (discussed in the next section of this chapter). To gather metrics, use *Tools → Metrics*. You'll be presented with a dialog box, as shown in Figure 6-15.

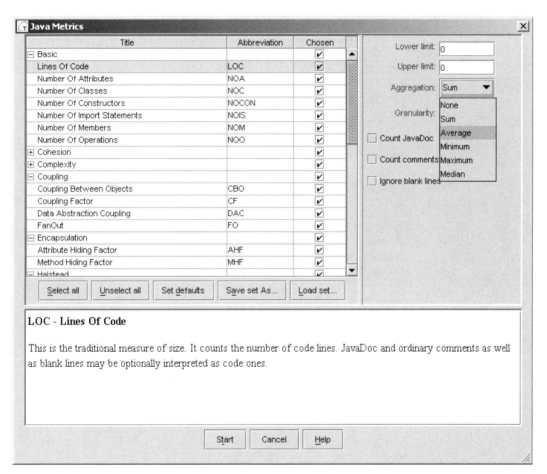

Figure 6–15
Some of the metrics available.

There is so much information that you can capture, the first task is to decide which metrics you want to track. In a small team environment, we recommend that the project manager and a couple of the more senior developers review the available metrics and determine which are most applicable to them. There is certainly some overlap; it might not need, for example, measures of both CC (Cyclomatic Complexity) and MSOO (Maximum Size of Operations) in the same metrics set. When you have identified the metrics that you wish to capture, use *Save set As* so that it can be easily run in future.

It is useful to vary the metrics you use over time so that you get a balanced view of different measures. You may find, for example, that the Halstead Effort measure of complexity gives a slightly different view of the complexity hot spots compared to using Cyclomatic Complexity (see side-bar).

It is a good idea to split out the metrics into two broad categories. The first would be for use by the project manager to give a feel for "progress." Some traditional measures do not necessarily apply for object-oriented development. For example, using the number of lines of code *added* over a given period for team productivity is not helpful if you are doing substantial refactoring with a view to simplifying the design. The total lines of code could go down from one day to the next, even though substantial progress is being made by refactoring behavior into superclasses from multiple subclasses. Maybe lines of code *changed* (i.e., added, deleted, or modified might be a better measure). Whatever the measures are, it is important for the project manager to have these progress metrics available. Figure 6-16 and Figure 6-17 show how easy it is to make the progress visible by gathering such information—most important if the project manager has to justify his and his team's existence to bosses, shareholders, and clients.

In fact, it isn't even necessary to export the data to a spreadsheet. Together can create a presentable enough bar chart for any given metric; just choose *Bar Chart* from the speed menu. This will display a dialog similar to that shown in Figure 6-18.

The second category of metrics would be for the architects to keep an eye on the integrity of the application. Is the application still simple enough to maintain? Example metrics in this category might be HD (Halstead Difficulty), or CBO (Coupling between Objects)—metrics that can be used to supplement Together's audit capabilities, which we look at in the next section.

As you have seen, Together ships with a large number of metrics out-of-the-box. It is also possible to define your own metrics, so if new measures are needed, we can add them in a very similar way to defining a new pattern or new audit.

It's important to remember that metrics are just numbers, and as such they don't say much by themselves. You always need to compare the numbers, either between modules (packages, classes, operations, etc.) or over time from one build to the next, tracking the important trends. If the measured complexity of the application is increasing, this probably means that corners are being cut in order to hit some deadline. After a while, you ought to be able to set ranges for metrics and then trigger a review if a metric moves outside of its defined range. Indeed, if these metric ranges are shared across projects, then over time they become valuable in defining a corporate standard. The appropriate ranges can be entered for each metric that the project uses and the ranges are then used by Together to define the red circle on Kiviat graphs such as that shown in Figure 6-19. Here we can see that the class analyzed has high values for FO (Fan-Out), RFC (Response For Class) and NORM (Number Of Remote Methods).

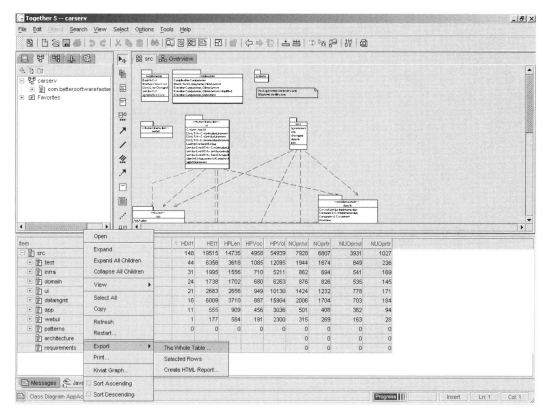

Figure 6–16
Together lets metrics be exported.

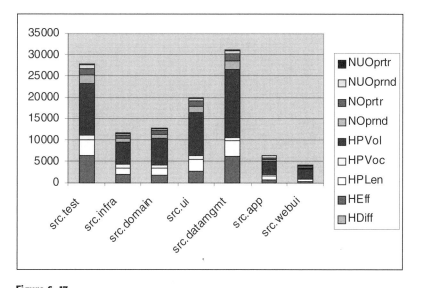

Figure 6–17
Any modern spreadsheet can rapidly create a chart from the exported metrics.

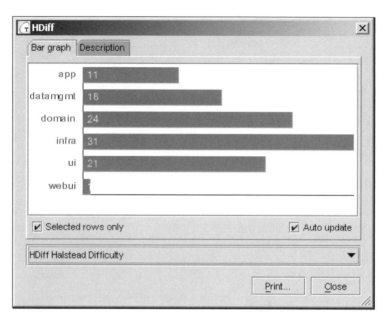

Figure 6–18

Together can generate bar charts for a given metric.

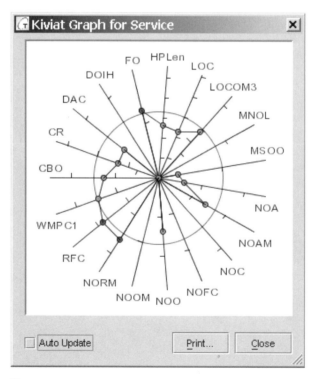

Figure 6–19

The circle defines the acceptable range of different metrics.

We recommend that you start by monitoring just a few metrics for a project that is already partly implemented. Use this set of metrics to identify possible refactorings. When this small set of metrics is under control, then identify a further set, and introduce them one at a time. You might perhaps have a "metric of the week" feature so that the developers are aware of each new metric that is being measured.

How Fast Is That?
Dan Haywood

We made the point that metrics are just numbers and need to be put into context. In my "other" job as a Sybase performance specialist, I often have occasion to measure throughput of some Sybase database, and the question often asked is, Can it go any faster?

It's a surprisingly difficult question to answer, because every system will have a different hardware configuration (server vendor, number of CPUs, their speed, memory, i/o cards, physical disk layout, network cards, and so on). So, there usually isn't an absolute number to aim for.

But, you can look for bottlenecks, make a change, and measure again. It's all to do with ongoing monitoring and comparison. The same is true for metrics; you'll need to come up with your own ranges based on previous measures.

When should metrics be captured? It will vary depending upon the reporting cycle. The project manager might wish to capture her metrics each week, whereas the architects might wish to run their metrics more often. It's also worth taking advantage of the fact that it is possible to run metrics from Together's batch mode as part of a nightly batch processing. Using the UNIX `crontab` *or the Windows* `AT` *scheduler, the code is compiled and then the metrics are run. The metrics output can then be emailed to the project manager or interested parties.*

Audits

Have you ever been given the job of defining project coding standards (knowing full well that you'll never have any practicable way of enforcing them), or—with the shoe on the other foot—been asked to ensure your code is compliant with the project standards and been landed with a large and impenetrable standards document to untangle? It can be disheartening.

The irony is that human beings are very poor at doing these sorts of rote checks, whereas computers are superb at them. This is the essence of Together's audits feature: accessing the model and code elements of the complete project and performing some common reporting task.

Together ships with numerous (mainly code-based) audits. Together iterates over each code feature and records violations in the code wherever they occur. Hence these audits directly address one of the aims of this book: to deliver better software.

We'll talk about audits in more detail in a moment, but for now, let's just see them in action. To perform an audit, use *Tools* → *Audit*. You'll be presented with a dialog, as shown in Figure 6-20.

By default, some of these are automatically chosen, others are not. For example, all of the audits in the Critical Errors group are chosen, while none

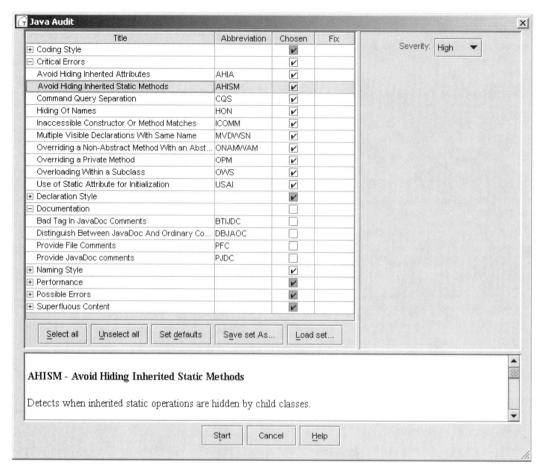

Figure 6–20
Together ships with numerous code-based audits.

of those that check documentation are selected. Try out the default audits on the *CarServ* case study—and prepare yourself to be shocked. We were. And we thought our code was good quality!

Okay, so these are the choices made by the TogetherSoft engineers, in some cases based on the Sun Microsystems Java coding standards. You may agree with all of them, but more likely you will find some either too lax (who are we trying to kid?) or too onerous. That's fine. In fact, if you look at all of the audits, you'll find some contradict others. In some cases judgement is required to decide which principle is more important in the particular context.

Just as we did for metrics, in a small team environment, we recommend that early on, two or more senior developers should identify the code-based standards that you wish to impose and then define a set of standards. Referring back to Figure 6-20, just make your selections, and for selected audit, customize it if you need to. (For example, the Avoid Hiding Inherited Static Methods is marked as of high severity if violated. You may decide it is only low severity.) Then, save your custom set using *Save set* As.

Audits should be run continually, or at least whenever a feature has been unit tested and is ready to be checked in and deployed. You'll recall that the metrics feature can be run from Together's batch mode, and the same is true for audits. The results of any violations may be automatically emailed to the developer, project manager, or a senior developer with responsibility for ensuring architectural integrity. Use the QA *Audit/Metrics Command Mode* to set this up.

Audit and metrics results are important inputs into reviews and inspections. When you've reviewed the violations and decided that the remaining ones are acceptable, it is worth storing the audit report under version control. That way, when changes are made to the package and the report produced again, you can focus on just the additional audit violations rather than on those that have already been reviewed and accepted.

Custom Audits

Since Together's audit module is extensible, if you have a coding standard that is missing from the set that ships with Together, you can write your own. It is remarkably easy to do, and there's an example of this in the sidebar "Customizing an Audit to enforce Hungarian Notation" later in this section.

In a small team environment, it is not going to be appropriate to have every team member get to grips with Together's open API. After all, while it is a Java API, it is nevertheless proprietary (these remarks are true for all the customizations that you might want to apply to Together). Even so, it is certainly worthwhile to select one or two individuals (perhaps those most interested in process issues) to learn the QA API. You can then start to automate your own coding standards. What sort of things might be worthwhile? Here are some ideas:

- A spell checker for variables, to get rid of all those obscure abbreviations that programmers love to use. The only valid variable names might be the formal names of classes and interfaces (that is, types), plus perhaps a well-defined list maintained in some flat file. Or, you could use role names of associations to supplement the list.
- Micro-tuning of performance; there are many performance-tuning books that detail such micro-tuning; a particular favorite is Dov Bulka's (2000). Be careful with this idea, though; many performance changes tend to obfuscate the code.
- Ensure that all user-defined properties are defined as needed to support some development process.

Some of the audits within Together support "autofix"—they can correct the audit violation for you automatically. Equally, when we write custom modules, we may be able not only to get the module to detect inconsistency or incompleteness, but to have it correct the information itself. Clearly, not every audit is able to provide such a feature—writing an autofix to remove cyclic dependencies would certainly be challenging! Writing an autofix to link code to the use case it is designed to implement would be impossible. Nevertheless, we expect that Together will become more and more sophisticated in this area—refactoring with a purpose.

Customizing an Audit to Enforce Hungarian Notation
Dan Haywood

Audits can be used to enforce standards such as naming conventions. A classic example of a strict naming convention is the Hungarian notation for primitives (Simonyi & Heller 1991). This notation—if you've not encountered it—encodes the data type as a prefix of the name of primitive variables. This means that an integer variable would need to begin with an "i," for example. To be honest, this is not a good naming convention for Java code—it was originally developed by Microsoft for the C Programming language, which is not as strongly typed as Java—but it will suit our purpose to explain how to implement custom audits.

The QA functionality is shipped as a module, but this module then acts as its own mini-framework. In other words, to create a new audit plug-in, you must write a class implementing the appropriate interfaces and install it into the directory:

```
%TOGETHER%\modules\com\togethersoft\modules\qa\audit\XXX.
```

where `%TOGETHER%` is an environment variable whose value is the directory to which you have installed Together (e.g., `c:\together-soft\together6.0`) and XXX is the name of a subpackage that will contain your new audit plug-in. Together's own documentation is pretty good but not particularly well advertised. So, to start off, hunt down and read what TogetherSoft has already written. You'll find it in `%TOGETHER%\modules\com\togethersoft\qa\doc\index.html`.

The audit framework is based upon implementing an adapter pattern. The class diagram for our Hungarian audit plug-in (with supporting classes from the QA framework) is shown in Figure 6-21. The «patternInstance» objects on the diagram are a way of documenting the use of patterns in the design, as discussed elsewhere in this chapter.

You can find the code for our HUNGARIAN audit plug-in and its helper class on the Web site at www.bettersoftwarefaster.com. Download the `hungarian.zip` file. This will extract to the following directory structure:

```
hungarian\
    src\            // source
    diag\           // diagrams
    classes\        // compiled code
    html\           // description of audit
    bat\            // batch files (install)
```

Open the project, but before you go any further, look at the dependencies on the QA module framework. The project's classpath (which can be viewed or set on the Search/Classpath tab under Project → Properties) has a reference to `openapi.jar` and `qa.jar`. These are both provided by TogetherSoft, the first being Together's open API, the second being the classes that make up the QA audit and metrics framework.

You should now be able to compile the code. All being well, your code will compile into the `classes` directory. To install the code into the appropriate subdirectory under `%TOGETHER%\modules`, run `bat\install.bat`. This will copy over the classes and a description of the audit from the `html` directory.

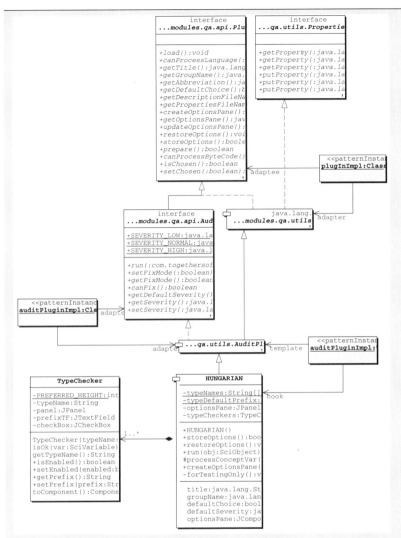

Figure 6–21
Class Structure for the Hungarian audit plug-in

Now, let's have a look at the code. The two classes that make up the plug-in are HUNGARIAN *and* TypeChecker. *By convention, audit plug-ins are capitalized. The name of the class must also be the name of the subpackage in which the code is delivered; in our case, the package is* com.together-soft.modules.qa.audit.HUNGARIAN.

The HUNGARIAN *class extends from the* AuditPlugInImpl *adapter, shipped as part of the audit framework. This adapter provides support for (a) traversing each code element of every class in turn, (b) allowing customization from the GUI, (c) allowing such customization to be saved to a persistent file, and (d) organizing the plug-in with respect to the other audit plug-ins.*

The essence of the HUNGARIAN class is two methods:

```
public boolean run(SciObject obj) {
    procGoal = PROC_OPERS | PROC_ATTRS;
    process(obj);
    return true;
}
```

and:

```
protected void processConceptVar(SciVariable var) {
    super.processConceptVar(var);
    for(int i=0; i<typeCheckers.length;i++) {
        if (! typeCheckers[i].isOk(var)) {
            AuditViolations.add(this,currMbr,var,
                "'" + typeCheckers[i].getTypeName() + "' " +
                "variables start with '" +
                typeCheckers[i].getVarPrefix() + "'");
        }
    }
}
```

The process() method is inherited from the superclass adapter and starts off the traversal. The inherited attribute procGoal indicates what code elements are to be recursed over. The process() method uses its value to call various processXXX() methods in the superclass to be called. These are the hooks—they are no-op implementations in the superclass, but the subclass (our plug-in) can override any that it needs to check. For our plug-in, there is only one hook we need to implement: that of checking any "conceptual variable" (instance variables, local variables, or arguments).

Every overridden processXXX() method must call the super class's equivalent method. This is to ensure that a full traversal of the code elements takes place. Thereafter, the method can do its checking. Our processConcept-Var() method takes the passed-in SciVariable and hands it to each instance of an array of TypeCheckers (the other class in our custom audit module). The HUNGARIAN constructor sets up an array of these, one for each primitive. The checker then indicates if the variable passes or fails its test. If it fails, then the HUNGARIAN constructor adds the information about the current variable to AuditViolations, a singleton collecting parameter.

The audit framework also allows customization from the GUI. This is accomplished by implementing createOptionsPane() and getOption-sPane(). This is optional—again, there are no-op implementations in the superclass template.

Swing components should be used to build the GUI, but there are two approaches you can take. The first is to use vanilla components (or perhaps your own toolkit), or alternatively you can use the customized Swing classes available in the com.togethersoft.modules.qa.utils package in the qa.jar file. These components are not exhaustive, but some common GUI functionality is available. You'll notice that no Java source code is delivered; however, the byte code has not been obfuscated, so you can use a Java decompiler to work out what is going on.

In our case, we have provided customization so that users can (a) decide which of the eight primitives they wish to check, and (b) change the prefix to check for. None of the widgets in the qa.utils package quite fit, so we used our own.

To make customization persistent (that is, remembered from one instance of Together running to the next), it is necessary to implement `storeOptions()` and `restoreOptions()`. In our case, we want to save the checkbox state and the prefix. This is done by spinning through each `TypeChecker` and getting/setting its state. The state is made persistent simply by calling `getProperty()` and `setProperty()` inherited (yet again) from our superclass adapter. This code is shown below:

```
1   public boolean storeOptions() {
2     for(int i=0; i<typeCheckers.length;i++) {
3       putProperty(
4         typeCheckers[i].getTypeName()+".enabled",
5         typeCheckers[i].isEnabled());
6       putProperty(
7         typeCheckers[i].getTypeName()+".prefix",
8         typeCheckers[i].getPrefix());
9     }
      return true;
11  }
12
13  public void restoreOptions() {
14    for(int i=0; i<typeCheckers.length;i++) {
15      typeCheckers[i].setEnabled(
16        getProperty(
17          typeCheckers[i].getTypeName()+".enabled", true));
18      typeCheckers[i].setPrefix(
19        getProperty(
20          typeCheckers[i].getTypeName()+".prefix",
21          typeDefaultPrefix[i]));
22    }
23  }
```

Finally, there are a couple of simple methods, `getTitle()`, `getGroupName()`, `getDefaultChoice()`, and `getDefaultSeverity()` that are used for organization—again, all optional.

The persistent configuration is stored to a file `qa\config\current.adt`. If you look at the contents of this file (it's in ASCII), then you'll see the properties being saved away, using a property of the form `Audit.XXX.PPP`, where XXX is the name of your plug-in (e.g., `"HUNGARIAN"`) and PPP is the name of the property (e.g., `"boolean.prefix"`).

Note: Beware that the audit framework does not tidy up old properties that have become defunct; we suppose that could lead to some subtle bugs over time. For example, in an earlier version of our HUNGARIAN audit, we saved properties named only `boolean`, `int`, and so on; these older properties were not removed when we enhanced the design such that the properties were now `boolean.prefix` and `boolean.enabled`, and so on.

Compiling the Model

The audits and metrics we have so far discussed have been code-based; they check that coding standards have been enforced and that measures for appropriate metrics are within range. But we can go further than this by ensuring that any design element is complete and conforms to our standards. What those standards may be will depend upon the development process that you are using and what you believe to be worthwhile.

We like to draw an analogy here with code. Your compiler will tell you when your code is syntactically complete; if it isn't, then you'll get compile errors. Similarly, your unit test suite will tell you when your code is semantically complete such that it meets its specification; if it isn't, then your tests will fail. Relying on just code-based audits is a little like only checking that your code compiles. Writing additional modules that check the rest of the repository tests the full scope of your development process.

Here's an example of what we mean. One company we know wanted to ensure that every public operation in every class appeared in at least one interaction diagram, and equally, that every object instance on interaction diagrams had a target class and message links that were associated with concrete operations. A module could certainly be written to perform such checks. It may not be a standard that can be enforced universally, though, and so a useful enhancement might be to allow a property to be defined on operations, to indicate if they are simple enough not to require a design diagram. This would reduce the volume of diagrams needing to be created and reviewed. In any case, a module can certainly be written to perform those checks.

Other Ideas

We're sure you can think of many more modules that you might want to develop using Together open API that will help to measure and, if possible, correct the quality of the project and its code. Here's a few to get you started:

- Check and add custom javadoc tags into code, such as `@author` or `@version`.
- Check that any object appearing in an activity diagram, class diagram, or interaction diagram also indicates the class from which it is instantiated.
- Check that any messages in sequence diagrams are associated with an operation of the class of the object receiving the message.
- Ensure that every parameter type and return type in interaction diagrams exists.
- Make sure that the names of events in state chart diagrams, and indeed in sequence diagrams, are correct.
- Check that every sequence diagram is hyperlinked to the use case that it realizes.
- Automatically add hyperlinks from every class to any class diagram in which it appears.
- Add in hyperlinks from class to sequence diagrams where they appear.
- Make components in deployment diagrams hyperlink to components of same name in component diagrams; make packages hyperlink to subsystems of same name in component or deployment diagrams (or both).

- Make hyperlinks bidirectional; display every hyperlink in a dialog, and for those selected by the user, add a corresponding link in the opposite direction.[33]
- Ensure that there are shortcuts for all diagrams in the package class diagram in which they are contained.

Our minimum metamodel suggests some more. For example, all functional requirements selected for this build should have at least one functional test.

We think that this is exciting stuff, because it is in this way that we can start to build a workable and enforceable software development process—lightweight or heavyweight, you choose. Here are two lessons we've learned from building computer systems: (a) to build anything big, you need a process, and (b) no one ever follows the process! Except here, we have a way to make sure that the process is being followed. And those team members who just love to develop processes can help out the rest by developing the Together modules to make the process easy to follow and audit.

To assist in developing such modules, you would be advised to develop some framework—or use ours! The RwiSupport framework, documented in Appendix F, provides a mechanism to iterate over the RWI (read/write interface) of Together's open API, providing quite detailed information on all elements within the Together "repository." Later in this chapter there are some examples that use the RwiSupport framework.

For any team environment the combination of QA audits, metrics, and custom modules become key tools if your aim is to develop better software faster. The code is going to be better if you are auditing it. And over time, you'll develop your software faster, because quality measurement requires fewer manual steps resulting in more complete and accurately documented code that is easier to maintain.

The next two sections are closely related as a means for continuously measuring quality. Generating up-to–date, in-step and cross-referenced documentation is an important stepping stone to effective inspections of the requirements, design, implementation, and tests. In this section on document generation we consider three main topics:

Generating Documentation

- Hyperlinking: cross-referencing related information
- Design Patterns: recording the use of recognized idioms
- Together's Document Generation: the mechanisms for producing documentation

Cutting code will build us a system, but unless that code and its tests are related back to the design and requirements, there is no way of knowing if the system is as specified. The minimum metamodel defines a basic set of elements (at implementation, design and requirements levels) that should exist within the single model of our system. Maintaining this set of ele-

---

33. Some features like this might, we suppose, appear in the product anyway. Only implement it if you can't wait!

ments—in other words, documenting the design—is critical if quality is to be preserved.

We have another reason for discussing document generation in this chapter. We can use custom modules based on Together's open API that will check for completeness of the design as part of our white-box quality measurement.

Hyperlinking

Together keeps class diagrams and code in-sync at all times. You can also forward or reverse engineer interaction diagrams, so these have a strong correlation to the code. However other diagrams that you create in Together will *not* give rise to any code directly, so in order to maintain effective links between them and their implementation you need to link them back to the code.

The way to do this in Together is by using hyperlinks, from the Properties inspector. However, before we go ahead and just hyperlink everything to everything else, it's worth stepping back and thinking about different types of links that can exist between model elements.

Model elements get linked together in a variety of ways as a system is specified and implemented. For example drawing an *include* link between two use cases, or referring to an operation on an interaction diagram results in a relationship between the elements. These are "semantic links", that is links that have a well-defined meaning. In some cases Together provides ways to navigate between elements that are semantically linked. Select an object on an interaction diagram for example, and Together will open the object's class in the text editor. Right-click in this text editor and choose *Select in Diagram*, and the appropriate class diagram will be opened with this class selected. However there are many other cases where we want to link model elements, and most importantly navigate between them when browsing the design, than are directly supported by Together. This is where we use hyperlinks. Whereas hyperlinks are fairly weak semantically (they tell the readers that the elements are linked without telling them why), they are very convenient since they allow almost any model element to be linked to any other and so require no special configuration of Together.

There are two particular ways we use hyperlinks:

- Realization: one artifact is realizing another at a lower level. For example, a collection of sequence diagrams might show the scenarios of a use case, and so are the realization of that use case.
- As a convenience in navigation: for example, to other sequence diagrams which are other scenarios for the same use case.

Realization

As a general principle, we try to link from design to implementation, and from design to requirements, and from tests to requirements. In other words, the realization and the higher level specification are linked together through at least three levels. These are the dependencies identified in the minimum metamodel, discussed in Chapter 1.

In an ideal world, realization links would be bidirectional—or more specifically, they would be stored persistently in one direction and dynamically generated to be navigable in both directions. This would allow a link defined in one direction to be traversed in the other, so that for example you could navigate from a requirement to its implementation without having to change the requirement file when it has been implemented. At the time of writing, Together does not do this, so you'll need to be a little diligent and put in the opposite link manually.

So, what are the hyperlinks that we should create? The links that we recommend are shown in Figure 6-22.

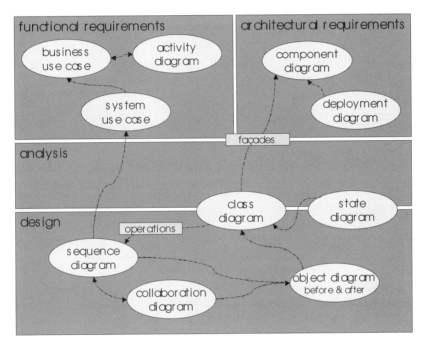

Figure 6–22
UML documents should be hyperlinked from design back through to requirements.

Let's go through these in turn.

- Link business use case diagrams with activity diagrams, and because use cases and activity diagrams are to some extent recursive, a link in the opposition direction may also be useful.
- Link system use case diagrams up to business use case diagrams to show which business processes the software addresses.
- Link the deployment diagram to the component diagram to indicate the platforms where the components will run.
- From the class diagram, link those classes that represent façades of subsystems up to components. It's also sometimes useful to link such façades to system use case boundaries, or system use case boundaries to components (neither shown in Figure 6-22).

- Link state chart diagrams back to class diagrams, though this link is also captured as one of the properties of the state chart diagram.
- Link sequence diagrams to system use cases to show which system functionality they implement.
- Link sequence and collaboration diagrams together in both directions; they are two different views of the same information.
- Link the interaction diagrams to object diagrams to explain the preconditions and postconditions for an example object configuration. Link the object diagram to a class diagram, highlighting the specific classes involved in the interaction.
- Also link operations of classes to sequence diagrams. If you use Together's *Generate Sequence Diagram* feature, then the hyperlink will be put in place automatically.

You'll appreciate that in Figure 6-22 we have shown just the UML diagrams, but the functional requirements and architectural requirements also have corresponding tests. So this figure does map quite closely onto the minimum metamodel in Figure 1-4.

Convenience in Navigation

The other type of hyperlink is as a convenience, just to make the documentation easier to navigate. We gave the example earlier of hyperlinking a collection of sequence diagrams that represent different scenarios for a common use case.

Here's another example. Often, package class diagrams (the implicit class diagrams for each package)[34] provide a high-level overview of the contents of that package and filter out detail so that only class names are shown, not members.[35] The *CarServ* case study does this throughout; Figure 6-23 shows the package class diagram for the datamgmt package. Although there are quite a large number of classes on the diagram, it is still quite useful as an overview of all the classes and the other packages and class diagrams within this package. From here, we can hyperlink to the more detailed views.

We like to have shortcuts for a number of class diagrams along the top of the package class diagram, but as an added convenience, we can hyperlink each class to the class diagrams in which it appears. If you have the *CarServ* case study open, try this out. Right-click on ServiceDM (slightly below and left of the center of the diagram) and you'll see that it is hyperlinked to two or three different class diagrams where it also appears.

We think it would be really good if you could click a button and Together would automatically add in these convenience hyperlinks. Well, Together

---

34. Package class diagrams are the class diagrams that exist for every package and have the same name as the package itself. We discuss their differences from regular class diagrams in Chapter 7.

35. Together tip: To show classes as here without the compartments for operations and attributes, rather than filtering the properties using the *Diagram Options* dialog, simply select all the classes on the diagram and choose *Hide All* from the right-click speed menu.

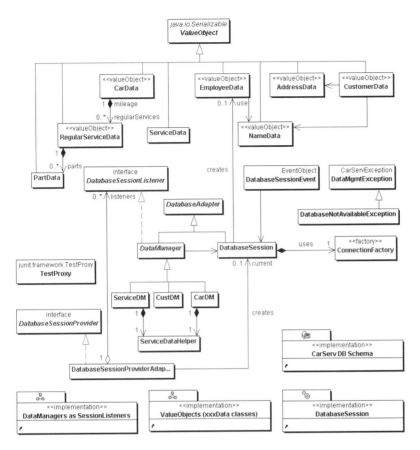

Figure 6–23
A package class diagram showing simple class icons and shortcuts to related diagrams.

doesn't do that out-of-the-box, but it can be programmed to do so through its open API. See the sidebar "Class-to-Class Diagram Hyperlink Module" to understand how it is done.

Class-to-Class Diagram Hyperlink Module

The class-to-class diagram hyperlink module automatically adds hyperlinks from every class to any class diagram in which it appears. This enhances the quality of the delivered documentation by making it easy to navigate through the many class diagrams that generally exist in a moderately sized project. The module itself uses the RwiSupport framework (see Appendix F for details).

For completeness the module should also remove hyperlinks that were generated by a previous run and which are now obsolete, but we haven't implemented this yet. Note that all the relevant classes need to be checked out of version control before running the module so that the hyperlinks can be added.

The following diagram shows the classes we have created to implement the module:

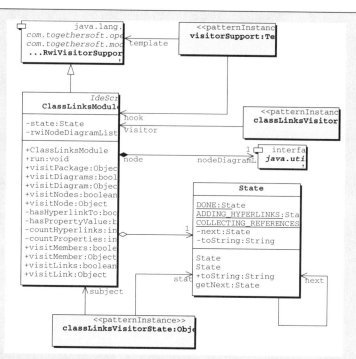

Figure 6–24
Class diagram for hyperlinking module.

You can see that we've used the subclass design to create the ClassLinks-
Module. *The module is stateful, so we've used the Objects for State pattern
(State pattern: Gamma et al. 1995) to keep track of the current state.*

*The first step is to collect references (shortcuts) held in each diagram, holding
them in a map containing lists of diagrams by node. Here's the code that does
the job:*

```
1   public Object visitDiagram(RwiDiagram rwiDiagram) {
2     for (RwiNodeReferenceEnumeration enum =
3         rwiDiagram.nodeReferences();
4         enum.hasMoreElements(); ) {
5
6       RwiNodeReference rwiNodeReference =
7         enum.nextRwiNodeReference();
8
9       if (rwiNodeReference.isImported()) {
10        RwiNode rwiNode = rwiNodeReference.getNode();
11        if (RwiSupport.isRwiNodeClassOrInterface(rwiNode)){
12          List diagramList =
13            (List)rwiNodeDiagramListMap.get(rwiNode);
14          if (diagramList == null) {
15            diagramList = new LinkedList();
16            rwiNodeDiagramListMap.put(rwiNode,diagramList);
17          }
18          diagramList.add(rwiDiagram);
19        }
20      }
21    }
22    return null;
23  }
```

The second step is for each node to add hyperlinks, if necessary, to the diagrams held in the diagram list for that node. Here's the code for that step (some error handling has been omitted):

```
 1   public Object visitNode(RwiNode rwiNode) {
 2     List diagramList =
 3       (List)rwiNodeDiagramListMap.get(rwiNode);
 4     if (diagramList == null) {
 5       return null;
 6     }
 7     for (Iterator iter = diagramList.iterator();
 8          iter.hasNext(); ) {
 9       RwiDiagram rwiDiagram = (RwiDiagram)iter.next();
10       if (!hasHyperlinkTo(rwiNode, rwiDiagram)) {
11         rwiNode.addProperty(RwiProperty.HYPERLINK,
12           RwiSupport.uniqueNameOf(rwiDiagram));
13       }
14     }
15     return null;
16   }
```

To build and install this module, first download `classlinks.zip` from the Web site at www.bettersoftwarefaster.com, and then extract:

```
classlinks\
   src\            // source and the Together project file
   diag\           // diagrams
   classes\        // compiled code
   manifest\       // manifest to describe module
   bat\            // batch files (install)
```

When you load up the project, you'll notice from the project properties that the project references `rwisupport.jar` in its classpath, so if you didn't build this JAR file already, then you'll need to; see Appendix F. Then build the `classlinks` project.

The `install.bat` script assumes that `%TOGETHER%` environment variable is set up to point to the Together installation, e.g., `c:\Together-soft\Together6.0`. Set this up if necessary. Then, run `bat\install.bat` (to copy the class files under `%TOGETHER%`.

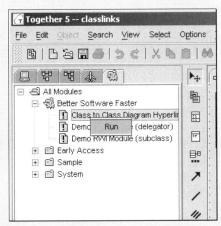

Figure 6–25
Invoking the custom module.

Some Provisos

One place that you might want to add a realization hyperlink is to state transitions (on state chart diagrams) with system events (e.g., as enumerated through the technique we introduced in Chapter 4, "The Stakeholder Step: Specify Requirements"). At the time of writing, Together doesn't support hyperlinking either to state transitions or to operations. But, an implicit semantic link (based on a naming convention) could be checked for and verified with a custom-written module. This would look for all design elements with `shapeType` property of `TransitionLink` (that is, the state transitions) and check that their event property was set to the name of a defined system event.

You may also have wondered why it is that when you add a hyperlink from an operation or a class (say, the `BookInCommand` class in the app package of the *CarServ* case study) to a use case (say, `Book in Car`), there is no JavaDoc tag added to the code. The answer is that this type of link is actually added to the other side—that is, to the `xxx.dfUseCase` file that contains the use case that you've referred to. If you compare the `System Use Case.dfUseCase` file before and after adding this hyperlink (it is just a text file), you will see the following changes made:

```
1  /**
2     @shapeType Hyperlink
3     @_modelType link
4     @_ref <oiref:java#Class#com.bettersoftwarefaster.
              carserv.app.BookInCommand:oiref><oihard>
5     @_reversed
6  */
7  class link14 {
8  }}/
```

While we don't need to understand all this, it is clear that this data defines the link from the `BookInCommand` class to the `Book in Car` use case of which this hyperlink is a member. Note the `@_reversed` tag, which shows that this is a hyperlink *to* this use case, not from it.

This way of handling hyperlinks suggests to us that bidirectional hyperlinks (navigable in both directions) ought to be simple for the TogetherSoft engineers to implement, and this is certainly an enhancement that we're looking forward to using.

In the meantime, it is worth remembering that if you hyperlink code to use cases (or any other design artifact that does not have a source code representation), then it won't be the code that is modified, but the design artifact. If you have your software under code control (and you will, of course), then you need to check out design artifacts (the `xxx.dfUseCase` file or the appropriate file if using standalone design elements) in order to hyperlink through to them. An unfortunate side-effect of this implementation, is that the version control system might indicate that a review of a requirement change is necessary when no change has really taken place,

Design Patterns

Identifying and documenting *instances* of design patterns in your design can be a very powerful technique in assisting others to understand your design. Typically, this means annotating a class diagram somehow to point out to the reader that there is an instance of some pattern. Together doesn't keep track of patterns and pattern instances directly, but it's simple enough to do yourself, and the *CarServ* case study uses this technique throughout.

UML talks about patterns as parameterized collaborations (Fowler 2000a) and this is also suggested by Together's *Apply Pattern* dialog box, which makes the parameters of patterns visible. When explaining a new design it is useful to relate the role the classes play in these parameterized collaborations. The JUnit authors (Beck and Gamma) describe the design of the JUnit framework in just this way; search out the "Cook's Tour" article for example—under `%TOGETHER%\lib\junit\doc\cookstour`—for an informative read.

This is why we sought out a way to make the use of patterns visible in Together. Our technique for documenting pattern instances is as follows. First, we create a `patterns` package to hold the definitions of patterns, such as `Observer`, `Template`, and so on. This package is somewhat equivalent to having a `requirements` package to hold use cases. Then, for each pattern that we have used, we'll either fill in the description of each of those patterns or, more often, just hyperlink to some favorite definition on the Web or our own intranet.

Then, we annotate our class diagrams with objects, each of which instantiates some class in the `patterns` package; these are our pattern instances. The experienced reader, who knows the patterns, gets to understand the design by looking first at the pattern instances, and only second at the classes.

As we've already said, the *CarServ* case study has lots of examples. In Figure 6-26, we have the `CommandManager` class diagram in the `infra` package.

This describes the `Command` subsystem. There are four instances of patterns shown in the diagram, and they are represented as objects stereotyped «patternInstance». The pattern instances indicate which classes are playing which roles with respect to the pattern of which they are an instance.

For example, the `CommandManager` class plays the role of the Subject in an instance of the Observer pattern. This object keeps track of a list of observers—in this case, `CommandHistoryListeners`. The pattern itself is represented on the diagram as an object, instantiating the class `patterns.Observer`. We're sure you get the idea.

Documenting patterns this way is a good way to get a feel for pattern density; in general, more patterns across a smaller number of classes is good. Beck and Gamma talk about high pattern density as common for mature frameworks: "Once you discover what problem you are really solving, then you can begin to 'compress' the solution, leading to a denser and denser field of patterns where they provide leverage."

The corollary of this is that if you can't spot any patterns in your design, then you should be worried. Effectively, what you are saying is, "I have such a unique problem that I've had to come up with a unique solution: one

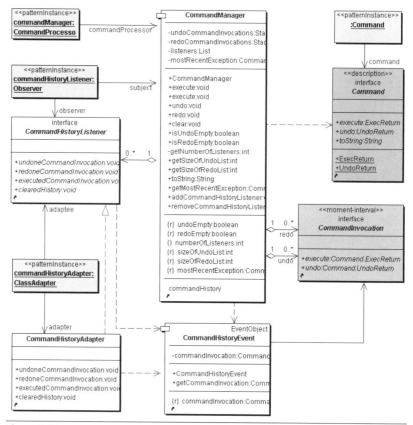

Figure 6-26
Pattern instances make it easier to understand a design.

that's never been done before." We think project managers should be concerned with such a report. So, the presence of patterns is a reassurance—though you do need to make sure you are applying the appropriate patterns, not just patterns for patterns sake.

If you decide to document pattern instances this way, then you'll need to customize Together. By default, Together does not allow associations to be drawn from objects to classes. This *can* be changed by editing the `model.config` file in Together's `config` directory, but a better approach still is to provide a separate `.config` file, named such that it will be loaded after `model.config` to override the appropriate config definition. The file `zzzBSwF.patternInstances.config` does precisely this. Download the file from the *www.bettersoftwarefaster.com*, and install by copying into `%TOGETHER%/config` (see Appendix C for more details).

This `.config` file also overrides definitions in `view.config` so that patterns and pattern instances are highlighted in a different color: We like to use this technique to color in notes as well. The `.config` file `zzzBSwF.coloredNotes.config` does this. Again, you can download this from *www.bettersoftwarefaster.com*.

We look at the stereotype of the instantiated class of the pattern instance to color in the icon. This means that the «patternInstance» stereotype isn't used directly—but, it is helpful for those who are using Together without the customized colors. It would be nice if Together could automatically change the stereotype of objects that instantiate classes stereotyped «pattern» to «patternInstance». And of course you can, by writing an open API module. See the following sidebar for the details of how to do this.

PatternInstance Module

The PatternInstance *module applies the* «patternInstance» *stereotype to any objects instantiated from a class whose stereotype is* «pattern». *To install the module, the file you need from the Web site is* patterninstance.zip. *This can be installed in a similar manner to the* classlinks *module you saw earlier in this chapter. The module's class diagram is shown below.*

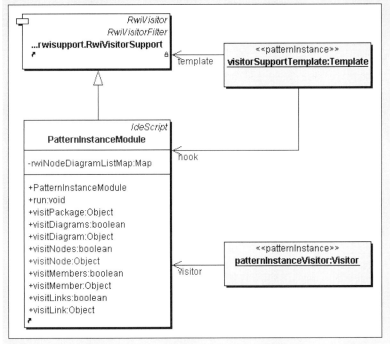

Figure 6–27
The Pattern Instance Module itself uses the Visitor and Template Patterns.

We also generated a sequence diagram (right-click Generate Sequence Diagram*) from the code for* PatternInstanceModule.visitNode()*; this is where the action happens. The sequence diagram is shown in Figure 6-28.*

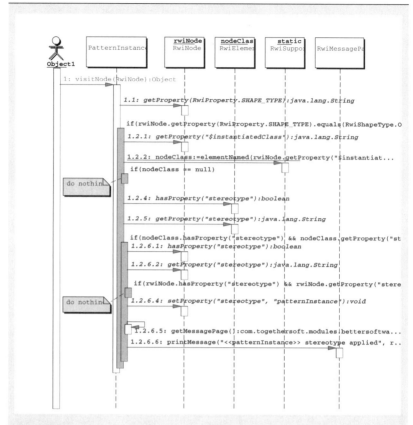

Figure 6–28

Sequence Diagram for `PatternInstanceModule.visitNode`

This diagram shows that each RWI node passed to the module is checked to see if it is an object. If it is, then the instantiated class for that object node (if any) is obtained.

The properties of this node are then checked; if it has a stereotype of <<pattern>>, then the stereotype for the original object node is set to <<patternInstance>>.

Together's Document Generation

Creating hyperlinked design documentation would be of little use without being able to export the information somehow. We shouldn't expect that the user of the documentation set necessarily has access to Together.

You can generate a JavaDoc-compliant web site using *Project* → *Documentation* → *Generate* HTML. In fact, the web site is a superset of the javadoc documentation, since it adds a number of features, including GIFs of the diagrams, image-mapped to provide direct hyperlinks.

For a large project, you'll find that generating the HTML can take a little time. Fortunately, it is possible to generate the HTML from the console. For any platform, the following will work:

```
TogetherCon.exe \
-script=com.togethersoft.modules.gendoc.GenerateDocumentation \
-d fully_qualified_project_dir\rtf  project_file.tpr
```

On Windows, you can use the equivalent umldoc program:

```
umldoc.exe -d fully_qualified_project_dir\rtf  project_file.tpr
```

Thus, we can create a simple batch/shell script to do this generation, and run it every night. We recommend that you do this after compiling the code and generating any metrics and audits.

As you probably know, it's also possible to generate RTF (rich text format) output for subsequent printing from your favorite word processor; this is *Project* → *Documentation* → *Generate Using Template*. You can filter out unneeded detail by creating your own template using *Project* → *Documentation* → *Design Template*. We usually start with the supplied `ProjectReport.tpl`, which will report on everything, clone it, and then remove the elements that we don't need.

And in case you haven't found it, it's also possible to generate the documentation in PDF format. To do this, it's *File* → *Print Documentation* then select *Send to*=PDF. Very nice.

Documenting Existing Code

To implement your application, you'll need to use numerous APIs, either part of the J2SE or J2EE platform (`java.util`, `java.sql`, `javax.servlet.http`, and so on) or indeed third-party packages (JDOM, Apache, etc.). If you're using an API that's new to you, then Together's reverse engineering capabilities can be very helpful. We often use reverse engineering ourselves in this way: Pointing Together at the source code for the JUnitX framework got us up and running quickly, and was the basis of much of the detail behind its presentation in this chapter and Appendix B.

Often, it is possible to obtain the source code, and you'll get the most information from Together if you do this. However, Together can also reverse engineer byte code, whether it is in a JAR file or not. Another option is, if the source code isn't available but hasn't been obfuscated, then you could always run a decompiler over it first.

Table 6-2 shows what information Together makes available when the code being reverse engineered is source code, byte code, or within a JAR file.

Table 6–2

Information shown from reverse-engineering different resources

Resource		Classes in Explorer Pane?	View/ Modify Source?	Associations Between Classes?
Source code		Yes	Yes	Yes
Byte code		Yes	No, shows a locked icon	No, except dependencies arising from operation signatures
JAR file	JAR file in a directory on project path	Yes, but shown residing in JAR file		
	JAR file added *as* a project path	Yes, providing separate path for diagrams is defined		

Source code also allows sequence diagrams to be generated, whereas byte code does not.

There is nothing to prevent classes on the classpath (as specified by in Project → Properties on the Search/Classpath tab) from being added as shortcuts to class and package class diagrams. The main difference between adding a JAR file as a Project Path and adding it in the Search/Classpath is that with the former, the contents of the JAR file will be parsed. In other words (provided its contents have been added as shortcuts to a diagram), dependencies between the classes in the JAR file will be shown. This does not happen for classes from JARs simply on the classpath. Another difference is that classes held in JARs defined on the Project Path appear in generated documentation.

Reviews and Inspections

All the automated quality measurement facilities in Together and other tools can be invaluable. What they can't be, though, is a complete replacement for what the Royal Navy likes to call the "Mark One Eyeball"—people have got to look at and examine the products if you are going to remove the majority of defects from them.

In fact, the automated facilities like audits, metrics, and customized document generation are inputs to the review process, and they help reviewers—including the author—to find and remove defects at the earliest possible stage. Removing defects early pays for itself many times over, so deciding the right time to review artifacts is crucial—too early, and there are too many defects and reviewers time is wasted; too late, and others have built on the errors and wasted their efforts.

Reviews can take many forms and include:

- Self: The author or developer reviewing his or her own work prior to submission.
- Pair: Working in pairs, one of the key practices of XP.
- Walkthrough: Informal review with peers.
- Formal reviews, such as Critical Design Review (CDR): Review events as part of a formal process.
- User review: Presentation to and feedback from users.

Inspection, sometimes called Fagan Inspection after Michael Fagan, who instituted the practice at IBM in the 1970s (Fagan 1976), is a particular way to carry out reviews based on a number of key practices. The focus of the inspections is to find defects and to predict the remaining level of defects based on statistical analysis of the inspectors' reports. Another key feature built into inspections is process improvement, as not only are defects sought, but systematic sources of defects are sought as well. This is very helpful. A comprehensive guide to software inspection is provided by Gilb & Graham (1993).

There is, though, a significant problem to address with iterative processes and reviews. We expect the large documents like the requirements specification to change more or less continuously through the lifecycle of the project. New requirements will arise during the project, and requirements which initially had only an outline specification will get a more complete definition nearer to the point in the project when it will actually be implemented. The problem is that reviews of summary documents for complete phases go out of date more or less immediately, and then the review process has to be repeated. Large reviews are too expensive to be economic if they have to be repeated continuously, and they are not effective if the artifacts are changed without further review.

XP has an interesting solution to this problem, and it is certainly in step with the theme of this chapter, which is continuous quality measurement. It is called pair programming. Kent Beck has explained the philosophy of XP as taking practices that we know are good in software engineering, such as testing and in this case peer review, and turning the dial to the maximum. If peer review is good, why not do it continuously by programming in a pair and not accepting any code into the code base that has not been produced by two people working together, one with their hands on the mouse and keyboard and the other reviewing—actively watching, questioning, understanding, and searching for defects to remove? While there are many admirers of the XP process, not all of them actually adopt the process, and this is one of the practices that is hard to switch to. It is often cited as the reason why a project chose not to adopt XP but to use another process. Pair programming, strictly applied, means that at least all the code is reviewed (as it is produced). Whether this is as effective as, say, Fagan Inspections for removing defects is difficult to say, but it is a continuous quality measurement process as opposed to discrete events. When the pressure to deliver is on, it is certainly possible for the project manager to drop an inspection to "catch up" some time—meaning that the change doesn't get reviewed. Pair programming on the other hand means every change is reviewed as it happens.

"We Don't Pair Program Because…"

This isn't a book on XP and pair programming, but we thought we might just address one objection often made: "We don't pair program because the customer won't accept a 50 percent reduction in the amount of code being written."

There have now been enough XP projects run for some rule-of-thumb metrics to have emerged, one of which is that the coding throughput is not down by 50 percent on most of them, but more like 15 percent. In other words, two programmers working in a pair will get 85 percent of the code written that would have been done by the programmers working by themselves.

The Continuous Step:
Measure the Quality

Still can't sell that reduction to the customer? Well, think on: The quality of the delivered code should be substantially higher than that of single programmers since the review process is occurring simultaneously with the development, so the amount of time spent reviewing code and/or fixing production defects is much reduced. Net effect: Pair programming may well give you a higher overall development throughput than single programmers.

If you don't adopt pair programming but still agree with us that all changes to the artifacts of the requirements, tests, design, and implementation need to be reviewed, how do you overcome the iteration problem? The solution is not to review summary documents like the Use Case Model or the High Level Design as one document. Instead, each use case and feature, each collaboration design, each class or package, and each feature set functional test specification must be separately specified and reviewed. The configuration management system is essential to plan and implement this approach effectively. Document generation is also important so that the summary documents can be easily produced when individual elements are changed.

Reviewing the Build Against the Initial Design

One project manager we talked with highlighted the value of design reviews taking place at the point when the code is being promoted to build. He said, "In practical use we find that developers can still move away from design frameworks if they are not marshaled, or their work is not reviewed. In order to be able to do the required auditing, we now take a snapshot version of design artifacts at the point of handover, by marking a configuration in the version control system. We then compare this configuration to the modified class diagrams, etc., created from the build configuration as part of the automated build process.

"This allows us to easily spot differences—and structural differences in particular. The debate is then had over whether the design has been improved or the build needs to be refactored to fit the design. We have had examples of both, and this benefits the designers and the builders as they learn best practice from each other's experience.

"This approach also addresses one of the issues analysts and designers raise, that builds should not be able to corrupt their models. Though the original models are accessible through version control (and therefore uncorrupted), in the build configuration the model diagrams reflect the 'reality' of what has been implemented. The fact that Together makes model and implementation one and the same was a major factor in selecting Together over other development platforms in the first place."

This experience highlights the importance of design (and other) reviews in the development process. Not only is the software and documentation improved, but knowledge is also transferred between team members, improving future results as well.

Another important aspect to understand is the dependencies between the artifacts. The minimum metamodel shows not just the relationships between the essential model elements, but also the minimum set of dependencies that we wish to exist between them. Look again at Figure 1-3 in Chapter 1. This shows that a design (or interaction) and a functional test are both dependent on the requirement. This is to be expected—if the requirement changes, we expect to have to update the design and the test specification. However, the code is not directly dependent on the requirement in this model. This is so that reusable code can be purchased or designed independently from specific functional specifications. The consequence of this from a review standpoint is that not everything has to be re-reviewed—only those things that are actually changed or that are directly dependent on the change.

What's Next

In this chapter we have looked at how continuous quality measurement is achieved with Together and how it is an integral aspect of software development. We measure quality in either a black-box fashion (not looking inside) or white-box fashion (probing the internals to the lowest level). We use testing, metrics, audits, document generation, and inspection to establish the quality status of our product, from unqualified status through developer quality, alpha quality, beta quality, and GA quality status.

We have also seen how Together's open API allows custom modules to be written that can check for different aspects, particularly the completeness of the non-code artifacts (use case diagrams, sequence diagrams, etc.), with respect to any given development process.

In the next chapter, we look at the detailed design and implementation: how to effectively turn the specification artifacts into real and working code.

chapter 7

The Micro Step:
Design and Implement

*There are two ways of constructing a software design.
One way is to make it so simple that there are
obviously no deficiencies. And the other way is to
make it so complicated that there are no obvious
deficiencies.*

C. A. R. Hoare

*A good object has a clearly defined role in the overall
structure of objects.*

Trygve Reenskaug (creator of the Model-View-
Controller concept)

*A designer knows he has achieved perfection not
when there is nothing left to add, but when there is
nothing left to take away.*

Antoine de Saint-Exupéry

*Abstraction—the process of forgetting information
so that things that are different can be treated as if
they are the same.*

Barbara Liskov

We now explore the main activities and issues involved in actually designing and then implementing a given functional requirement, expressed,
for example, as a use case. Our starting point is a valid build for which the currently included requirements all have valid functional tests that pass and in
which the existing code has valid unit tests. We contrast this "micro" step for
design and implementation with the "macro" step, considered in the next
chapter, where the overall architecture of the system is considered. We also
look at the features and setup of Together to assist this process, and how we
can configure it to suit our project's needs.

At this point in the book you might be expecting us to explain the process of taking a requirements specification document as a whole and turning it into executable code. But then again, maybe you know us well enough by now not to expect everything in the expected order!

We are looking at the micro process—that of turning *one* functional requirement into runnable code—*before* considering the macro level of architecture and frameworks. There are two reasons why we are doing this:

- First, we learn more naturally from the bottom up, with the detail before the summary, the instance before the class. Looking at the step of implementing one requirement is an important prerequisite to understanding how you might undertake implementing a thousand functional requirements. More is different, most certainly—but let's at least start by looking at the process for one.
- Second, in small projects the macro process may be dealt with less formally than is necessary on large projects—the micro process is therefore essential to the small team, whereas arguably the macro is less essential.[36]

So, the steps we consider here are shown in Figure 7-1, which is yet another variant of our basic development process (see also Chapter 1, Figure 1-5, Chapter 5, Figure 5-1, and Chapter 6, Figure 6-4).

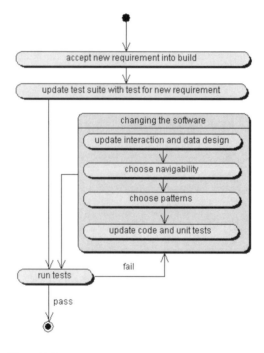

Figure 7–1
The micro development process.

---

36. As we'll argue in the next chapter, it is still something we believe is important, even in small projects.

The diagram shows more specific details for dealing with the scenario of implementing a new functional requirement. Before this, we need to agree on and specify a fair test of the requirement if this was not previously agreed during requirements capture.

In this chapter we will consider a worked example, looking at various aspects to consider. We then provide some more general advice and tips for you to consider in the following areas:

- Effective interaction design
- Effective class diagrams
- Patterns
- Documenting existing code
- Configuring Together

Enough preamble; on with the chapter!

We start by looking at the implementation of one new functional requirement, focusing on

- Accepting the new requirement into the build
- Defining a functional test to validate that requirement
- Designing the user interaction
- Designing the object interaction
- Designing the persistent data

Accepting a New Requirement into the Build

Requirements are not generally captured one by one. Use cases and features are discovered through interaction with users and stakeholders, and many will exist before any are implemented. During the active life of a system, new requirements are always being found and specified, so there will always be requirements in our model that are not yet implemented. In order for the rules of the minimum metamodel to be fulfilled—specifically, that every included requirement must have a valid test that passes and a design using implemented and tested classes and operations—there must be a mechanism for indicating whether a requirement is included in a particular build.

There are a number of mechanisms for doing this. If the feature list is being kept outside of Together, such as in a spreadsheet, then this may indicate whether the feature has already been implemented, is to be implemented in the current build, or possibly in which future release the feature is planned to be implemented. Alternatively, the feature list can be kept within Together, and the same sort of information can be tracked, typically by defining some new custom properties of use cases and sub-use cases. We discuss how to configure Together to add new properties at the end of this chapter, and Appendix E provides the detail.

The advantage of using Together to hold the features list is that it becomes possible to create custom pen API modules to ensure that the rules of the minimum metamodel are followed. In other words, if there is an included feature that does not have a corresponding test, then the custom module can flag this up. Although such modules are not yet included in the delivered features of Together ControlCenter, nor have we implemented them as a companion to this book, it would be straightforward and cost-effective to do so. Using Together to store the requirements is therefore a worthwhile first step.

As an example of a new requirement for this chapter, consider the first sentences for the normal flow of the Service Car use case:

1. The service manager asks for the customer's name and zip code, and enters this information into the system.
2. The system verifies that the customer is known, and displays the cars that are known to be owned by the customer.

If you look at the case study code, you'll find this was implemented as a lookup dialog.

The example enhancement is to modify this lookup functionality. Since the lookup is performing somewhat more than that implied by the wording within the Service Car use case, the first step is to make the flow more explicit by introducing a new Lookup Customer sub-use case. If you like, we are refactoring the existing requirements in order to make them easier to modify. We end up with:

Service Car

1. Include: *Lookup Customer*.
2. The system displays the cars that are known to be owned by the customer just looked up.

Lookup Customer

1. The service manager asks for the customer's name and/or zip code, and enters such information as provided into the system.
2. The service manager then requests to view all customers whose details match those entered.
3. The system displays the details of the matching customers, and the service manager selects one of them.

The use case diagram is now as shown in Figure 7-2.

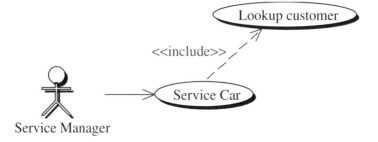

Figure 7–2
The Service Car use case includes the sub-use case of looking up the customer and entering details.

Now we can introduce our new feature request, which is to allow customers to be looked up by street address as well as by their name and their zip or postal code. After all, there could be many Smiths or Joneses in the system, and it is possible not all of them know their zip or postal code.

The new words for the Lookup Customer use case are now:

1. The service manager asks for the customer's name, **address,** and zip code, and enters such information as provided into the system.
2. The service manager then requests to view all customers whose details match those entered.
3. The system displays the details of the matching customers, and the service manager selects one of them.

At the point a requirement is accepted for implementation within the next timebox, it is useful to get together the implementers (FDD calls them the feature team) with the stakeholders or definers of the functional requirement for a feature walkthrough. The main purpose of such an event is to get a full understanding of what the users really need and to understand the impact on the user interface design, the program design, and the persistent data design.

Too-Clever Lookups
Dan Haywood

The worked example used in this chapter is based on enhancing the lookup of Customers for CarServ; in fact, all we will actually be doing is adding an extra field to a dialog box. The idea of bringing together all the implementers and stakeholders to evaluate the impact on the user interface will therefore seem rather heavy-handed; and of course, for such a small enhancement, it would be.

And yet...I remember seeing an application where the mundane process of doing lookups on customers had been enhanced to a quite remarkable level of sophistication. Once a customer had been looked up through the appropriate dialog box, the user could "drag" the customer's details into a holding area; a little stickman icon showing that customer's name would then be shown. If the user needed to access that customer's details again, she could simply drag the stickman icon over to the application, and the lookup would automatically be performed. Nice, huh?

There's a punch line (you knew there would be). Unfortunately, the people who came up with this cunning bit of UI wizardry were the implementers, who thought it would be "cool." When the users saw this holding area and those funny little stickman icons, (a) they were confused, and (b) when they understood what it did, they decreed that it was of no use—the users hardly ever had recourse to look up the same customer's details twice anyway.

So, that was a waste of money, pretty though the user interface was. If the stakeholders (users) and implementers had sat down earlier, it could have been avoided.

Following the walkthrough, it may be necessary to update the estimate for implementing the feature so that this feeds into the ongoing plan for the whole system. Another output of the feature walkthrough should be an understanding of the sequence of system events that occur. Indeed, this is precisely what we have done with the refactoring of the Service Car use case above. We pick up on this shortly when we look at designing the user interaction.

Defining the Tests

Having identified the requirement, the tests to validate the requirement must be defined. This should be done prior to, or at least independent from, the design process. Given that this requirement will primarily impact the user interface, we might initially define a manual test that could later be automated using Together's visual test builder, described in Chapter 6. Alternatively, we could define a series of automated tests from the start, provided there are interfaces defined in the specification that can be used to write the tests. Since we have defined suitable interfaces, this is what we do here.

There are four classes that are impacted by the new requirement, one in each of the following packages: `datamgmt`, `domain`, `app`, and `ui`. Each of these has just one public method that is impacted:

- `datamgmt.CustDM.findCustomers()`
- `domain.CustomerFactory.listCustomers()`
- `app.CarServApp.listCustomers()`
- `ui.LookupCustomerDialog.<init>()`

The `findCustomers()` and the two `listCustomers()` methods take just three arguments: `lastname`, `firstname`, and `zipcode`. The new specifications for these methods should be that they take four arguments: `lastname`, `firstname`, `address`, and `zipcode`.

The changes required for `datamgmt.TestCustDM` are

```
1  public void testFindCustomersViaAddressStreet()
2        throws DataMgmtException, TestAccessException {
3    CustomerData[] actualCustomers =
4      custDM.findCustomers(null, null, "oolyback", null);
5
6    assertEquals(TestData.nigellaLawson(), actualCustomers[0] );
7  }
```

The other `testFindCustomerXXX()` methods also need changing, but only to pass in a null for the address.

The test cases within the `domain` package do not directly test `list-Customers()`, because if `CustDM.findCustomers()` works, then it shows that `CustomerFactory.listCustomers()` also works. However, the `CustomerFactory.listCustomers()` method is called in a couple of places within `domain.CarTestCase` (the common base class of domain test cases) to set up the fixture, so the `setUp()` method of `domain.CarTestCase` does need changing to pass through four arguments rather than three.

Turning to the app package, the `app.TestCarServApp` does invoke `CarServApp.listCustomers()`, so will need some minor modifications to pass through the four required arguments. In this test case the `CarServApp.listCustomers()` method is not as exhaustively tested as the `CustDM.findCustomers()` method was; really, this is just confidence testing at this stage.

Finally, the *CarServ* case study has no unit tests for the user interface, so (in the absence of a visual test script) changes to `ui.LookupCustomer-Dialog` will need to be signed off during user acceptance testing.

Designing the User Interaction

Since we have used use cases to specify the required functionality, it is natural to use sequence diagrams to play out the scenarios embodied within those use cases. The sequence diagrams need not contain any of the objects within the system; the focus is more on the interface between the actors and the system. We prefer sequence diagrams over collaboration diagrams because we like to take the scenario text and copy it as a number of notes on our new sequence diagram. This then describes what needs to happen at each step. We then add an actor to the sequence diagram, and while we are at it, we hyperlink to an actor in the use case diagram that uses this use case.

Other specification inputs include the activity diagrams (if any) and system events for the use case we are designing. The former makes sure that we don't lose sight of the overall business process, and the latter is mostly to ensure that we use consistent terminology.

Figure 7-3 shows the (albeit somewhat trivial) sequence diagram for the Lookup Customer use case.

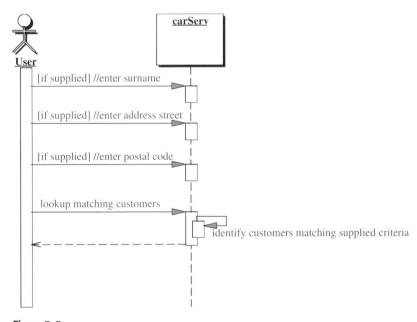

Figure 7–3
A sequence diagram makes the user interaction clear.

This may seem somewhat dry and sterile, and if working with users—who quite possibly are nontechnical and not versed in UML notation—then some other way to design the user interaction may be in order.

One technique is to storyboard the user interface in a way similar to that done by movie scriptwriters and directors. That is, the user interface dialogs are literally drawn up using pen and flipchart. This technique offers a number of benefits. First, it is easy and quick to do; second, both the user and the programmer contribute; third, the user does not need to be constrained by convention or by what (the programmer thinks) is technically possible. These storyboards may be discarded once used.

On the other hand, sometimes it can be as easy for the programmer to sketch out te user interface and interaction directly on the computer. Together v6.0 introduced the GUI Builder feature that has this as its goal.

The GUI Builder allows a user interface to be designed by dropping Swing or AWT user interface components onto the screen. Each such component is added as a field of the class being designed (a subclass of a container such as JDialog or JFrame). The properties of those components are then set in a method called initGUI(). Some Java IDEs that support GUI design work similarly, though choose a different name for the initializing method. With that in mind, the configuration options for Together's GUI Builder lets different method names be indicated as that containing the GUI composition code, to support GUI code originally built using one of those IDEs.

Together's own wizards for creating GUI container classes (*File* → *New*) creates classes that already support the initGUI() method. The following code is generated for a new JDialog:

```
1   package ui;
2   import javax.swing.*;
3   import java.awt.*;
4   import java.awt.event.*;
5
6   public class LookupCustomerDialog extends JDialog {
7     public LookupCustomerDialog(Frame parent, boolean modal) {
8       super(parent, modal);
9       initGUI();
10      pack();
11    }
12    private void initGUI() {
13      addWindowListener(
14        new java.awt.event.WindowAdapter() {
15          public void windowClosing(
16            java.awt.event.WindowEvent evt){
17              closeDialog(evt);
18            }
19          }
20        );
21    }
22
23    private void closeDialog(WindowEvent evt) {
24      setVisible(false);
25      dispose();
26    }
27  }
```

With the GUI Builder feature enabled (it is an activateable feature), the designer pane can be toggled to show the GUI Designer. This brings up a representation of the container class, plus a toolbar. Figure 7-5 shows the sketching out of the fields that make up the prompt section of the Lookup-CustomerDialog in the CarServ case study.

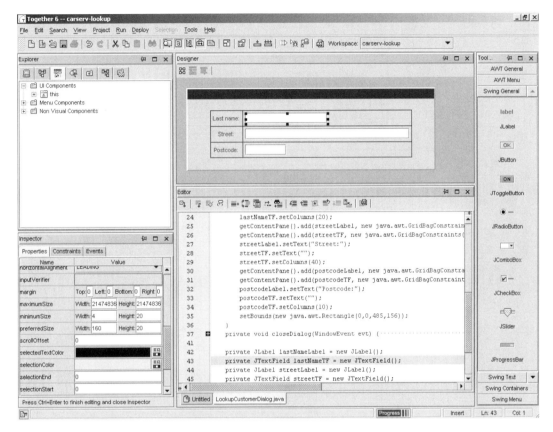

Figure 7–4
Together's GUI Builder being used to design the carserv LookupCustomer dialog.

There are a few things to note in the above figure:

- the editor pane has been split so that you can see both the member variables, and part of the implementation of the `initGUI()` method;
- the inspector pane shows some of the properties of the `lastNameTF` text field;
- to the right you can see the toolbar palette of other user interface components that can be added to the dialog container;
- the first method call within the `initGUI()` method sets the layout manager to be a `java.awt.GridBagLayout`.

When components are being added to the container, guidelines and area shading are overlaid on top of the visual representation of the container class to indicate where the component may be added. For example, if a `BorderLayout` is in force, then five different areas are shaded, corresponding to this layout manager's north, west, south, east, and center regions. On the other hand, if a `GridBagLayout` is in force, then a number of different areas appear, such that the component can be added relative to existing components in the grid.

The above discussion shows GUI Builder being used to generate code from a GUI design, but—as you might have expected for Together—the GUI Builder feature can also reverse engineer existing code and render the user interface for a container class based on the contents of its initializing method (`initGUI()` or equivalent).

At the time of writing, the GUI Builder feature did not support custom subclasses of standard GUI components. For example, within the *CarServ* case study, the `infra.MnemonicButton` is a subclass of `javax.swing.JButton`, and `infra.HeadedTable` is a subclass of `javax.swing.JTable`. The GUI Builder does not allow such JavaBeans to be imported into the toolbar, nor support the rendering of such JavaBeans in its interface.[37] However, we do expect to see such enhanced functionality in subsequent Together versions.

There is another way to define user interfaces, namely, to apply best practice—in other words, to apply a pattern. When implementing for the J2EE architecture (predominantly Web-based applications, though standalone Swing applications are also supported), Sun's J2EE patterns may well help. These are available as patterns within Together, as Figure 7-5 shows. Within the *CarServ* case study, there is extensive use of one common pattern in particular, namely the Observer pattern (Gamma et al. 1995). For example, it is used to enable the user interface after the user has signed on, as shown in Figure 7-6.

Getting back to the worked example, to make the address lookup enhancement, the `ui.LookupCustomerDialog` class needs to be changed. The changes amount to not much more than adding a new field and calling the updated version of `CarServApp.listCustomers()`.

Designing the Object Interaction

In the case of the worked example, there really isn't a lot of object interaction; a single class from each tier interacts with a single class in the next tier. That is,

```
ui.LookupDialog calls
app.CarServApp, which calls
domain.CustomerFactory, which calls
datamgmt.CustDM.
```

The enhancement does not change this interaction flow.

---

37. For this reason (if no other) the *CarServ* case study doesn't use GUI *Builder* feature. We happen to like creating user interfaces using custom JavaBeans.

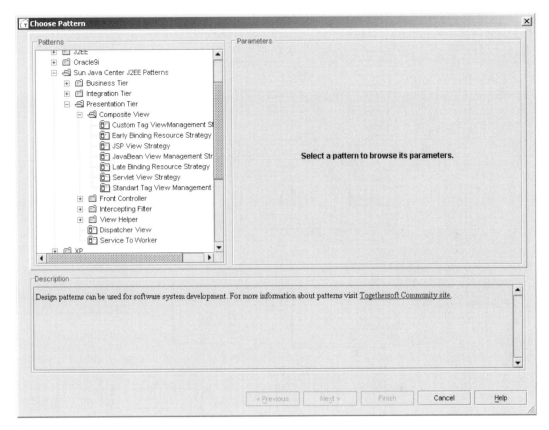

Figure 7–5
Together supports Sun's J2EE patterns.

If only all design were that easy! We have much more to say about making the correct interaction choices; it is, after all, one of the hardest of the object orientation disciplines to learn. But rather than discuss this in the context of our admittedly simple worked example, we've deferred this until later in the chapter.

The change required in `domain.CustomerFactory` class is simply to accept the additional `addressStreet` argument in its `listCustomers()` method and pass this onto `datamgmt.CustDM.findCustomers()`. Similarly, the change required in `app.CarServApp` is to take the additional `addressStreet` argument in `listCustomers()` and pass this through to `domain.CustomerFactory`.

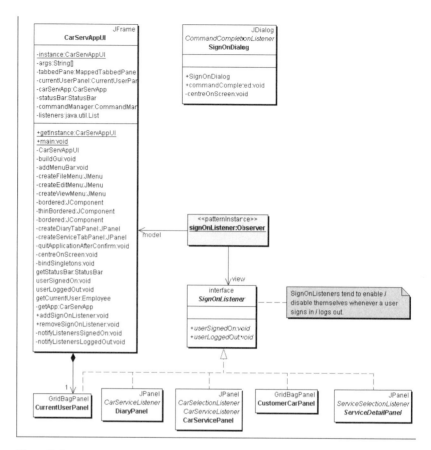

Figure 7–6

The Observer pattern is used throughout the *CarServ* user interface.

Designing the Persistent Data

When running through the changes to the unit tests, we started at the back-end persistence layer. After all, all dependencies lead to the back end. Figure 7-7 shows the database schema for *CarServ*.

As you can see, luckily the `adr_address` table already contains the `adr_street` column, so it looks like the information required is already present; we just need to provide the ability to query on it.

The changes needed to the `CustDM` class revolve around the implementation of the `getFindCustomerPS()` method; as you will have been expecting, essentially an extra `AND` clause is required in the `SELECT SQL` statement. The extra parameter of the `findCustomers()` method binds the argument to the SQL placeholder in the `findCustomerPS` prepared statement.

If the database schema *had* needed to be changed, then implementing the requirement would have needed some changes to the schema (`ALTER TABLE` statement) and might also have needed changes to the data itself.

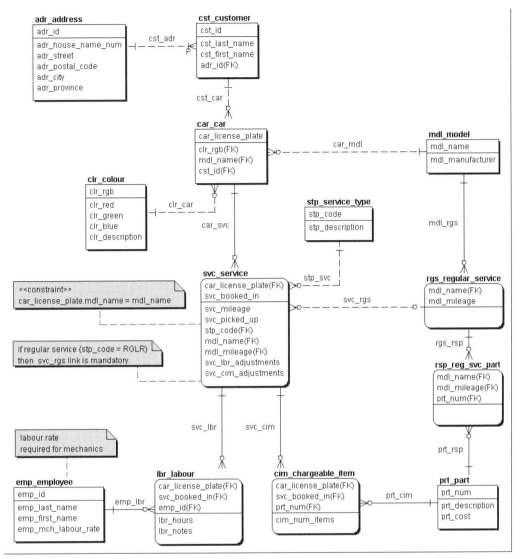

Figure 7–7
Database schema for the *CarServ* case study.

For example, if the street column hadn't been present, then it might be possible to determine the street name based on the already present postal code. Actually implementing the enhancement might then require some scheduled downtime to allow the Database Administrators to apply the change.

This section concludes our worked example of applying an enhancement. You can download the enhanced version of CarServ from *www.bettersoftwarefaster.com*, the file being `carserv-address.zip`. The remainder of this chapter provides various more general advice and tips for you to consider in your own development processes.

Having reviewed the design and implement step for just one simple requirement change, we now consider some general advice for this stage of development, first looking at how to design effective object interactions. Object-oriented programs execute functionality by sharing responsibilities between a number of objects which must collaborate to achieve the desired result. In a good design, each object will have a clearly-defined role in each scenario it participates in, which we can show on a sequence diagram. As well as considering sequence and collaboration diagrams in this section, we'll also look at navigability between objects and the dependencies that arise between the classes.

When modeling object interactions, and depending upon the complexity of the scenario, we may decide to have a number of sequence diagrams, with each sequence diagram dealing with a single system event. Each of these should be hyperlinked to the underlying use case.

Before and After

It is often useful to draw an example object configuration as at the start of the system event that triggers the scenario. This technique is based on that described in the Catalysis method (D'Souza & Wills 1998). The idea is to show an object diagram with a number of objects in their starting configuration, before the object interaction takes place. New objects and new links are then added to the object diagram, and links and objects that will be destroyed when the interaction has completed are also annotated. Any objects or links that will be created and then destroyed as part of the interaction—that are transient—are also similarly marked.

In other words, this single object interaction diagram shows both the "before" state and the "after" state. Or, if you prefer, it shows the pre-conditions and the post-conditions for the interaction.

We can hyperlink the object diagram to a sequence diagram, and then get down to doing the design. The mission—if we choose to accept it—is to get the object configuration from the before state to the after.

One of the contributors to *www.togethercommunity.com*, Paul Field, developed a `.config` file for Together that allows the lifetime of objects and links to be denoted, allowing the example object diagram to be easily annotated. A modified version of this `.config` file is available from *www.bettersoftwarefaster.com*. Download and install the file `zzzCatalysis.beforeAfter.config` into `$TGH$/config` directory, and then reload the configuration or just restart Together.

When you then create your objects and links, you will find a new property called `lifetime`. The values of this property are `new`, `destroyed`, `transient`, or `noChange`. The semantics of these values are shown in Table 7-1.

Table 7–1

Semantics of `lifetime` Property for Catalysis Before and After Object Diagrams

lifetime	before interaction	after interaction	notes
new	did not exist	exists	
destroyed	existed	no longer exists	
transient	did not exist	does not exist	is created during the interaction, but is removed before the interaction completes
noChange	existed	exists	

As an example of all this in practice, consider a drawing package that has different shapes on a picture. These shapes can be selected, and the user can request to create a group of shapes from the currently selection, as for example is being done in the partial screenshot shown in Figure 7-8. Figure 7-9 shows the before and after object diagram for this example, created using the `.config` file given above.

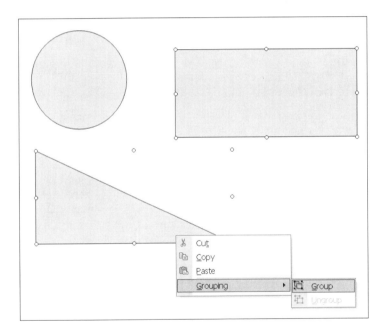

Figure 7–8

Partial screenshot of a graphical editor application grouping two objects.

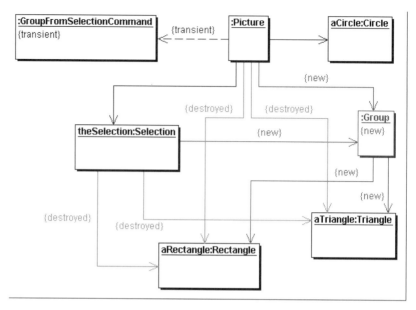

Figure 7–9
A single object diagram can show both the before and after state of an interaction.

Choosing Between Designs

To choose the best design, we'll draw up the interactions as we think works best, but to be honest, we often do some trial and error using a whiteboard before we commit ourselves to documenting any of these into Together. Good tool though Together is, no tool can ever have the immediacy of a whiteboard and some marker pens. Moreover, several of us can brainstorm different designs without crouching around a screen. Also, if we spent 20 minutes drawing up a lovely picture in Together, we know we'd start getting emotionally attached to it, no matter how good or bad it was.

Class/responsibility/collaboration (CRC) cards are another popular, non-CASE tool technique (Beck & Cunningham 1989); modeling in color builds on this (see Chapter 3, "The First Step: Model the Domain").

To help choose the best design, we look at two things:

- Navigability
- Dependencies

Dependencies Between Classes

Let's take a temporary detour from the CarServ case study to look at showing dependencies on class diagrams.

The following diagram (Figure 7-10) shows four different types of relationship between the classes. A `Person` *may be an* `Employee` *in a* `Company`*. The* `Company` *has a* `Map` *of* `Employees` *and also of* `Desks`*:*

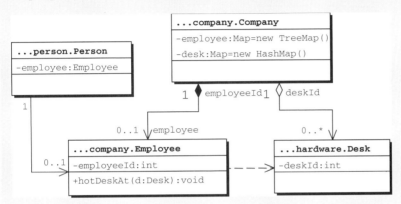

Figure 7–10
An example class diagram.

This company operates a hot-desking policy so that when the `Employee` *clocks in, she is allocated a desk to sit at for the day. The* `Employee` *does not hold an ongoing reference to this desk (there is no instance variable here), but nevertheless depends upon the concept of* `Desk` *because it appears in the* `hotDeskAt` *operation—in fact, in the method signature.*

The dotted line indicates the dependency between `Employee` *and* `Desk`*. Together does not show these by default, but can if configured through the options dialog box; check View Management → Dependencies → Show between Classes = true. In some cases it is most important to show these links in order to understand the design and a number of the book's class diagrams, in this chapter particularly, use this option.*

To explore these issues, let's consider two different designs from the *CarServ* example. We want to schedule a car in for a service, and this means instantiating a new `Service` instance. Figure 7-11 shows a simple view of our domain model.

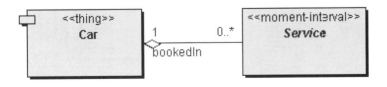

Figure 7–11
The domain model diagram for Cars and Services does not show navigability.

We can think of a couple of designs:

- The Car is asked to instantiate a Service; it creates and then remembers the Service. The Service does not know what Car it relates to.
- The Service is passed a Car object as a parameter of its constructor and it remembers this Car that it belongs to. The Car does not know about the Service object.

Figure 7-12 shows a sequence diagram for the first option, and Figure 7-13 shows the corresponding implementation class diagram.

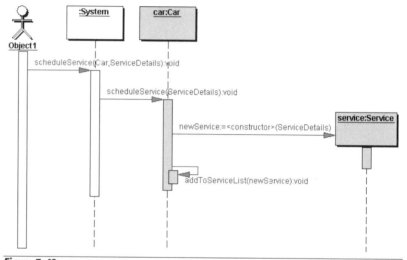

Figure 7–12

The Car is responsible for instantiating and holding Services.

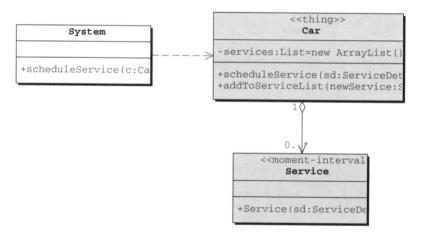

Figure 7–13

The navigability is from Car to Service.

Similarly, Figure 7-14 shows a sequence diagram for the second option, and Figure 7-15 shows the corresponding implementation class diagram.

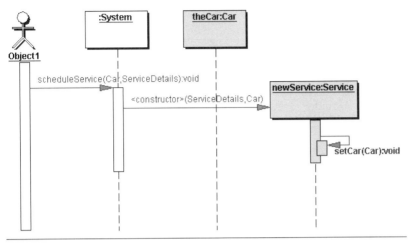

Figure 7–14
The System instantiates Service, and Service remembers the Car.

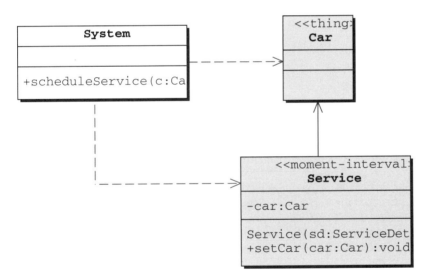

Figure 7–15
The navigability is from Service to Car.

These designs both have navigability in one direction only: Either the Car knows about the Services, but not vice versa, or the Service knows about the Car, but not vice versa. There is, of course, another design, where navigability is in both directions. We'll discuss this shortly.

Which of our two designs is the better? Considering just navigability, it is not clear which to go for, and we won't know which solution to adopt until we consider some other use cases. For example, will it be necessary for a Car to know if it has been booked in for a Service? If so, then the navigability implied by our first design looks more appropriate, since it also supports this additional requirement. If not, then either design may do.

Looking at dependencies (the dotted lines) can also help us decide between designs. A lot of design decisions are guided by the desirability of *loosely coupled, highly cohesive* components, principles first explained by Yourdon and Constantine (Yourdon and Constantine 1979). We can see from Figure 7-14 and Figure 7-15 that there are more dependencies in the second design—from System to Service—and so it is more highly coupled than the first design. This tips the balance and indicates we should go for the first design.

Bidirectional Associations

For any given scenario, there will be one navigability direction that works best. However, for a number of scenarios that involve the same two classes, you may find that the best navigability direction varies from one scenario to the next. In other words, you have a requirement for bidirectional navigability.

To see this, let's consider just two features that our *CarServ* application might need to implement. First, we might want to list all Services that a given Car has had; second, we might want to know what Car a given Service related to. These requirements will probably give rise to a bidirectional relationship.

There are a number of ways to model this in Together, and we'll look at these later in this chapter when we look at effective class diagrams. For now, we just want to visit the topic from the perspective of interaction design.

The problem with bidirectional associations is that they increase coupling within the design. If either class is modified, then there is the possibility that the other class will also need modification; at the very least, some impact analysis is required. And, of course, it is impossible to remove either class, because the other class has a dependency.

On the other hand, is that so severe? If the two classes reside within the same package, then probably not. After all, packages usually map onto deployment units, so there is no great hardship in changing both classes rather than one.

Another perspective on this is that classes are to packages as methods are to classes. A class is an association of methods: any method can call any other method, and all methods have access to common data (the instance variables). So, in the same way, any class within a package can call any other class within that package, and any instance variables with package-level visibility can be accessed.[38]

---

38. Indeed, in Java, any package of classes could even be rewritten to be a single class using Java's nested static classes.

When the bidirectional association is between classes in different packages, then it is a different story; these should almost certainly be avoided. We talk more about how to do this in Chapter 8.

Assigning Responsibility for Maintaining Associations

So far, we've talked about the changes to navigability implied by different designs, but we haven't talked about assigning the responsibility for maintaining associations.

Navigability and responsibility are not necessarily the same thing. In fact, they are orthogonal concepts, as shown in Table 7-2. We've shaded in the cells that are just symmetrically restating some other combination.

Table 7-2
Navigability of Associations and Responsibility for Maintaining Associations

	A responsible	B responsible	Either A or B responsible
A navigability to B	1(i). A manages and aggregates B	1(ii). A aggregates B, but B attaches to or detaches from A	1(iii). A aggregates B's, but B's can unilaterally remove themselves
B navigability to A	2(i) B aggregates A, but A attaches or detaches itself to B symmetrical to 1(ii)	2(ii) B manages and aggregates A symmetrical to 1(i)	2(iii) B aggregates A's, but A's can remove themselves symmetrical to 1(iii)
A and B both have navigability to each other	3(i) A manages and aggregates B's; B knows which A aggregates it	3(ii) B manages and aggregates A's; A knows which B aggregates it symmetrical to 3(i)	3(iii) Mutual registration and de-registration

With the exception of option 1(ii) (and the symmetrical option 2(i)), they are all quite common. Option 1(iii) (and 2(iii) initially might look unfamiliar, but in fact the common Observer pattern (Gamma et al. 1995) uses this.

Option 3(iii), the Mutual Registration pattern (Henney 1999), may perhaps be less familiar also. This has the class diagram shown in Figure 7-16.

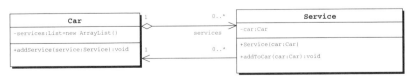

Figure 7-16
Class diagram for the mutual registration idiom.

The code for the `Car` class is:

```
1   public class Car {
2     public void addService(Service service) {
3       if (services.contains(service)) {
4         return;
5       }
6       services.add(service);
7       service.addToCar(this);
8     }
9
10    /**
11     * @link aggregation
12     * @associates <{Service}>
13     * @clientCardinality 1
14     * @supplierCardinality 0..*
15     * @supplierRole services
16     * @constraint {ordered}
17     */
18    //other operations
19    private List services = new ArrayList();
20  }
```

Similarly, the code for the `Service` class is:

```
1   public class Service {
2     public Service(Car car) {
3       addToCar(car);
4     }
5     public void addToCar(Car car) {
6       if (this.car = car) {
7         return;
8       }
9       this.car = car;
10      car.addService(this);
11    }
12
13    /**
14     * @clientCardinality 0..*
15     * @supplierCardinality 1
16     */
17    // other operations
18    private Car car;
19  }
```

The detach methods would be implemented similarly to the attach methods.

Changing Perspective

Although we can see navigability and dependencies from sequence diagrams if we look hard enough, we find them easier to spot if we look at the interaction from another perspective, namely, as a collaboration diagram. Figure 7-17 and Figure 7-18 demonstrate this, showing the same interaction first as a sequence diagram and then as a collaboration diagram.

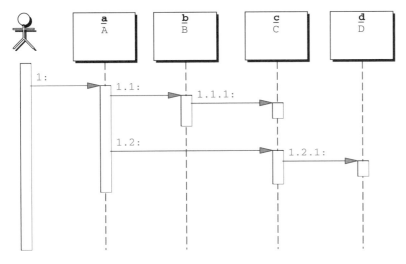

Figure 7–17
Interactions shown as sequence diagrams emphasize time.

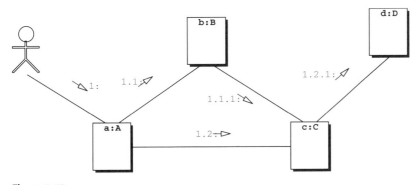

Figure 7–18
The same interaction as a collaboration diagram emphasizes relationships.

Incidentally, we created the collaboration diagram by cloning the sequence diagram and then choosing *Show as Collaboration* from the diagram's speed menu. If both views are useful, then we keep both and hyperlink them together.

There is an interesting way of visualizing the quivalence of these two diagrams as orthogonal projections of a three-dimensional figure, as shown in Figure 7-19.

When we're laying out the collaboration diagram, we try to follow the layout of the corresponding classes in the appropriate class diagram—and we'll hyperlink to that class diagram. Sometimes, we create a new class diagram just for the purpose. We then have a nice visual check that we haven't introduced new dependencies between classes; that is, the interactions that we've defined follow well-established links. We'll consider changing the design if there are new dependencies created, or if we've introduced a bidirectional dependency.

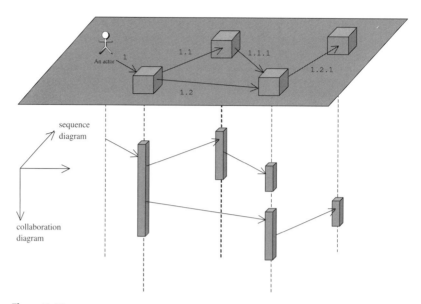

Figure 7–19
Sequence diagrams and collaboration diagrams are two views of the same interactions.

Avoid Detail in Interaction Diagrams

We're almost tempted to argue that sequence and collaboration diagrams are specification and analysis artifacts rather than design artifacts. That would be overstating our position, because they *do* belong to the design process, but we think they work best when documenting the responsibilities that we have assigned to particular classes.

For example, Figure 7-20 shows the `Book in car` sequence diagram from *CarServ* case study.

There's not much detail, but it still tells us something useful: in this case, that it's the responsibility of the `Service` to book in the `Car`, not the `Car` to book itself in for a `Service`. The notes that you see are cut and pasted from the text of the corresponding use case.

On the other hand, Together allows sequence diagrams to be reverse engineered from the code; you may well have tried this back in Chapter 2, "The Last Step—Deploy and Run!" when we were introducing the *CarServ* example. And there is no doubt that it can be very powerful, provided that you don't swamp the diagram with detail. Figure 7-21 shows another sequence diagram for booking in a car, but this one was generated from the code. It corresponds to just the `bookInCar` interaction from Figure 7-20.

With just seven objects and a similar number of interactions, this diagram is perfectly understandable. However, if we hadn't done any filtering, we would have ended up with a diagram with over 60 objects and over 350 messages. We were going to show you the results, but honestly—what would be the point? The diagram is completely unusable.

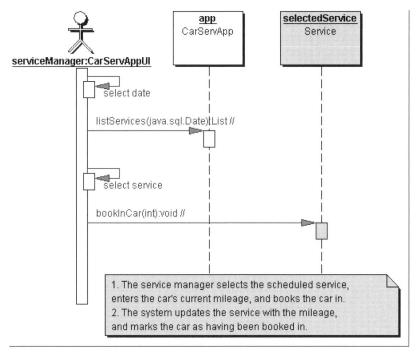

Figure 7–20
Booking in a car, described at a specification level.

So, to get the correct number of objects and messages will take a little trial and error. For ourselves, we hardly ever show framework and library classes (including the JDK), and show the implementation only of the application classes that are closest to the action. You'll find that the *Generate Sequence Diagram expert* remembers your previous choices, so it's quite easy to try out a number of different combinations. Then, when you are happy, you can delete all the rejects.

After you have reverse engineered your diagram, you may be able to further simplify it. Together isn't always able to determine that two references (in two operations in different classes) necessarily refer to the same object. So, where you do know this to be the case, you can edit the generated diagram to show more precisely how the code works. If you try to replicate our `BookInCommand.doExecute` sequence diagram in Figure 7-21, you'll note that we've done this. And Together sometimes (and somewhat unfortunately) uses a single object when in fact there are two; this often happens with objects that have no name (that is, the return value of some method call)—in this case Together names these objects `anonymous`. If this happens in several different operations, then you'll get the effect.

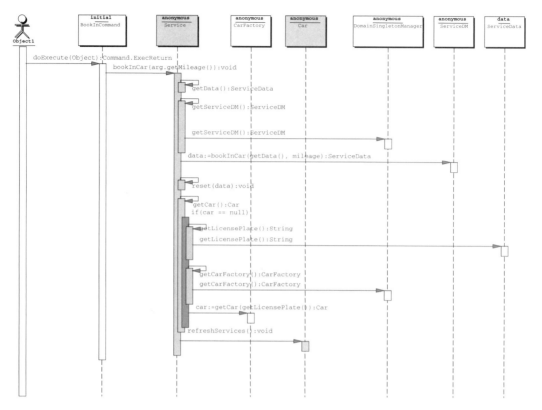

Figure 7–21

Booking in a car again, but this time at an implementation level.

Statement blocks

Together uses statement blocks to define scopes and shows these as shaded blocks on an object's lifeline. We think these also work well for higher level domain model diagrams. For example, it is quite common to iterate over some collection, but perform more than one task on each member within the collection. Using statement blocks has distinct advantages over other ways of showing conditional or iterating paths in UML sequence diagrams; see Figure 7-22.

Statement blocks can also be used to show conditionals, which can be a convenient shortcut compared to drawing two sequence diagrams, one for each scenario. There is a good example in *CarServ*, in the `ScheduleXxx-Service.doExecute` sequence diagram. This shows how either a regular or an ad hoc service is instantiated, dependent upon some factor. An abbreviated version is shown in Figure 7-23.

Invoking Class Methods

Interaction diagrams show interactions between objects, not classes. How then to show class methods being invoked? In the early stages of

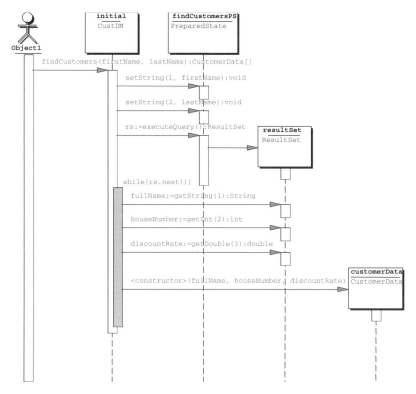

Figure 7–22
Together's statement blocks are elegant and accurate.

design, it's quite typical to have lookup functions (e.g., against a Map) as class methods. The usual signature is something like

```
public static SomeClass lookup(int someClassId);
```

Later on, these static methods often move into a method on some sort of a factory class; see Factory pattern (Gamma et al. 1995). Should we show these lookup methods on a class (or factory) separately from the regular instance methods? We counsel against this. Generally (unless you want to explain how factories are being used to instantiate objects), it's going to be too much detail. Rather, just "overload" the object on your sequence diagram as also representing the class. You could perhaps define some stereotype for sequence diagrams to ensure that `lookup()` and similar methods are correctly interpreted by the reader.

Having said all that, if you use Together to generate sequence diagrams, then you'll find that it will generate separate objects, one for static methods (called "static") and then regular instances. We normally find ourselves deleting that static object.

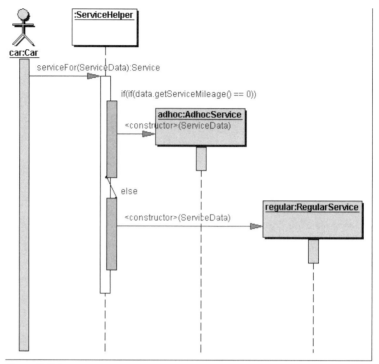

Figure 7–23
Statement blocks can show alternate outcomes.

Asynchronous Interaction

UML defines a number of different message types, shown in Figure 7-24. The three message types that are of most use to us are

- Synchronous call: This is the default interaction drawn by Together and implies a simple (synchronous) method invocation; that is, the client blocks until the server completes the method.
- Asynchronous: The client continues processing while the server continues its processing.
- Delivery delay: Can be applied to any of the above options; specifies a delivery time of the message. Doesn't tend to be used for intraprocess interactions, but can be useful for sending interprocess messages, for example, if using Java RMI, CORBA, or JMS. It is useful for diagrams that show timing constraints, since not only the execution time, but also the communication time constraints, can be specified.

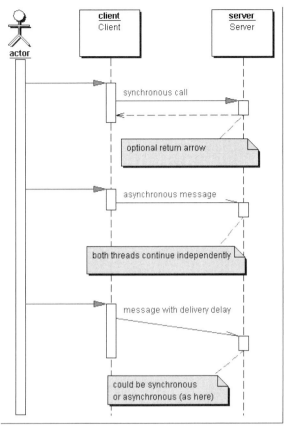

Figure 7–24
There are various UML interaction types.

These are all pretty easy to implement in Java, though implementing asynchronous messages takes a little more effort than synchronous messages. Often, asynchronous messages are accompanied by a callback method, as shown by the sequence diagram in Figure 7-25.

The implementation of `client.doAsynchronousMethod()` is:

```
1  public void doAsynchronousMethod() {
2    new Thread() {
3      public void run() {
4        server.asynchronousMethod();
5      }
6    }.start();
7  }
```

The implementation of `doAsynchronousMethodWithCall-back()` is pretty much the same:

```
1  public void doAsynchronousMethodWithCallback() {
2    new Thread() {
3      public void run() {
4        server.asynchronousMethodWithCallback(Client.this);
5      }
6    }.start();
7  }
```

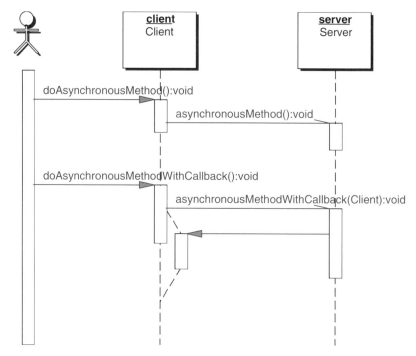

Figure 7–25
Asynchronous message calls.

The corresponding `server.asynchronousMethodWithCall-back()` implementation is:

```
1  public void asynchronousMethodWithCallback(Client c){
2     c.asynchronousMethodWithCallbackCompleted();
3  }
```

Note that the `withCallback()` method in Figure 7-24 also shows the UML notation for concurrent threads. If you try to reproduce this sequence diagram, you'll discover that it is only possible to set up multiple threads when the message type is asynchronous; this reflects the implementation.

Together also supports additional aspects of real-time system development, incuding enhanced sequence diagrams, however this is outside the scope of this book, so here we have just considered these three types of messages.

Effective Class Diagrams

Another important aspect of detailed design is documenting the class structure. In this next section, we consider several aspects of class modeling:

- preserving the domain model view
- package class diagrams versus class diagrams
- illuminating the corners of design
- class symbol compartments
- bidirectional associations
- qualified associations

Preserving the Domain Model View

In Chapter 3, "The First Step: Model the Domain" we used Modeling in Color, Coad archetypes, and other techniques to create a domain model. The domain model identifies the types relevant in the domain, their relationships, attributes, and possibly some operations. This domain model will have been documented in a package class diagram (or possibly several, if multiple packages have been defined).

Waterfall methodologies take the deliverables from the specification phase, and then start creating a parallel set of deliverables that are the implementation of this specification. In Together this would equate to creating two separate Together repositories, one to hold the domain model types and the other the implementation. In fact, some users of Together do use this approach, and use hyperlinks (via URLs) to link the implementation back up to the domain model.

However, we feel that is not playing to Together's strengths. We have been on many projects where the analysis and design/code repositories have been separate entities. After the first phase of the project has been delivered, there is never any time to go back to the analysis repository to make those updates and modifications that turned up during implementation. As the project continues, the analysis and implementation views get further and further apart, and ultimately no one trusts the information in the analysis view at all.

So, as we elaborate our domain model into implementation, we will *not* be creating new classes that correspond to the domain model types. Rather, we shall be adding detail to those existing types; the type becomes the implementation class. All that is changing is our perspective and our interpretation.

This solves the two models problem, but it creates another: The original analysis can get lost in all the implementation detail. Suppose you had a new employee just about to join your project—you would want to give her some documentation to read so she could start getting acquainted with the problem domain. A key part of this documentation would be a domain model type diagram. This is fine if you haven't started on design. More likely, though, you will have added a number of new implementation classes, private helper methods, and so on; your poor new employee will not be able to tell what is important in the diagram and what is not.

The solution is to create class diagrams over and above the package class diagrams. These class diagrams are logical views of the repository that specifically show just the domain model types, their associations, and (if you wish) the public operations.

There are several examples of such diagrams in the *CarServ* case study. One of the most important is the `Overview` class diagram in the `domain` package; see Figure 7-26 (a larger version of it is also in Appendix G).

We like to label such class diagrams to indicate that they should only include classes that represent the implementation of domain model types. One way to help enforce this is to introduce some sort of property or stereotype to label the classes accordingly. We prefer properties over stereotypes because we use stereotypes for the Coad archetypes (modeling in color), discussed in Chapter 3.

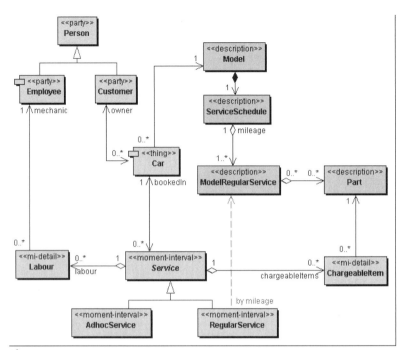

Figure 7–26

Class diagrams can be used to filter out implementation classes, showing instead just the important domain model classes (types).

The property that we use is `represents`, as in "represents domain model" or "represents implementation." Since properties are modeled as JavaDoc tags, it is easy enough to do the labeling:

```
1  /**
2   * @represents DomainModel
3   */
4  public class Customer {
5    // …
6  }
```

```
1  /**
2   * @represents Implementation
3   */
4  public class CustomerFactory {
5    // …
6  }
```

You might also have a value of `ModelAndImpl` for classes that represent the domain model and have a realization in the implementation. Or, you could decide on the policy that "domain model" implies implementation. It's up to you.

If this solution appeals, then you might like to create a custom inspector to maintain this value easily and to assign the property to class diagrams themselves. We discuss this later on in the chapter (and show the detail in Appendix E). You could also create an open API module (in the manner of "Compiling the Model," in the previous chapter) to check that no classes that represent Implementation appear on a diagram that represents the Domain Model.

Package Class Diagrams Versus Class Diagrams

We use packages to organize and partition our domain model, and indeed the full set of design and code artifacts. Packages have an implicit class diagram; you might have noticed that we term this the *package class diagram*. In Together, a package class diagram can be recognized by an icon of four small rectangles. It is also possible to create explicit class diagrams, (distinguished by an icon of just three small rectangles).

The effective use of these two different diagram types becomes key as we add detail, so we need to understand how they work. What's the difference?

- A package class diagram is a view of the classes and interfaces of the directory that corresponds to that package. Classes and subpackages of the subject package appear automatically on the diagram.
- A class diagram is a view of explicitly selected classes. No classes appear by default.

Classes *can* be excluded from package class diagrams using filters or by being explicitly hidden. Model elements from other packages may be explicitly added to package class diagrams, if required.

Figure 7-27 shows three classes physically residing in a `src` directory. A package class diagram (suffix `.dfPackage`) will automatically be created and will reside in either the `src` directory or in a separate `diag` directory having a one-to-one correspondence with the `src` directory.

The package class diagram provides a default visual representation of the classes in the `src` directory. Every file that exists in the `src` directory will automatically have a representation in the package class diagram. If a file is deleted from the `src` directory, then its representation will be removed from the package class diagram. Further, if you remove its representation from the package class diagram, *the file itself will be removed*. In design pattern terms, you are manipulating the model directly, as in the Observer or Model-View-Controller pattern (Gamma et al. 1995).

We can optionally create a class diagram. A class diagram is itself a file (suffix `.dfClass`), and as such, it will reside in some directory. The package class diagram for that directory may or may not have a shortcut representation to the class diagram, though by default it will not. To add a shortcut for the class diagram in the package diagram, use *Add Shortcut* from the speed menu.

Any class—from any package—can be represented in this class diagram by adding it as a shortcut, using *Add Shortcut.* from the speed menu. In Figure 7-28 we have done precisely this. Note the shortcut symbol in the bottom left of the `domain.CarServApp` class.

This means that the class will have two visual representations, one in the class diagram and one in the package class diagram for the package in which it resides.

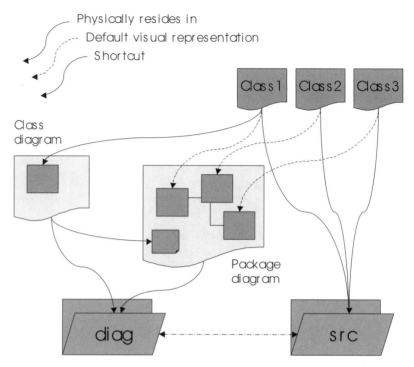

Figure 7–27
Relationship between packages, classes, diagrams and directories.

Figure 7–28
Classes from other packages can be shown as shortcuts.

Together allows us to add new classes on a class diagram. This new class (or more specifically, the file of this new class) will then reside in the package that the class diagram itself lives in. However, if you were to immediately "delete" this class from the class diagram, you would *not delete* the class. You are merely removing its visual representation in this class diagram. To delete the class, you would need to go to the package class diagram (or the file system itself) and delete the class there.

How should package class diagrams be used? Well, there are two schools of thought:

- The first is to keep as little information as possible in package class diagrams, and to concentrate on the class diagrams. Under this approach, package class diagrams are effectively little more than derived data.

- The second is to use them to provide a "default view" (a table of contents) to all classes within the package, and then use diagram options to hide those features that are not required. For example, attributes, operations, and various helper classes (such as Exception classes) could be hidden.

If the first approach is used, then the package class diagrams are mostly ignored. Instead, additional class diagrams (such as Overview) are explicitly created to navigate the repository. This is the approach predominantly taken within the *CarServ* case study.

If the second approach is used, then it becomes less necessary to create Overview class diagrams and instead just use the package class diagrams. If any new classes are defined, then they will by default appear in the package class diagram. They may then be explicitly hidden (or their detail hidden) if necessary. The *CarServ* case study also does this to some extent; having enabled dependencies for regular class diagrams, we explicitly hide dependencies on package class diagrams using *Tools* → *Options* → *Diagram Level* then under *View Management* → *Show* → *Dependencies = false*.

On package class diagrams, you may also wish to hide members of classes using *View Management* → *Show* → *All Members = false*. Alternatively, you can hide all detail by selecting the classes and choosing *Hide All* from the speed menu. There is a difference between these options; the former will not show the attributes and operations, but will show the compartments. The latter will hide the compartments as well.

If you favor the second approach of using package class diagrams as a default view, then you may also be tempted to add various other adornments, such as notes and shortcuts to sequence diagrams and the like. However, do note that behind the scenes, all of this information is being stored in the underlying `xxx.dfPackage` file, and by default Together does not offer to check this into source code control. You will therefore need to ensure it is checked in to avoid inadvertently losing information.

If you decide to put the `xxx.dfPackage` file into source code control, then note that it will need to be checked out whenever a new class is added to the package. That isn't completely true: The class can be added; it's just that it won't appear on the package class diagram until the `xxx.dfPackage` has been checked out.

Illuminating the Corners of the Design

Since class diagrams allow us to show some subset of classes, they are a good way of focusing in on a small corner of the design to explain some point. We'll often have several class diagrams in each package focusing on different points. There might also be class diagrams that assemble classes from multiple packages; these we can put in the root package of the project. There are plenty of examples of this in the *CarServ* case study.

Since the point of such a class diagram is to show detail, we will show all operations and attributes, and we will also make sure that "dependencies between classes" is enabled through the options dialog (*View Management* → *Dependencies* → *Show between Classes = true*). For the diagram itself, check that *View Management* → *Show* → *Dependencies = true* (it should be).

The scope of Together's dependency checking can be set to be either *All*, *Diagram local* or *None*. For the sort of dependencies being discussed here, *Dia-*

gram local is sufficient. However, in Chapter 8, we shall be revisiting dependencies from an architectural standpoint, when checking across diagrams is required.

It is also possible to limit dependency checking to either *Declarations only* or *All usages*. The former checks only the signature of methods, whereas the latter also checks the implementation. Whether you need to enable *All usages* instead of *Declarations only* will depend first on the style of your programming (do you often tend to instantiate and discard objects within a method?) and also on the speed of the computer you use for development—clearly *All usages* requires more processing power.

For ourselves, we try to run with dependency checking at *All usages* wherever possible. We *turn off* dependencies for package class diagrams, because the number of dotted lines can be overwhelming, but turn them on for class diagrams when we want to see the detail.[39]

For example, Figure 7-29 shows the implementation of the `Customer-Factory` class, used to instantiate `Customers`. The only classes shown are those that provide additional appropriate context.

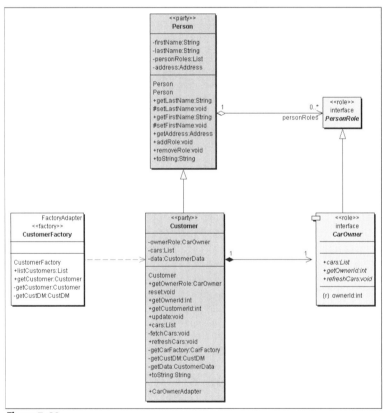

Figure 7–29

Class diagrams can narrow in on a particular corner of the design.

39. And there's an exception for every rule: We turn on dependencies for package dependencies when the package is a super-package—that is, one containing only more packages.

Add Linked

Together has another feature with which it is definitely worth being acquainted. Suppose you've been doing some coding (rather than drawing) and have added associations to classes in other packages. When you go to view the class diagram, you'll find that Together, by default, won't show those classes that reside in "foreign" packages. However, you can ask Together to add those classes. Click on the class that has the associations, and then right-click *Add Linked*. Together will then search for references, superclasses, subclasses, and implemented interfaces to any distance that you specify. From the list of classes and interfaces that Together then presents to you, you can then add classes selectively.

When learning a new API, this can be very helpful to get to grips with some code that we've just reverse engineered. For example, add a shortcut to a class like `java.util.ArrayList` and see what interfaces it implements. Conversely, start with `java.util.Map` or `java.util.Collection` and find their respective subtypes.

Of course, it is also useful when you are creating a specific class diagram in order to "illuminate some corner of a design."

Class Symbol Compartments

Within UML, it is legitimate to create additional compartments within a class symbol to capture user-defined features of the class. Together uses this technique extensively for its representation of JavaBeans. With Java-Beans, properties and events each have their own compartment. (A property is a combination of a `getXxx()` and/or `setXxx()` method; an event is the presence of both the `addXxxListener()` and `removeXxxListener()` methods). Another occasion when Together creates a separate compartment is to show member inner classes and nested static classes.

Unfortunately, perhaps, Together does not show any iconic or textual stereotype to indicate the nature of the information held in the new compartment, so you do need to know what you are looking at.

On the other hand, there's nothing to stop you from explicitly adding your own stereotypes. Figure 7-30 shows a Clock class that is both a Java-Bean and has inner/nested classes. There is no ambiguity because of the stereotypes that we've added.

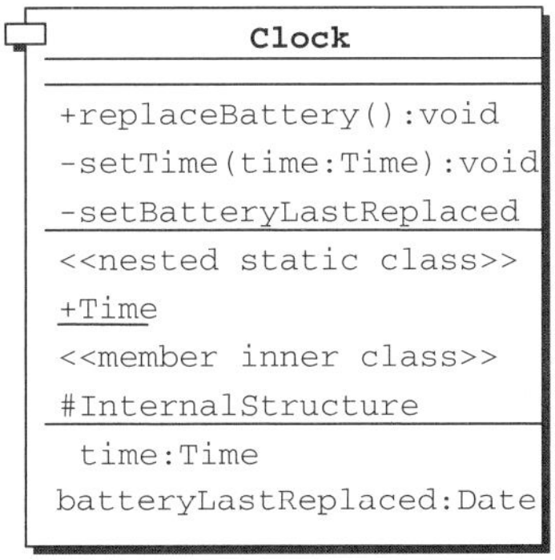

Figure 7–30
Stereotypes distinguish inner and nested classes from JavaBean properties.

It is worth noting that Together also uses stereotypes for Enterprise Java Beans. Together uses stereotypes to allow manipulation of all the classes that constitute the EJB (the Remote interface, the Home interface, the Bean itself and Primary Keys for Entity EJBs) using a single visual representation. Session beans define three additional compartments, entity beans define four, and it all works rather nicely.

Bidirectional Associations

UML allows links to be drawn with a navigability arrow on either side. In mainstream object-oriented programming languages (OOPLs) such as Java, there is no such thing as a bidirectional reference, so two distinct references—one in each class—are needed. One approach to modeling this in Together is to manually draw the two links, as shown in Figure 7-31.

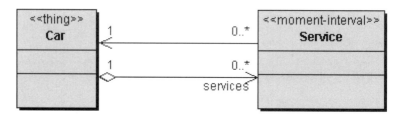

Figure 7–31
Drawing two links is one way of showing a bidirectional navigability.

However, there is an issue with this—namely, one of referential integrity. If an instance of `Car` refers to an instance of `Service`, then that instance of `Service` should point back to the same instance of `Car` (assuming here only a single analysis association). Therefore, we need at least one constraint—on the aggregated class—to ensure this referential integrity. Figure 7-32 shows the bidirectional association with these constraints.

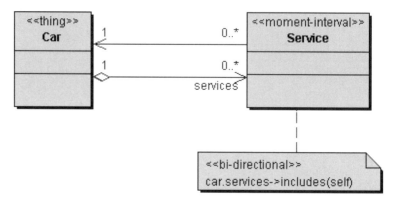

Figure 7–32
But, a constraint is required to ensure that the semantics of bidirectional associations are preserved.

We've expressed the constraint using the Object Constraint Language (OCL). For more details on OCL, see, for example, Warmer & Kleppe (1999a). As you can see, we like to stereotype this constraint as «bidirectional»; this saves us actually having to read the rest of the text.

On the other hand, Together supports a pattern called convert to bidirectional, which offers another more economical way of representing bidirectional links. The idea is to draw a single (unidirectional) link and then convert it. The pattern works best if converting a one-to-many link (from Car to Service) rather than a many-to-one (from Service to Car). The pattern dialog box is shown in Figure 7-33.

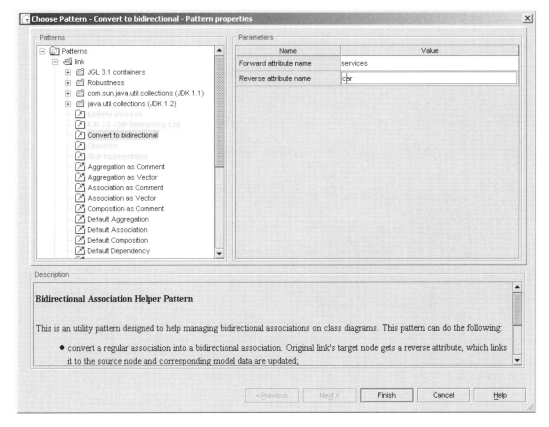

Figure 7-33
Bidirectional links can be created using the convert to bidirectional pattern.

The resultant class diagram is as shown in Figure 7-34. As you can see, we have removed the aggregation diamond, but only because it can be hard to distinguish the diamond from the navigability arrow.

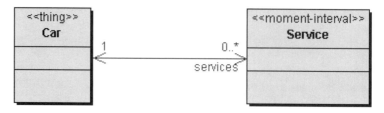

Figure 7–34
Bidirectional associations made easy.

Behind the scenes, JavaDoc tags are inserted into the code. The hard work is done in the source class of the original unidirectional link:

```
1   package domain;
2   import java.util.*;
3
4   public class Car {
5
6     /**
7      * @associates <{Service}>
8      * @clientCardinality 1
9      * @supplierCardinality 0..*
10     * @supplierRole services
11     * @constraint {ordered}
12     * @bidirectional <{domain.Service#car}>
13     */
14    private List services = new ArrayList();
15  }
```

In the other class, the tags are somewhat more straightforward:

```
1   package domain;
2
3     public class Service {
4
5     /**
6      * @bidirectional
7      */
8     private Car car;
9   }
```

This is pretty cunning, though if the JavaDoc tags get inadvertently edited, then it will break the link. In particular, note that if the `Service.car` instance variable were to be renamed in the source code, then the `@bidirectional` link in the Car class would need to be edited also.

Qualified Associations

Occasionally, it is worth showing not only that an association between objects of two classes exists, but how that association can be navigated, given an object of one of the classes. UML calls the "key" shown on such associations the qualifier. For example, if one of the objects holds a hash table containing a set of the other objects, the qualifier would indicate the hashkey that returns the single required object rather than the whole set.

Together supports the concept of such qualified associations, rendering the qualifier within braces. That is, a "client qualifier" (the @clientQualifier tag) can be specified, and this adorns the connection as {clientQualifier}. The braces distinguish it from a client role (@clientRole tag) adornment.

Figure 7-35 shows an example from *CarServ*. Each Model has a ServiceSchedule, which defines by mileage (7500, 15000, 22500, etc.) the set of parts required for replacement at that service. The ModelRegularService objects are held in a Map, keyed by mileage.

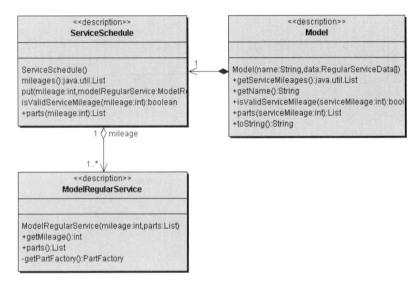

Figure 7–35
Qualifiers are shown as adornments to the association.

Let's now turn our attention to the role of patterns in design and implementation.

Using Patterns

We've been quoting Gamma et al. (affectionately known as the Gang of Four, or even just as GoF) whenever we discuss patterns, and you probably know that their book, *Design Patterns* (Gamma et al. 1995) is the seminal work on the subject. The GoF book describes what constitutes a pattern and then catalogues 23 patterns, categorizing them as structural, behavioral, or creational.

There are, of course, many more patterns than just these 23; see for example (Buschman et al. 1996). We also have domain-neutral analysis patterns (Coad, North, & Mayfield 1997; Fowler 1997), idioms (Coplien 1992; Warren & Bishop 1999), and anti-patterns (Brown et al. 1998). Good online references include *www.hillside.net/patterns* and *www.antipatterns.com*.

These days we're starting to see patterns everywhere, and not just in software architectures. Dan's wife is a keen (and very good!) cook, and has just bought a cookery book called *Appetite* by Nigel Slater (Slater 2000). It is an interesting read, because it is a cookbook without recipes. In fact, Slater is positively against recipes: "I have never believed in the foolproof recipe…food varies, and that's what makes it so interesting." He goes on to list all the different variables that could have a bearing on the way you need to cook, for example, some fish. We get the same thing in software; every system is a little different from the next. Slater then gives us some patterns. For example, "Use your nose…you will find that the smell a dish gives off as it cooks can be a good clue to its progress." If Slater had called his book *Cooking Patterns*, then I guess that one would be called the "Use your nose" pattern. Slater even has some anti-patterns: "There is a branch of cookery I call Cluttered Cooking…so choc-a-bloc full of ingredients that the main ingredient has been lost." We have to admit that we like the way that "cookbook" approaches have been discredited—even in cookbooks!

Cheeky Chappies!
Dan Haywood

I was teaching a course on object-oriented design and Java patterns, and one of the students asked me if I knew about the Lava pattern. I had to admit that I didn't, but we went looking on the Web to see if we could locate it. Well, we didn't find anything in the regular sources, but we found one called Lava flow on the AntiPatterns site. I asked if this was it, and she said yes, that was what she meant.

This anti-pattern describes that lump of code that you don't think actually does anything, but the guy who wrote it has left or moved on, and you dare not change or remove it in case it breaks the application. When the code was originally written, it might have been fluid and molten, but it has now become solidified and impenetrable; just like lava flow. I'm sure you've all see this anti-pattern one place or another.

So, I had to ask: Why did you want to know about this pattern. The answer? Because she had some contractors working on their system and they had taken to documenting the patterns in their code. Very laudable, except that the pattern that they were citing was this one. The subtext is clear: We're the worst sort of contractors whose aim it is to write working code but keep all the dark and hidden mysteries of how it actually works strictly to ourselves. Oh, and we'll be leaving this project soon, and then you'll have no idea what this code does!

What do patterns mean in Together? If you've used Together at all, we're sure you will have tried *Class by Pattern* and *Link by Pattern* in class diagrams. So, you'll appreciate that what patterns get you in Together is code generation—but not just any old bit of code; instead, you'll get some code that you know addresses a particular problem and context with a particular solution, consequences, and trade-offs.

You can apply patterns to a class, a link or a member. The patterns vary in scope, from the very large analysis patterns (e.g., Coad Components, The Four Archetypes), to traditional design patterns (e.g., GoF, Observer) to simple idioms (Main Class).

We find that sometimes the pre-canned patterns that ship with Together put in too much detail. For example, the Composite pattern puts in manual dependency links between the leaves, components, and composite. We prefer not to have these links, but that's okay—we just delete them.

It's also possible to develop your own patterns. A good example of this would be variants of the Observer patterns that call framework classes from your own project's architecture. We'll talk more about developing your own patterns in the next section, "Customizing Together."

And, finally, before we leave this subject of patterns, let us remind you about the technique of documenting pattern instances (UML collaborations) as a useful way of enriching your design. We explained this technique in Chapter 6.

Patterns as First-Class Citizens?

When you apply a pattern in Together, your classes will be modified and (depending on the pattern chosen), some manual pattern link dependencies may be added. However, there is no other direct record that a pattern was applied.

The technique that we described in Chapter 6 of documenting pattern instances (UML collaborations) goes some way to promoting patterns to first-class citizens. In other words, there is documented evidence that a pattern has been applied.

If this technique appeals, then you might agree with us that it would perhaps be nice if Together could create these pattern instances directly when applying one of its own patterns. On the other hand, Together is process-independent, and having such behavior in the tool would surely be forcing one particular process on the Together user community.

That said, it is possible to have one pattern call another, for example, a TestCase pattern calling a TestProxy pattern. So, it certainly would be possible to provide wrapper patterns for the more common patterns that call the underlying pattern, and then document themselves by creating a pattern instance. If you feel inspired and do implement this, please share it on www.togethercommunity.com!

Patterns are closely related to the subject of this next section, refactoring, or the art of changing your design without changing what it does.

Beck's *Extreme Programming Explained* (2000), effectively the manifesto for XP, places a heavy emphasis on refactoring. "If design is good," says Beck in the preface, "we'll make it part of everybody's daily business (refactoring)." The object of a refactoring is to transform the code in such a way that it has the same functional characteristics, but has a better and more flexible design. In other words, if your code is ugly or fragmented, redesign it by applying well-defined refactorings (and use your unit tests to make sure it still works).

Refactoring with Together

The Micro Step: Design and Implement

Martin Fowler gives names and describes how to perform over 70 refactorings (2000b).[40] Fowler has purposefully used a cataloging approach similar to that adopted by the Gang of Four with the *Design Patterns* book (Gamma et al. 1995), hoping that we'll get to know these refactorings by name. Here is a small selection:

- *Convert unidirectional association to bidirectional.*
- *Encapsulate field*; in other words, convert an instance variable into a JavaBean property.
- *Move method*; that is, move a method from one class to another.
- *Extract method*; extract some code from a large method and create a new helper method from it.
- *Rename class.*
- *Replace conditional with polymorphism*; in other words, replace switch statements with some sort of Strategy or State pattern.
- *Remove parameter*; if a parameter is not used in a method, then remove it.

Given that we have this catalog of refactorings—proven ways to transform your code—wouldn't it be great if a tool could apply these refactorings for us? Then, applying these refactorings would be just a matter of selecting a refactoring from a dialog box. In fact, for Java, Together does support many of these refactorings in a similar way to the Refactoring Browser for Smalltalk, which was the first language to have this kind of support.

Of the refactorings listed above, some are supported within the normal way of working in Together. The *encapsulate field* refactoring is effectively the same as the *Property* member pattern.

However, if you use the normal mechanisms in Together for some refactorings—rename method or class, for example—the rename is comparatively shallow. Renaming a class directly in the graphics editor changes its constructors and the physical file name (including, in recent versions of Together, moving the old file from source code control and adding the new one). However, this operation does not carry out a full impact analysis to change all other code that would be impacted by the rename.

The solution is to use Together's refactoring support. This carries out the impact analysis so crucial to making many refactorings painlessly and ensuring all the affected code is updated. The following refactorings are supported in version 6.0 and more are promised.

For Classes and Interfaces

- extract interface
- extract superclass
- move class/interface
- rename class/interface

For Information Purposes

- show ancestors

---

40. Beck's book introduces the theory, and Fowler's book the practice; they are two sides of the same coin.

- show descendants
- show implementing classes (for interfaces)

For Operations/Methods

- extract interface
- extract superclass
- rename operation

For Information Purposes

- show overrides

For Attributes

- encapsulate attribute
- extract superclass
- pull up attribute
- push down attribute
- rename attribute/property

There are also refactorings that you can do on a block of code statements, like Extract Operation; see Figure 7-36 and Figure 7-37.

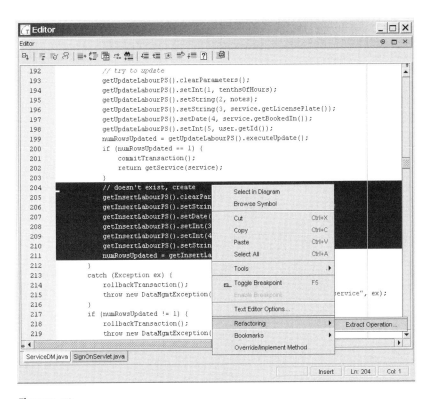

Figure 7–36
Highlight the code to extract…

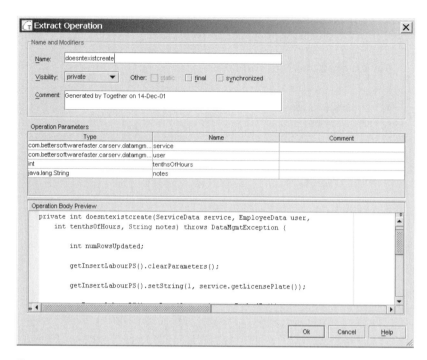

Figure 7–37
... and complete the dialog appropriate to the refactoring.

We think that Together's evolution into a refactoring browser is pro-found and that it could literally change the way you code. No longer do you need to put up with badly named methods, gigantic switch statements, or huge method bodies. Just apply a refactoring, retest, and move on. This is what computers are for: automation of the mundane to free humans for more creative work.

Customizing Together

Finally in this chapter, we consider the ways in which Together can be config-ured to provide tailored support to your team's design and implementation activities.

By now you'll have come to appreciate that Together can be customized in many different ways to support practically any development process:

- In Chapter 3 we showed how to modify `.config` files to annotate bean properties either as read-only, read/write or write-only.
- In Chapter 6 we showed a `.config` to support documenting and coloring of pattern instances, and another to color in notes.
- In this chapter we showed another `.config` to support document-ing before and after object diagrams.
- In Chapter 8 there is another example of modified `.config` files to support documenting package dependencies.

There are many more examples on *www.togethercommunity.com*. To take one at random, Tom Lee of Togethersoft UK posted a `.config` that allows the shape of an activity to be changed dependent upon its stereotype. By the way, Appendix C summarizes all the `.config` customizations that we've used within this book.

We have also looked at Together's open API and its ability to write custom modules using Java:

- In Chapter 6 we showed you how to implement an audit.
- In Chapter 6 we also developed two custom modules that checked the consistency of the design artifacts within the Together repository; these both used the *RwiSupport* framework discussed in Appendix F.
- In Chapter 8 there is another custom model to check the consistency of design artifacts (again, relating to package dependencies); this also uses the *RwiSupport* framework.

The sky is the limit when it comes to using the open API, and many examples are available from *www.togethercommunity.com*. Tim Shelley (also of TogetherSoft UK) posted a module to enhance the capabilities of sequence diagrams. Another one (posted by Dan) dumps all the properties of any element—useful when building or debugging new modules.

There are plenty of other ways that Together can be customized. We've mentioned in several places that templates can be defined and also noted earlier in this chapter that custom patterns can be written. These two customizations are similar in that they are both accessed through the *Choose Pattern* dialog from the speed menu, though templates are much simpler to create either using the *Code Template Expert* or by directly editing the files under `$TGH$/templates`. Appendix D gives some motivation and examples of some templates that we often use ourselves.

Again, there are plenty of examples on *www.togethercommunity.com*; indeed, templates seem to be a favorite contribution. For example, Dave Astels (of Saorsa Development) provided a link template to implement aggregate associations as arrays.

Templates are simple text files with macro entries, but patterns are much more powerful, since they are written in Java and have access to the full Together open API. Here are some ideas for patterns that you couldn't write using a simple template:

- A *value object* class pattern to automatically add an implementation of `equals()` and `hashCode()` to an existing class using either all private nontransient attributes or perhaps those identified by some tag, such as `@value`.
- A *Memento* class pattern to automatically create a new memento class (a snapshot, similar to the `datamgmt.xxxData` classes in *CarServ*) from an existing domain class.
- A *mutual registration* link pattern to take a bidirectional link and add the appropriate methods in both classes to support the mutual registration pattern (Henney 99).
- A *listener* method pattern to automatically create the `addXxxListener()` method, `removeXxxListener()` method, the `XxxListener` class, the `XxxEvent` class, and the `fireXxx()` methods in a single step.

- A *create table* class pattern; patterns don't necessarily need to generate or modify Java code, so a pattern could generate `create table` SQL statements in a `.sql` file to simplify building a persistence layer using an RDBMS. This could be enhanced further to generate SQL/J code; there is a brief discussion of this technology in Chapter 8.

Looking on *www.togethercommunity.com*, we found fewer patterns, probably because they take more effort to write. Nevertheless, Dave Astels (again) has posted a *Forwarding Wrapper* pattern to allow a new class to extend an existing one through delegation, not inheritance.

Many custom modules and patterns rely on additional information being defined. For example, the value object pattern suggested above might use an `@value` property. Together offers several ways to allow custom properties to be defined:

- The easiest of these is using the *Inspector Property Builder*. This is just a graphical user interface to the most common facilities of the `inspector.config` configuration files.
- Alternatively, a `.config` file can be created manually that uses the syntax of `inspector.config`. This allows certain additional options to be accessed.
- For the most sophistication, Together's open API can be used. This provides even more control.

Appendix E shows how to create custom inspectors using all three of these techniques. Incidentally, though we didn't point it out at the time, the `.config` to support before and after object diagrams also installed a custom property.

What's Next

In this chapter we have looked at the micro step of designing and implementing software using Together. A key part of this process is in designing the interaction while preserving the domain model view. Together's patterns, documentation generation, and its customizability make it an efficient platform for development.

In the next chapter, we take a step back from the detail and look at some of the architectural issues of building software.

chapter 8

The Macro Step: Architecture

Man is a complex of patterns and processes.
R. Buckminster Fuller

*Each pattern describes a problem which occurs over
and over again in our environment, and then
describes the core of the solution to that problem, in
such a way that you can use this solution a million
times over, without ever doing it the same way twice.*
Christopher Alexander

Patterns generate architectures.
Ralph Johnson

Software is hard… it needs to be softer.
Robert Martin

We now step back from detailed design and look at how a team can manage
architectural issues. The term software architecture is used in many different ways in software engineering methods and processes. We emphasize
that architecture is the repository of the team's vision—or at least that of its
leaders—and that it is emphatically more than documents. Architecture is
software. It should also include the patterns that guide the use of architectural
software. Understanding the separation not only of the overall divisions of systems into packages with well-defined interfaces and dependencies, but also
between architectural software (dealing with fundamental mechanisms and
policies) and feature-set software (dealing with particular functionality), is a
key to improving the architectural robustness of systems.

In this chapter we consider first the nature of software architecture and
its importance. We look at whether projects should lead first with architectural considerations, based on nonfunctional requirements, or with the
implementation of features based on the functional requirements. We consider the derivation of and responsibility for architecture and then look at
four specific topics relevant to defining software architecture:

- defining architectural constraints with deployment and component diagrams
- managing dependencies
- the interaction between architectural tiers
- managing versions and configurations

What Is Architecture and Why Is It Important?

The first thing to realize is that in the software engineering context, architecture is a metaphor. We understand what architecture is in relation to physical buildings and structures; certain of the functions and practices of architects are relevant by analogy to the key role that software architects play in the design of software systems. The analogy is useful, although like any analogy, it can be taken only so far.

Architects define the overall layout, the building materials, and the principal divisions of space, light, and structure. In software, architects are interested in the principal divisions of a large program. They are interested in the infrastructure software that provides mechanisms for persistence, distribution, process threads, messaging, transactions, and security. They are interested in the policies, patterns, and power tools that enable a disparate team of developers to produce systems that are coherent, understandable, and maintainable. Architecture is thus an expression of the vision and leadership of the key designer or designers.

In the best systems, architecture exists and is communicated in the structure of the software itself as well as in the way the team communicates and interacts. Without it, teams will find that there is no road map to the location of functionality and data types, and therefore no clear way forward, as the system must evolve to handle new functional and level of service requirements.

Good architecture can enable what TogetherSoft in its own development team refers to as "massively parallel development." The focus of this book is primarily on small teams—with more than a pair and less than a dozen team members, but teams like that can grow—and grow very fast—if the architecture they produce is effective, relevant, and robust. Massively parallel development can occur where there is a well-defined platform, tailored for a specialized application area but nevertheless nonspecific in terms of the detailed functionality. Together itself has exactly this kind of architecture at its heart. More than half of the functionality of the product is added to the framework by very small "teams" of between one and three people working largely independently from other similar teams, all writing to the common open API and utilizing the common mechanisms (and the patterns of use these mechanisms imply). The result is a coherent product— a coherence that flows directly from, and in proportion to, the coherence of the architecture. Interestingly, TogetherSoft now has two architecture teams, both guided by the original vision of the software architect, working on current and future generations of the framework. The commitment to evolve and grow the architecture as well as the functionality of a software product is of course essential for its longevity.

Another characteristic of architecture involves patterns. Patterns are of vital importance to architects because patterns allow them to be involved in the *detail*, not just the big picture, of how buildings and software are made.

Building architects do get involved in details like the shape of the door handles (though they probably don't fit them to the doors), just as a software architects may be interested in which search algorithm is used in a performance-critical use case. But one of the most effective ways an architect can support detailed aspects without actually supervising or intervening in others' programming is by establishing patterns. For example, a particular specialized version of the Observer pattern could be specified as the means for synchronizing changes across a network of users or computers. The architect can go further than this, specifying framework classes and specific instructions to developers as to how the framework classes are accessed.

By encoding these instructions into Together patterns, the architecture is not just a document of policies and constraints: It is actual software delivered to feature developers that speeds their work and maintains the consistency of the software across the whole application. It means the patterns are tailored to the architecture and guide team members in how to use it, and they also ensure that the code generation can go much further than merely generating stubs based on mapping UML to Java. The generated code in many cases will even provide complete executable code.

An example of how Together can be tailored to specifically support a given architecture can be seen in the way it supports J2EE. We discuss this in Chapter 9, "The J2EE Architecture."

So, architecture is not simply statements of policy or guidelines for developers. Fundamentally, software architecture is *software*. It is software that addresses the generic mechanisms that the system will use, to implement for example persistence, the user interface, and interprocess communication. For the most part, especially in small systems, this software will be bought or may even come included in the JDK, the application server, or the operating system. However, small teams sometimes need to start by developing the architecture they need rather than by implementing the functional requirements. Which should you do?

Smaller teams have a choice whether to focus on architectural software first or on functionality first, whereas larger teams generally need to establish architecture early in order to coordinate the work of multiple disparate groups of developers.

Figure 8-1 shows three concurrent processes that are required by projects:

- Understand the business needs.
- Choose and/or construct architectural components.
- Implement system features.

Understand the business needs is essentially the requirements-capture process, which we discussed in chapters 3, 4, and 5. It involves modeling the problem domain, then identifying and prioritizing the functional requirements that are the input to the development process, *implement system features*. In many cases small teams can focus simply on these two processes. We would characterize this as a "functionality first" approach, where architecture is implicit, or inherited from other projects, or simply allowed to evolve by refactoring the software as new features are added.

The Macro Step:
Architecture

213

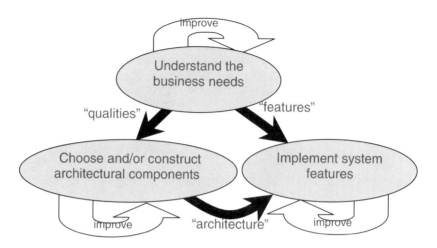

Figure 8-1

Three concurrent processes in larger projects.

One of the benefits of use case diagrams is that they provide a view of just the functionality required by the customer, and no more. One of the downsides, though, is that it can be hard to discover and reuse similar code needed in different functional areas, because their similarities are only identified later on. Expect to refactor the code in order to pull together those similar areas as they are discovered when using a "functionality first" approach. As we noted in Chapter 7, "The Micro Step: Design and Implement," refactoring is an essential activity and well supported by Together.

In larger projects it is worth separating responsibilities for all three separate processes shown in Figure 8-1. The second output from understanding the business needs is a view of the qualities (effectively, the nonfunctional requirements) that the system is required to have. Knowledge of the required qualities informs the choice of architecture. The process to implement the features of the system is then able to use both the features input and the architectural software on which the features are to be built, as delivered by the *choose and/or construct architectural components* process.

Starting from and emphasizing architecture could be termed a "framework first" approach. Rather than focusing on the specific functionality of the system, the nonfunctional requirements relating to the number and types of user, the performance, distribution, and volume of data access, the security requirements, and so on, are the starting point. Common functionality is therefore identified early and built into the logical framework of capabilities that the feature developers use to deliver the functional requirements. But there is a downside—such an approach can result in functionality being built that isn't required immediately, and therefore may never be—tricky to justify to the stakeholders on a cost/benefit basis. "YAGNI!"[41] we hear them cry.

41.   "You ain't gonna need it!";see Chapter 5.

Since functionality-first development favors spending the minimum of development time on architectural software, most of the architectural components are bought in package form (for example, the DBMS, perhaps an application server, and the operating system). All the team's efforts are focused on delivering features.

Both approaches are useful in their context. Here are some cases when the emphasis should be on functionality-first development rather than on framework–first development:

- The system is small. Any architecture, if developed, would only be small or trivial anyway.
- The system must be delivered quickly. Here, it's better to defer the cost of developing an architecture up front and, instead, do the work later as a refactoring exercise. The cost of refactoring may in the end be more expensive than the cost of building the architecture up front, but the penalty of a delay in time-to-market more than offsets this difference.
- The lifespan of the system is short. Developing an architecture up front would only reduce the lifespan of the system still further.

However, before you convince yourself that you don't need an architecture, remember that successful systems often grow, and that sometimes being second to market with a better solution beats being first to market with the second-best solution. Successful systems tend to carry on being used too, so that short lifespan may get extended!

Big Stakeholder-Oriented Systems
Dan Haywood

At Andersen Consulting I learned the architecture-first way of building systems, and for a while I was of the opinion that it was the only way to do so. Later in my career, I did lots of work for financial institutions in the City of London, and suddenly, hardly any of the systems I looked at spent development time on architecture. And yet they were making money for those financial organizations and so clearly had business value—even if they were pretty hard to maintain.

I realized that sometimes market conditions mean that highly stakeholder-oriented systems make lots of sense. Okay, because there is little bespoke architecture, it means that in the long run they may be more expensive to run, but in the short term they can be built more quickly, and so they start to deliver business value more quickly. When the business is a financial organization that makes millions a day, having a system—or even a particular feature—available a few weeks earlier than the competition can make a big difference.

Here's another reason why architecture development isn't—or at least hasn't been—very popular in these financial organizations: The most valuable commodity is the business (the trader), not the IT support. The business is often happy to pay the extra overhead it takes to run and maintain the system, because compared to the value of the business being done, it is inexpensive. The financial and political muscle often lies in the hands of the traders, who want new features immediately, rather than in an IT department, say, wanting to build a "nice architecture."

The Macro Step:
Architecture

Look at other businesses where the margins are much slimmer, and it will be a different picture. The systems I built at Andersen Consulting were for the government or utilities. Here, the end-users are not making millions a day in trades, and funding for new complex systems tends to be allocated once in order to gain cost savings over many years—hence the greater emphasis on building architecture first.

Naval Architecture
Andy Carmichael

The importance of software architecture as something to establish even before there is a clear view of detailed functional requirements was brought home to me on a project I participated in a number of years ago for the Royal Navy. Unfortunately, due to circumstances beyond their control, somewhere in the South Atlantic they had managed to "mislay" a few of their frigates, and they were naturally anxious to replace them as quickly as possible. Possibly to their surprise, they discovered that whereas they could build a ship from keel to launch in little more than four years, developing the software for the command and control systems aboard could take several years longer. Since putting the old software back was not an option, and putting to sea with no command and control system was not attractive either, they realized that the most important thing to establish was a new software and hardware architecture within which an increasing level of functionality could be implemented release by release. In this case, while the architecture was certainly influenced by knowledge of some of the functional requirements, it was primarily driven by the nonfunctional or level of service requirements.

In a world where we know requirements are changing incredibly rapidly in the business "battleground," we need to look for things that are more stable than the functional requirements. Often, this is the software architecture—or at least the sets of interfaces to the software architecture. Where architecture is successfully established, new functionality can often be added for a fraction of the cost one would anticipate in a more conventional (waterfall style) development process.

Responsibility for Architecture

Better
Software
Faster

Sometimes, a standard architecture has already been defined or purchased by others outside of the control of the development team. In this case the architecture provides the constraints on the design. If your project is just one part of a much larger program of work, or where company standards define specific platforms, it is likely some kind of full-time architecture group will set the limits on the architecture that you must work with. Architectural constraints might also include a defined development platform, process, and deliverables, or (at a more mundane level) a set of coding standards.

Many companies are painfully aware of the burden of maintaining their various computer systems and that the pain is increased because of the sheer variety of platforms (be that platform the hardware, operating systems, API, database, or development process). So, predefined architectural constraints define limits as to the type of platforms that are allowed. From the universe of possible technical solutions that might meet the requirements, only those that are implemented on the selected platforms can be considered.

There is always the chance that the constraints such an architecture imposes will be just too constraining, and it might be technically impossible to address the functional and nonfunctional requirements. For example, mandating the use of entity beans in EJB v1.0 would have created some interesting implications with respect to response times and throughput, had it been mandated for Chapter 1's online banking system from its original release!

If some constraints have been set externally, how are you to know that they are compatible with the requirements that must be met for your project? The ideal answer would be that the architecture group has built systems similar to yours already, or at least a technical prototype. However, it's notoriously hard to ensure that such prototypes fully test out the candidate architecture, so if this is the only evidence that the architecture group can offer to you (and they might not be able to even offer that), some contingency in your project plan is going to be advisable.

When to Deliver and Test Architectural Software
Andy Carmichael

On a large project involving several different teams, all delivering functionality for a customer service application, I learned an important lesson about getting architectural software delivered early. The project was approaching an important software delivery milestone: the first delivery of beta test software to the client. All the teams knew the deadline was tight, and yet everyone believed that they could get their work done in time to integrate the software and ship it on time. However, one week before the deadline, the project manager was forced to declare a one month slip in the delivery of the software. How could it have got so close to the deadline without his knowing that his teams simply would not make it?

In fact, the situation was much worse than he knew even then. It took the project six more months to achieve the software delivery. The analysis of the disaster, after the fact, showed that a major reason for the delay—and the lack of visibility of the delay—was that the architectural software, which handled client-server communications, transaction management, and database access, was also scheduled for delivery on the same date as all the functional requirements being developed by other teams! The first real integration of the software occurred only a few weeks before the original deadline.

Not only does this story underline the importance of continuous integration, but it highlights that architecture must be delivered and stable much earlier than the user functionality. There are just too many opportunities for wrong assumptions if developers must write software to stub interfaces, or worse, architecture specifications that are only paper documents.

Even if there is a full-time architecture group within the organization at large, should there be specific responsibility for architecture within our own development team with responsibility for defining and managing the architecture? We've stressed already in this chapter the need for vision and leadership in the team. It is in defining the architecture that this leadership is most clearly demonstrated, but that doesn't mean that all changes to architectural software are the responsibility of just one or two individuals.

In fact, everyone in a small team may need to be involved in architectural decisions. If a defect in the architecture has been noted, then one individual might work on defining some alternative refactorings, design changes or new patterns. A meeting involving everyone on the team helps to (a) ensure that everyone understands the current problem, and (b) determine the correct way forward. Leadership and consensus are both needed, though where it's not possible to achieve both, talented leadership is the overriding requirement.

Documenting Architectural Constraints

Component and deployment diagrams are somewhat underused aspects of UML, and we find this surprising. Here's why: If we were to ask you to describe your system, then you'd most likely draw a component or a deployment diagram. You'd probably sketch on the whiteboard a picture of a PC, a back-end UNIX database, probably a Web server, and maybe even indications of which chunk of software runs where. If you just draw the chunks of software (okay, let's call them components), it would be a runtime component diagram. If you put in the hardware, it would be a deployment diagram. You might not use the formal UML notation, especially if it is on the whiteboard, but it would be a component or deployment diagram nevertheless.

Describing how the architecture will look when it's deployed is what these diagrams are all about. More formally, we are constraining the design by specifying aspects of the architecture with which the design must comply. For example, you may want to build a Web-based application, and the database will be on a separate server to the Web server, with a high-speed network connecting them. Or, maybe you want to keep presentational services (servlets and JSPs) on one side of a firewall, with business logic (EJBs) on the other side. Equally, if EJBs are in use, then stored procedures might be proscribed. Figure 8-2 shows these constraints using a deployment diagram.

You may decide that all network interactions between Java applications will be using SOAP (RPCs encoded as XML documents) rather than RMIfor interoperability. Or, you might decide that your servlets must extend from the Java class `javax.servlet.http.HttpServlets` (so that they can be invoked using HTTP through firewalls) rather than just `javax.servlet.GenericServlet`.

Figure 8-3 shows these constraints captured with a component diagram.

Runtime component diagrams and deployment diagrams have a great many similarities. Are both needed? It depends on how much detail you need to convey. Even very simple systems can have some subtleties, which suggests two diagrams may be needed. Figure 8-4 shows a runtime component diagram for the *CarServ* case study (you may remember it from Chapter 2, "The Last Step: Deploy and Run!"). The diagram would start to look very cluttered if it was drawn showing the hardware nodes as well, and since that was not the purpose of this diagram, they were omitted.

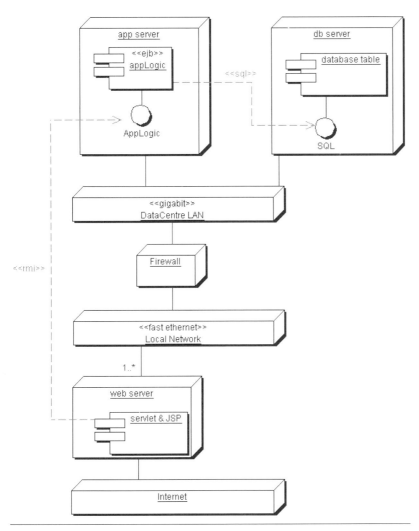

Figure 8–2

Deployment diagrams can capture numerous architectural constraints.

Note how this diagram shows the communication from client to server twice: once by indicating the low-level network connection (stereotyped «rmi») between the Cloudscape client JARs and the Cloudscape server, and then the higher level semantic dependency (stereotyped «sql») from the client-side application packages to the relational tables. There is also a subtlety on the server in that the Cloudscape server JARs load up a file (the CarServDB component) and in so doing, present the data held within that file as relational tables to be queried via SQL.

Component diagrams are also useful for showing compile-time dependencies, as in Figure 8-5. For the *CarServ* case study, this component diagram shows how each component (corresponding to packages) uses other components, some of which use the Cloudscape JAR files.

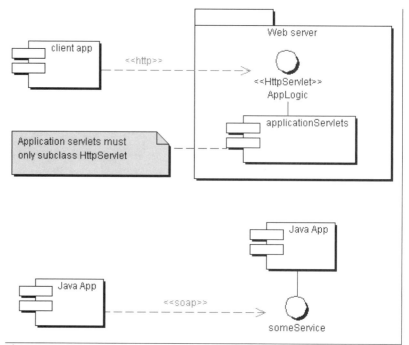

Figure 8-3

Runtime component diagrams can be used to communicate constraints.

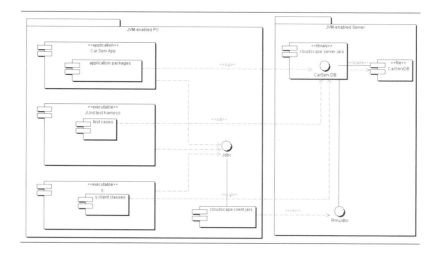

Figure 8-4

The *CarServ* application in client/server mode, as a runtime component diagram.

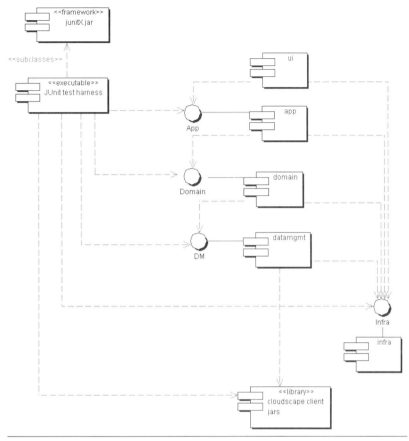

Figure 8–5
Compile-time dependencies show how software is constructed.

You may have noticed in Figure 8-4 that we have placed components within subsystems (same icon as a package). Strictly speaking, UML does not define any semantics for subsystems in component diagrams, but Together lets us draw this picture nevertheless, and you are free to use it however you wish.[42]

We tend to use containing subsystems in one of two ways. First, as in Figure 8-4, we use it just to indicate that components run on a certain platform. This is easy to understand. It would equally have been valid to stereotype the components, or even to introduce the platform (be it a JVM, a servlet container, or whatever) as a separate component in its own right and show the dependencies.

The alternative use for containing subsystems is to differentiate components versus the interfaces that they implement. For example, in the *CarServ*

---

42. We can perhaps look forward in the future to these types of diagram also being synchronized continually via a LiveSource link to the files used to build the software and actual hardware networks.

case study the `infra` package defines an interface `CommandHisto-ryListener`, which is called whenever a command is executed, undone, or redone. The Undo and Redo menu items implement this interface so that they can enable and disable appropriately. This design might be shown at a high level using a component diagram, as shown in Figure 8-6.

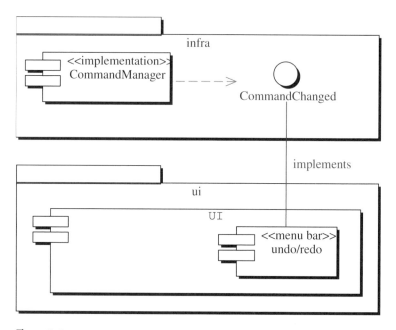

Figure 8–6

Subsystems can be used to distinguish implementation versus interfaces implemented by other subsystems.

This can even be extended to interfaces logically implemented by software running in different process spaces. As delivered, the *CarServ* case study is a client/server application, where the main business logic resides in the client-side application, but a variation on this architecture would be to move the business logic into a middle tier. In this case the reference objects would be shared and instantiated just once in the middle tier rather than each client instantiating its own copy. Thus, it might be decided that each client (that is, user interface) should be updated automatically whenever a `Car` or `Service` is updated by some other user.

Figure 8-7 shows a component diagram explaining this idea. Again, we've used stereotypes to indicate the underlying technology that we expect to realize this requirement; we've also indicated the use of Java Messaging Service (JMS) with a stereotype on the dependency link, «jms». Use of component and deployment diagrams like this encourages component thinking (Cheesman & Daniels 2000), which in turn improves the team's ability to build reusable software with reusable software.

These examples show how you can communicate very valuable information with these diagram types. They can be produced as early in the lifecycle

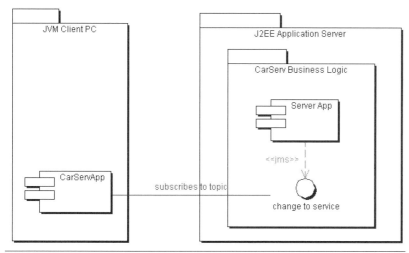

Figure 8–7
Interfaces can be implemented by software in different process spaces.

as the domain modeling stage or at the same time that you are capturing functional requirements. Although these diagrams do represent and contain design decisions rather than requirements, the high-level architectural constraints they contain do affect other early decisions (could you go out and buy a Cray supercomputer to calculate your portfolio, for example, or do you have to make do with the palm-top?). From the first builds, the architecture you are deploying to will affect other design decisions. It's as well to document these early and—most importantly—maintain the changes to the architecture as the project progresses.

Defining the major divisions of the software and their interfaces is a key responsibility of the software architect. It has been known for many years that one of the important considerations in packaging software for ease of maintenance is to ensure the dependency graph between the components is acyclic (Parnas 1979), with no mutual dependencies. This ensures that changes to less stable parts of the software can be made after other parts of the system have been completed and delivered. This is equally, perhaps especially, true of object-oriented systems. Therefore, when defining and reviewing architecture, we need to be able both to specify where dependencies should (and should not) exist and to find out where they actually *do* exist. Together provides some important facilities that help the software architect to do this.

Since in Java the main mechanism for identifying the major divisions of the software is the package, let's start this section with a look at package dependencies.

Managing Dependencies

Dependencies Between Packages

Here's a simple package dependency diagram, Figure 8-8.

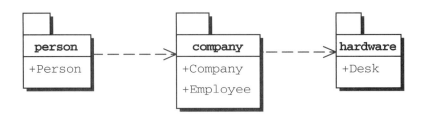

Figure 8–8
Together shows package dependencies derived from the class dependencies.

The dependencies in the diagram are derived directly from the code in the classes that the packages contain. We can see these in Figure 8-9, the example we considered in Chapter 7. As can be seen in this diagram, any relationship between classes implies a dependency between the classes and therefore their packages. We use the UML dependency link (the dashed arrow) only if there is not a more specific relationship, such as association, aggregation, or inheritance, that explains the usage more exactly.

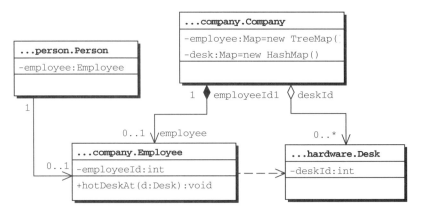

Figure 8–9
Together supports dependencies (and other link types) between classes.

Unlike with the class dependencies, Together doesn't attempt to keep the package dependencies up to date all the time—that would involve too much processing overhead on most hardware, and it would slow down normal working. However, to update the dependencies is simple enough—just right-click on the diagram and *Update Package Dependencies*.

It's also possible to *manually* draw dependencies between packages. We use these to define and check architectural constraints (see sidebar).

Dependency Inversion Principle

To build a "good" architecture, the packaging of software should display high cohesion (all the classes in a package closely relate to the purpose of the package and to the other classes in it) and loosely coupled (each package is as independent as possible from other packages). Object-oriented languages have facilities, particularly interfaces and abstract classes, that make it easier to design software with these characteristics, but sometimes this means transforming structures from the most obvious form to ensure undesirable dependencies are removed.

Robert Martin has discussed the interaction of two metrics for instability and generality that can be applied to packages (Martin 1995). Unstable packages have dependencies on many other packages, since they may have to be modified if the packages they depend on change. General packages are the least application-specific, and they provide reusable facilities that are relevant in many different situations. Architectural software needs to be general and stable. The concepts in these packages therefore need to be abstract and as far as possible independent of other packages. On the other hand, other parts of the application—for example, the user interface—can be much more concrete (that makes it more understandable), and it is likely

The Macro Step:
Architecture

to be dependent on several other packages (including generic user interface utilities that by contrast need to be abstract).

The goal of good architecture is to provide software that other developers can build on. It needs to be flexible, not rigid (able to be changed in a straightforward way); robust, not fragile (changes do not cause other parts to break); and reusable, not immobile (it is not so entangled with its original context that it can't be moved and reused in another context). In summary, architectural software should be cohesive, loosely coupled, abstract and general, stable, flexible, robust, and reusable. Achieving this requires appropriate dependencies through the package structure.

Other papers by Robert Martin define a principle for removing unwanted dependencies, the Dependency Inversion Principle (Martin 1996a, 1996b). This states that

- High-level modules should not depend on low-level modules. Both should depend upon abstractions (in Java terms Interfaces).
- Abstractions should not depend on details. Details should depend on abstractions.

Translating this principle into a Java context, it means that as far as possible the dependencies between packages should be from classes or interfaces *to* interfaces. Low-level packages (in our terms, architectural packages) should define interfaces that define the operations they require from objects of classes from other packages. When a reference is needed from a utility class to an application class, the utility class should instead define an interface that the application class can implement, and should reference that instead.

Let's consider this principle with an example we looked at in Chapter 7 when discussing interaction design and navigability. We concluded that although we would prefer all links having navigability in only a single direction from an implementation viewpoint, we often need bidirectional communication between the objects. In *CarServ* we might first want to list all `Services` that a given `Car` has had; second, we might want to know what `Car` a given `Service` relates to. The quickest way to find the objects for these scenarios is to use a bidirectional relationship between `Car` and `Service` even though it involves a little more development effort (or the judicious application of a Together pattern) to ensure the objects are updated correctly.

Do we care about the bidirectional dependency that will arise between these two classes? Well, perhaps—but only if the classes are in different packages. We need to make sure that our microdesign does not break the constraints defined by the macro-architecture. And we need to ensure there are not cyclic dependencies between the packages.

It may in some circumstances be possible to remove the bidirectional dependency by moving the location of classes, interfaces, or methods/operations (or perhaps removing them if they aren't actually needed). Together can help with a very useful feature; just right-click on the dependency line and choose *Show Dependencies*. The code elements (instance variables, arguments, local variables) giving rise to the dependency are shown in a tab of the message pane and can be viewed from either the dependents' or providers' perspective. Some of the refactorings supported by Together are also relevant (e.g., Move Class, Extract Interface, Move Method).

If the impact of moving or removing features is too large, then we can apply the dependency inversion principle by introducing abstractions—usually interfaces—in the package that we want to be independent.

Suppose that `Car` and `Service` are in two different packages. Architecturally, we decide that the `car` package should depend upon `service` package, but not the other way around. In other words, our architects are saying that we would like to reuse the functionality within the `service` package in some other context—perhaps servicing trucks or aircraft. We need to introduce an interface in this package that defines the methods this package needs; following the naming convention used throughout Java, let's call this `Serviceable`. We make `Car` implement this `Serviceable` interface, as shown in Figure 8-10. The resulting one-way dependency between the packages is seen in Figure 8-11.

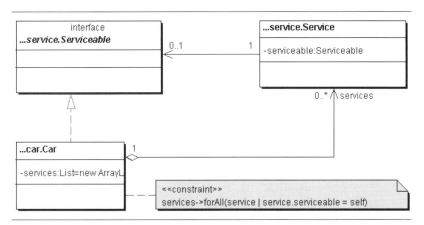

Figure 8–10
The car package depends on an independent service package.

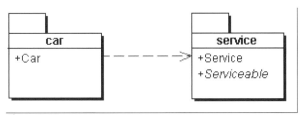

Figure 8–11
The corresponding package diagram showing the one-way dependency.

Equally, we could have decided that the `service` package should depend upon the `car` package, but not vice versa. Perhaps the `Car` class is being reused from another application that gives us facilities, say, for looking up model numbers and parts. This would have given rise to the design shown in Figure 8-12.

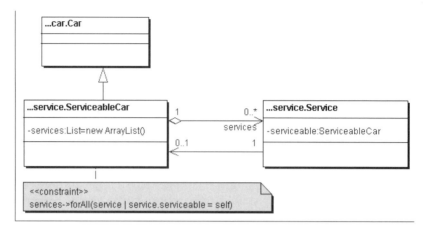

Figure 8–12
The service package made to be dependent upon an independent car package.

This technique is used in many of the familiar patterns, for example Adapter, Strategy, Observer, and many others from the Gang of Four (GoF) book (Gamma et al. 1995).

Mandating Dependencies

If the architect is responsible for defining dependencies between the various packages that make up the system, then it is the responsibility of the other developers to make sure that the microdesign of classes conforms to the macrodesign of the architecture.

The use of explicitly drawn dependencies is one way in which architects can simply indicate what dependencies are allowed and what are not. Consider, then, the package dependencies shown in Figure 8-13, which were drawn to shown the expected dependencies from an architectural viewpoint. The architect drew dependencies from:

- `testPackage5` to `testPackage1`, and
- `testPackage1` to `testPackage2`.

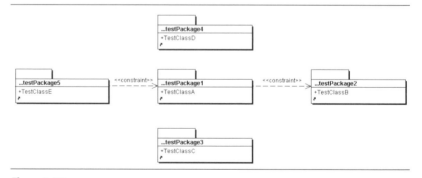

Figure 8–13
The package dependencies constraints defined by the architecture.

Figure 8-14 shows the architectural constraints as before, but it also shows the actual dependencies that were found by Together parsing the code in the packages' classes. From the actual code there are dependencies from:

- `testPackage1` to `testPackage5` (opposite direction), and
- `testPackage1` to `testPackage2` (same direction).

There are also dependencies between packages about which the architect said nothing:

- `testPackage1` to `testPackage4`, and
- bidirectional dependencies between `testPackage1` and `testPackage3`.

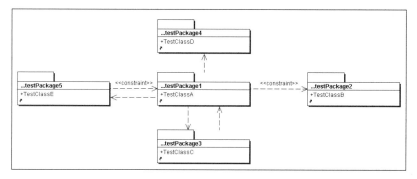

Figure 8–14
The actual dependencies derived from the code compared with the architectural constraints.

So, it is clear in this example that the actual dependencies derived from the code are at variance with the architect's vision of the software.

The color-coding and labeling of the dependency links, discussed in the previous sidebar, makes it much easier to see the discrepancies between the dependency constraints and the actual dependencies. A simple visual inspection can tell the architect that there are problems with the code introducing unwanted dependencies, that there are insufficient dependencies permitted within the architecture, or both.

Package Dependency-Checking Module

It would be nice if we could be informed by automatic audit when we have bidirectional dependencies between packages or when actual dependencies between packages do not follow the constraint dependencies manually drawn by the architect. This is precisely what the package dependency-checking module `PackageDependenciesModule` *does for us.*

Using the `RwiSupport` *framework (described in Appendix F), it iterates over packages, analyzes the dependencies, and reports any issues that need to be reviewed by the designer. Figure 8-15 shows the module at work.*

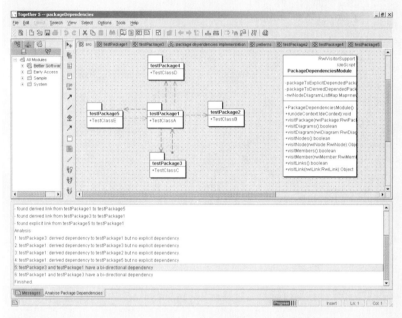

Figure 8–15
Running the custom module.

Try it out for yourself. Download the `packageDependencies.zip` *file from the Web site at* www.bettersoftwarefaster.com, *and extract:*

```
packageDependencies\
  packageDependencies.tpr    // Together project file
  src\                       // source
  diag\                      // diagrams
  classes\                   // compiled code
  manifest\                  // manifest to describe module
  bat\                       // batch files (install)
```

Copy the `packageDependencies` *directory to your hard drive, load up the project file and build. To install the module, first ensure that the* `%TOGETHER%` *environment variable is defined, e.g., to* `c:\Togethersoft\Together6.0`, *and then run* `bat\install.bat`. *Restart Together, and a new module should be installed. (Since this module depends upon the* `RwiSupport` *framework,* `rwisupport.jar` *must be available, as for the module in Chapter 6). Try running the module on a project of yours, and see how if fares.*

To consider how this module works, look at its class diagram shown in Figure 8-16:

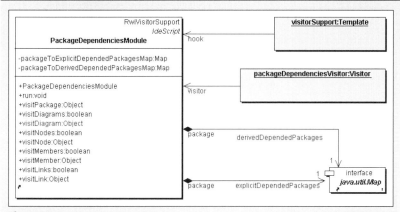

Figure 8–16
The PackageDependencyModule class.

Each diagram is visited and the links from each reference inspected to see if they are dependency links. As the model is traversed, relevant information is stored in two Maps. This is quite a common design—build up an internal model of the information under test. For example, the dependencies between the packages shown in Figure 8-14 would give rise to the object diagram shown in Figure 8-17:

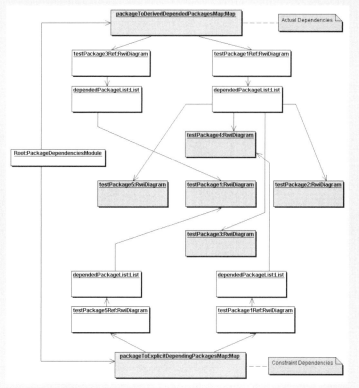

Figure 8–17
The objects visited and checked by the module.

Interactions Between Tiers

A useful and common architectural pattern is the layered or tiered framework with upper tiers relating to user interface and client-side processing, and lower tiers relating to server processing and data management (Booch 1996).

We have used this pattern in the case study example with four tiers being represented by the following packages:

- Presentation: ui
- Application: app
- Domain: domain
- Data management: datamgmt

As we discuss in the next chapter, this also conforms to a typical J2EE architectural structure. Let's now consider the three levels of interactions between these four tiers.

Presentation to Application

When using sequence diagrams to model the scenarios of a use case, an object is often used to channel interactions, acting as a unified interface to the application. We either stereotype or name this object `System`, as example in Figure 7-10 in the previous chapter. However, it's unlikely that your final implementation code will actually have a `System` class, so what does this object represent, and on which layer of the architecture does it reside?

It might seem a reasonable guess that the `System` class resides in the presentation layer. The presentation layer, after all, describes the actor's interactions with the software. But the interaction we capture in the use case should be abstracted away from the details of the actual user interface and so it would be inappropriate to place the `System` class here. There are often many ways for an actor to interact with the software to accomplish the same thing. For example, in our *CarServ* system we could have both a Java Swing application running on a PC and a ruggedized wireless LAN Palm Pilot user interface, to allow the mechanics to enter the hours they've spent on a service without leaving the workshop. They could achieve the same goal (that is, execute the same use case) through two completely different presentation interfaces.

So, instead, we think of the `System` class as the gatekeeper to the middle business logic layer—in effect capturing the complete potential interaction between the presentation and application layers. In design pattern terms, it's an example of a Façade pattern (Gamma et al. 1995). It acts as the logical application, the essence of the application, without respect to its presentation layer. This is just as well; user interfaces are after all fashion items and quite likely to change year by year.

What are the candidates to implement the `System` class? Larman (1998) has discussed this already; the following is based on his list:

- an actual system class
- a physical device
- a number of use cases
- a small number of façades

Some of these are probably better candidates than others. The first and second options—a system class or a physical device—are pretty similar to each other; in software terms one is really an abstraction of the other. We might be tempted to use a physical device if the nature of the interactions were quite technology-specific, perhaps swiping a Java Smartcard. The problem with this approach is that since all the interactions are concentrated through one class or interface, the abstractions from the problem domain (Car, Service, Customer, etc.) will not be separately visible.

Some have suggested the system class as a proxy for the actor doing the work, but this amounts to delegating responsibility to some sort of security context object for the current user, and again it loses visibility of the key abstractions identified in the problem domain model. We would rather that the system check with the security layer that the current actor has permissions to accomplish the use case, rather than try to model the actor directly with a class. Moreover, the J2EE architecture supports this security layer approach (the `ServletContext` and `EJBContext` methods provide methods such as `isUserInRole()`) so there are already firm precedents for not translating the system object into a proxy for the actor.

In some cases it can be effective to delegate to an object that is a manifestation of the use case being accomplished. This effectively involves designing a class for the use case which is instantiated when a user invokes the feature. Those ever-popular wizards that we see in modern applications are an example of this idea. After all, wizards allow you to accomplish a goal (for example, create a new project in Together) and each use case similarly describes a user's goal. This is a variation on the approach that we've used in *CarServ*, for handling interaction between the `ui` and `app` packages. In this case we've translated the use cases (or rather the system events occurring in the use cases) into a set of command classes..

Figure 8-18 shows the `System Events` class diagram in the `app` package, detailing the classes that implement the use cases (for example, `Book-InCommand`). The strategy that these classes follow is to define a nested static class (by convention, we called it `Arg`) that defines the information required for the command to do its work. Classes in the `ui` package subclass the command classes, providing an implementation of the `getArg()` method—an instance of the Template pattern, in fact (Gamma et al. 1995). Figure 8-19 shows a sequence diagram detailing how scheduling a service is implemented; note how the command object interrogates the argument object at the start, and then at the end, updates the argument with the created `Service` for display on the user interface.

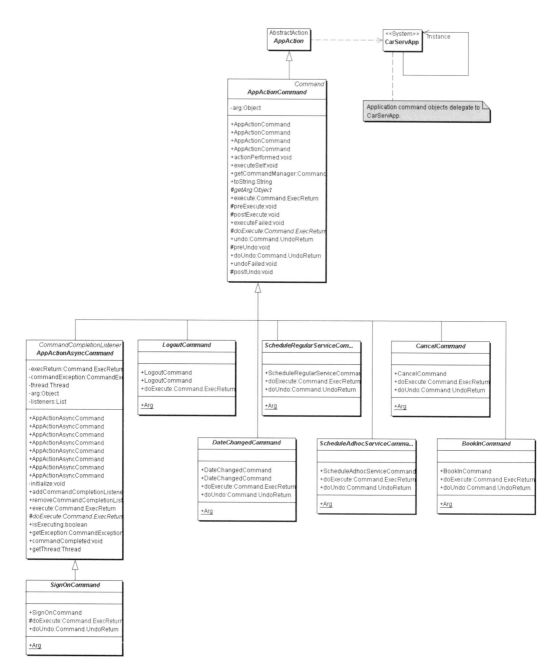

Figure 8–18
Command objects realize the interaction from the user interface.

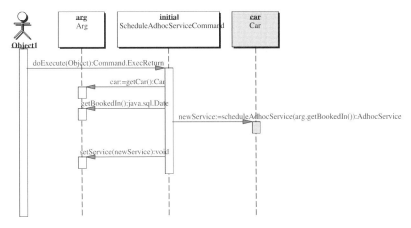

Figure 8–19
The Command object gets and sets information in the Arg object.

Application to Domain

In the interactions between application and domain packages, it's clear that the application objects should depend upon the domain objects, and not vice versa, as the application layer deals with more volatile functionality and the domain layer with more stable concepts. In J2EE terms, the application layer would be implemented as session EJBs, and the domain layer as entity EJBs.

The distribution of functionality across the application and domain layers can sometimes cause issues. We don't subscribe to the view that the domain layer should provide nothing more than getters and setters. After all, a `BankAccount` domain object probably ought not to provide a `set-Balance()` method. However, the `withdraw()` and `deposit()` methods, for example, may well reside here, as will other "business methods."

As a rule of thumb, the business methods that should reside in the domain layer are those that are always likely to make sense to any possible application within the domain. In other words, the business methods provided in the domain layer are likely to be of use to any and all of the application(s) accessing the domain objects.

Should the presentation layer always go through the application layer to get to the domain layer, or is it ever appropriate for the application layer to be skipped? We think there are occasions when the application layer can legitimately be bypassed. Every system we've worked on has had a bunch of reference data or decodes (for example, currency codes), and there is usually very little or no business functionality associated with this sort of data. We don't think there is anything wrong with providing a direct presentation layer interfacing with these domain objects. Indeed, we've built development tools to automatically generate such user interfaces.

Domain and Data Management

Another option for handling divisions between major areas of software is to "chunk out" the system's functionality into a number of subsystems, each with its own façade. We have used this approach for a different layer of the *CarServ* application, from the domain layer to the persistence or data management layer. The persistence layer (the `datamgmt` package) presents three façades, `CustDM`, `CarDM`, and `ServiceDM`. As you might expect, these data managers are responsible for handling (that is creating, finding, updating, saving and deleting) customers, cars, and services respectively. We've also tried to keep these data managers as loosely coupled as possible, reconstituting relationships between classes in the domain layer, not the data management layer. Figure 8-20 shows the three data managers in the `datamgmt` package, with their dependencies on the underlying data classes (instances of the ValueObject pattern) also shown.

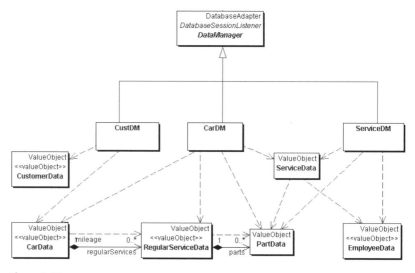

Figure 8–20
Three façades are used for the *datamgmt* package, `CustDM`, `CarDM`, `ServiceDM`.

In the *CarServ* case study, you'll see that we have rigorously kept to the conventional pattern, that the business domain objects depend upon the data management (persistence) layer. This means that the application layer does not need to know about persistence issues; the illusion is that the domain objects are just always "there." Behind the scenes, databases are being read from and updated. This is shown in Figure 8-21.

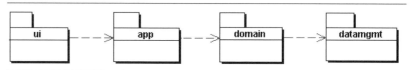

Figure 8–21
The domain package depends upon the datamgmt package.

However, if you look at the *CarServ* case study, you'll notice a lot of repetition. Pretty much the entire structure of the `domain` package is cloned within the `datamgmt` package with value object classes named in the form `"XxxData"`. So, another approach is to invert the dependency between the `domain` and `datamgmt` packages. This removes much of the repetition, because the `datamgmt` classes can extend from their equivalents in the `domain` package. This is shown in Figure 8-22.

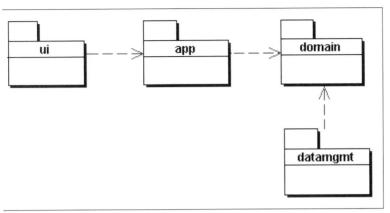

Figure 8–22
Or, is it the other way around?

The first approach (`domain` depends upon `datamgmt`) is that adopted in J2EE by entity EJBs under EJB v1.1 specification, whereas the second approach (`datamgmt` depends upon `domain`) is used within the more far-reaching EJB v2.0 specification.

In Figure 8-22 the `app` packages depend upon `domain` packages, but (by the principle of substitutability; Liskov 2001) actually refer to instances within the `datamgmt` package. This requires the application of some sort of Factory pattern (Gamma et al. 1995) to decouple the `app` package from the job of actually instantiating instances of classes within the `domain` package. In the J2EE platform and EJBs, this is done using the Java Naming and Directory Interface (JNDI), the EJB home interfaces and the EJB container. We'll consider this further in the next chapter.

We have already discussed configuration management (CM) in several chapters in this book, and it is well to remember that it is an essential foundation not only to the use of Together in a team but also to the whole development process. As well as aspects already discussed, configuration management also involves tracking compile-time and runtime dependencies, and goes hand-in-hand with release management.

You may notice some similarities here with our previous discussion of component diagrams and deployment diagrams. Component diagrams can be used to indicate either compile-time or runtime dependencies, and deployment diagrams indicate where the software should be deployed once it is released.

Configuration management should be set up as soon as possible in the project lifecycle. Iterative development processes that rely on frequent releases (XP, FDD, DSDM, and others) need solid mechanisms for compiling the code, building the release into packages, and pushing it out into production. Setting up this infrastructure early on when there is only a small amount of software means it is not too large an overhead. As the scope of the actual system grows, so can the sophistication of the CM infrastructure.

Parallel source code trees can be used, one for development and one for the current production code. This allows urgent defects found in the production code to be fixed and shipped as patches before the next formal release. These fixes must then also be applied to the development source code. Less serious defects are fixed only in the development source code and released according to the release schedule.

An automated nightly batch run is a good way of keeping control of the source code. This process can build the software and quite a lot more besides:

- Build all checked-in software, to ensure that it compiles.
- Depending upon the sophistication of the tests, run all automated tests to ensure that existing functionality has not been inadvertently broken by new changes.
- Generate HTML documentation.
- Run audits and metrics.
- Run custom-developed modules.

Together itself has built-in version control support. It acts as a source code client with your selected CM system or the one shipped with the product. It allows code to be checked in and out with simple right-click actions. Do be aware, though, that the source code client functionality built into Together follows the 80/20 rule—not every administrative function is available, just the commonly needed checkin, checkout, diff (compare with a previous version), and history functions.

Additionally, Together provides the ability to generate makefiles (*Project → Generate Makefile*), and this can be used to automate the compiles. Alternatively, there are some third-parties that use Jakarta's Ant.[43] Audits, metrics, gendoc, and custom-developed modules can all be run from the command line, as documented in Together's help documentation.

Moving and Renaming Model Elements Under Version Control

Together lets you rename classes very easily, and it will change the code and even the filename. Classes can be moved between packages just by dragging and dropping from any diagram that has representations of the source and target packages. Together effects the move of the underlying files and updates `package` statements and references to the class.

43. Together itself is also integrated with Ant, which means both that Ant scripts can be run from Together and that Together's functionality can be invoked from Ant scripts. This requires knowledge of both Ant and Together's open API, but the resulting build programs can be very powerful.

However, when the file is under version control and you want to move a file between directories (for example, move a class between packages), then you will need to take some additional steps. You have two options:

- In Together, check out the class, move it to the new package, and then create a new class in the new package. Then, uncheck out the original class and delete it from source control configuration.
- Don't check out the class in Together, but rather, use a more fully functioned source code client to actually move the class in the repository. When you then check out the class in Together, note that you'll need to check and possibly fix the `package` statement.

Which approach you use will depend upon whether you care about preserving the past history of changes made to the file. With the first option, you'll lose that history, and in the second you won't.

If you are carrying out really radical refactoring of package structures, the advantages of carrying it out in Together are really too great to pass up, even given the difficulty of the version management system recognizing the moves and keeping history. One possible solution that combines the options above is to make the changes in Together, then independently make the moves in the version control system, and finally check back in the files that were modified by Together, since these will have all the modified references.

What's Next

In this chapter we've considered architecture and architectural constraints, and looked at ways of defining and documenting architecture. In particular, we've shown the role that UML component diagrams and deployment diagrams play in addressing these issues.

We've also looked at ways to identify good architecture—for example, avoiding cyclic dependencies in package structures—and how modules can be developed using Together's open API that can help identify when architectural principles have been violated. Layered architecture and refactoring under version control have also been discussed.

In the next chapter, we look at Together's support for the de facto architecture for implementing enterprise applications on the Java platform—J2EE.

chapter 9

The J2EE Architecture

*It doesn't take much to see that the problems of
three little people doesn't add up to a hill of beans
in this crazy world.*

Humphrey Bogart

*EJB technology has removed the need to
write "plumbing" code.*

Bill Roth

*Anybody who has any doubt about the ingenuity
or the resourcefulness of a plumber never got
a bill from one.*

George Meany

This chapter looks in more detail at the J2EE architecture, which is a common standard for distributed systems defined by Sun Microsystems and
the framework of choice for many Java developments. We look briefly at the
features and advantages of using this framework, and then consider how
Together ControlCenter supports deployment of the built software to application servers supporting J2EE. The combination of powerful application servers
providing the infrastructure for running systems and Together's flexible
deployment facilities for development and deployment, makes for effective distributed systems and efficient development and maintenance.*

There's clearly a lot of interest in building enterprise applications with
Java. Many of Together's more advanced features (specifically, those in the
ControlCenter edition) are there to support J2EE development. We are not
looking to provide a full tutorial for J2EE in this chapter[44], rather to provide
an overview of how Together supports J2EE and simplifies the development
of J2EE systems.

Much of the J2EE platform is focused on server-side technologies—
servlets, Java Server Pages (JSPs), Enterprise Java Beans (EJBs), Java Naming

---

44. See for example Monson-Haefel (2000) or Haywood (2002) for such coverage.

and Directory Interface (JNDI) and so on. In fact, it might almost be worth characterizing the Java 2 Standard Edition (J2SE)—the JDK as was—as client-side development (the most obvious indication being the Swing GUI toolkit) and J2EE being oriented to server-side development. But while server-side applications bring many advantages in terms of cost of ownership, development of such applications can be somewhat harder because the feedback loop is longer. That is, in order to determine if your software works, you need to compile it, deploy it to a server-side process (which you need to remember to start), and then test it out.

Together provides support for all of these stages, and it is also bundled with Apache's Tomcat, the reference implementation of servlets and JSPs. Of all the J2EE technologies, these two are probably the most important in that they are mature and easy to understand, and they deliver immediate value. Together's bundling of Tomcat makes it easy to develop, deploy, and debug servlets and JSPs. There's currently lots of interest in EJBs also. Together has "first-class citizen" support for EJBs, and specifically supports an ever-growing number of application servers.

Using Together Makes it Easy

To show how Together makes it easy to develop J2EE applications, let's work through an example of using Together with servlets by building a small Web front-end for the *CarServ* application. You'll find the final code in the `webui` package of *CarServ*. This Web application is only a demonstrator, it's single-user and doesn't have all of the functionality of its Swing-based big brother, but there's enough in there so that you can appreciate Together's capabilities. So, first up, load the *CarServ* case study project.

Development

In the `webui` package, you will find four servlets, all subclassed from an adapter superclass. This is shown in Figure 9-1.

The abstract `WebUIAdapterServlet` superclass provides utility functions to simplify the rendering of common HTML elements (such as tables and forms). However, the structure of it was created simply using the *Reference* HttpServlet pattern, as shown in Figure 9-2.

The above pattern works well for Http servlets, which are the mainstay of Web applications. Together also offers a more general pattern that provides additional control, as shown in Figure 9-3.

In terms of the design of our *CarServ* webui application, all Http requests are directed at the `CarServWebUIServlet`; this acts as a controlling servlet. It then includes the output of the `SignOnServlet` (either a log-in form or a "logged in as:" message). If the user has logged in, then it also includes the output of the `DiaryTabServlet` or the `ServiceTabServlet` (corresponding to the two tabs in the Swing equivalent).

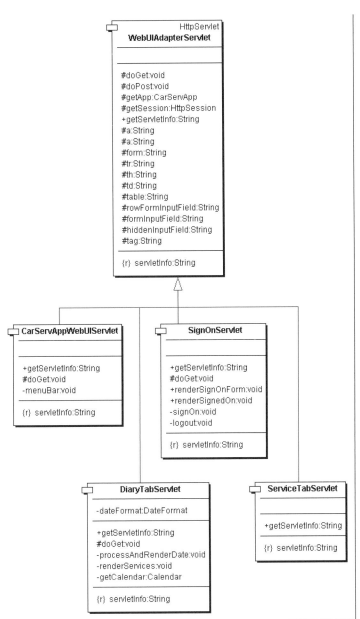

Figure 9–1

CarServ WebUI servlets.

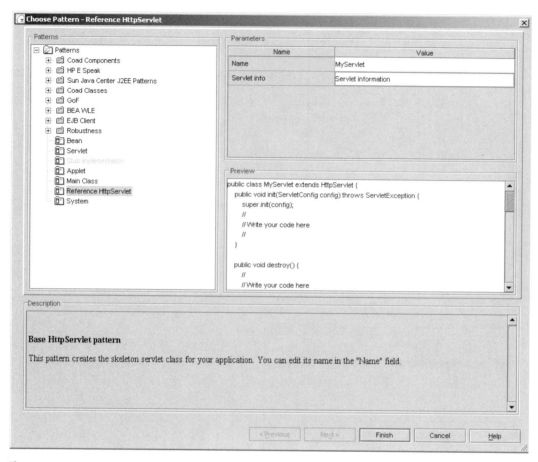

Figure 9–2

The *Reference HttpServlet* pattern allows servlets to be quickly created.

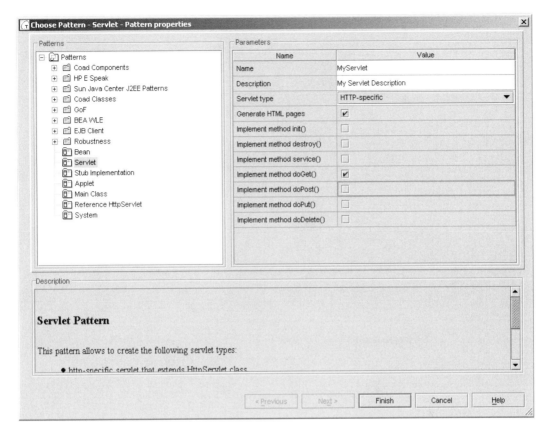

Figure 9–3
The *Servlet* pattern offers more customization.

Deploying to the Bundled Tomcat

The simplest way to test Web applications is to deploy to the bundled Tomcat servlet container.

Configuration

There are various properties that can be associated to servlets when they are deployed in a Web application. This information is specified on a *servlet* property page (this will appear in Together's properties inspector for any class extending HttpServlet). Figure 9-4 shows this inspector page.

This indicates that the logical servlet name (the `<servlet-name>` tag in the Web application deployment descriptor) is app and the URL to access the servlet (`<url-pattern>` under `<servlet-mapping>` in the deployment descriptor) is /app; this is relative to the Web application's context. We've also specified an initial parameter (`<init-param>` under `<servlet-name>`), though this information is not actually used by the application.

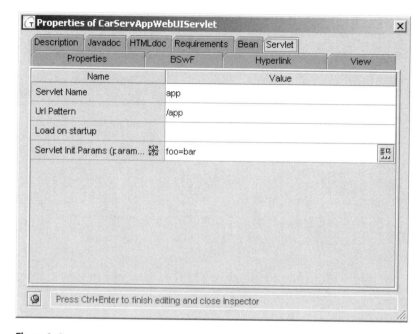

Figure 9–4
Servlet configuration can be captured as simple properties.

These properties are stored as regular JavaDoc tags in the source code:

```
1   /**
2    * @servletName app
3    * @webURLPattern /app
4    * @servletInitParam foo=bar
5    */
6   public class CarServAppWebUIServlet
7           extends WebUIAdapterServlet
```

If no servlet properties are defined, then Together will default to using the class name of the servlet as both the logical `<servlet-name>` and the `<url-pattern>`.

Deploy and Run

To deploy and run the servlet, a run configuration must be defined using *Run → Run/Debug Configurations*. Select `CarServAppWebUI` and hit the *Edit* button. Figure 9-5 shows the resulting dialog for our Web application.

Running this configuration will start up an instance of Tomcat and deploy the Web application under the default context. The Web browser is also started, pointing at the defined servlet. This is shown in Figure 9-6 using Microsoft's Internet Explorer as the browser. The application can then be run in a very similar way to the client-server version (Figure 9-7).

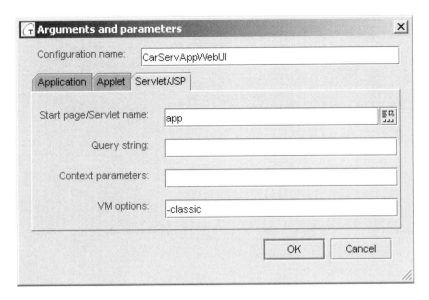

Figure 9–5
Servlets can be defined as a runtime configuration.

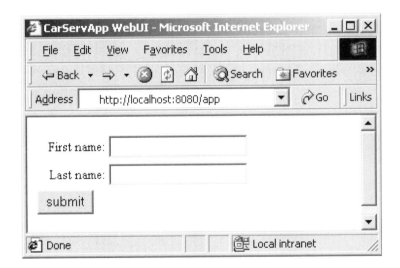

Figure 9–6
A Web browser is started automatically when a Web application is run.

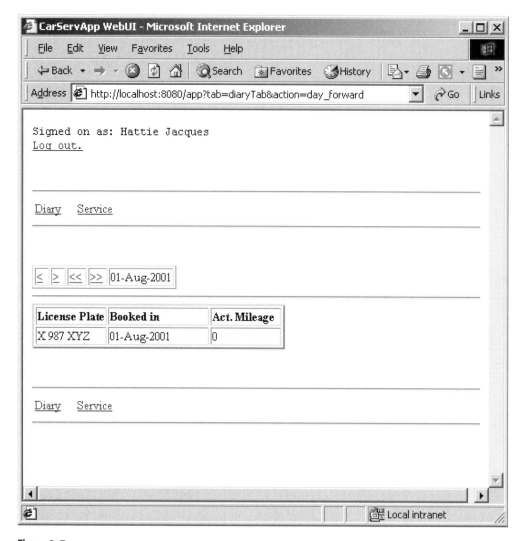

Figure 9–7

The somewhat minimal *CarServ* webui application.

Behind the scenes, Together temporarily creates a Tomcat configuration file `conf\serverNNNN.xml` and also a `WEB-INF\web.xml` deployment descriptor, both under the project root. When Tomcat is launched, it is pointed at the configuration file. The relevant fragment is:

```
1   <ContextManager debug="0" home="C:\carserv\"
2       workDir="C:\carserv\work" showDebugInfo="true">
3
4     … lines omitted …
5
6     <Context path="" docBase="C:\carserv\" debug="0"
7             reloadable="true" trusted="true" />
8   </ContextManager>
```

The deployment descriptor has the following form:

```
1   <web-app>
2
3     … lines omitted …
4
5     <servlet>
6       <servlet-name>app</servlet-name>
7       <servlet-class>
8         com.bettersoftwarefaster.carserv.webui.
9         CarServAppWebUIServlet
10      </servlet-class>
11      <init-param>
12        <param-name>foo</param-name>
13        <param-value>bar</param-value>
14      </init-param>
15    </servlet>
16
17    … lines omitted …
18
19    <servlet-mapping>
20      <servlet-name>app</servlet-name>
21      <url-pattern>/app</url-pattern>
22    </servlet-mapping>
23
24    … lines omitted …
25
26  </web-app>
```

The configuration file and deployment descriptor will be removed when Tomcat is stopped, but there's nothing to prevent you from copying the deployment descriptor when packaging up the application for system test or into production. However, an alternative approach is to use Together's Web application diagram, and we'll discuss this shortly.

Debugging

Deploying your Web application to the bundled Tomcat makes debugging trivial. Just set the breakpoint as usual, and run using *Run ◊ Debug* to launch the Debugger. Figure 9-8 shows Together having stopped at a breakpoint.

Deploying to an External Application Server

Although the bundled Tomcat application server is useful during development, the Web application will be deployed to an external application server when it is released into production.

Configuration

When using the bundled Tomcat, we showed you that a Web application deployment descriptor (`web.xml` file) is implicitly created. To explicitly create the deployment descriptor, Together's Web application diagram can be used, as shown in Figure 9-9.

Figure 9-10 shows the different elements that are available (note, our *CarServ* Web application does not use any of these additional elements; they are there for illustration only).

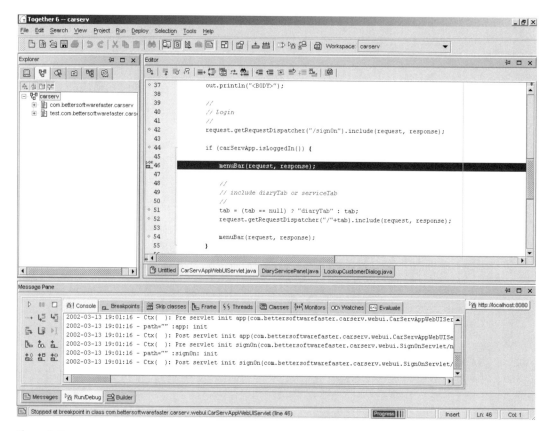

Figure 9–8
Breakpoints work in Web applications as for regular applications

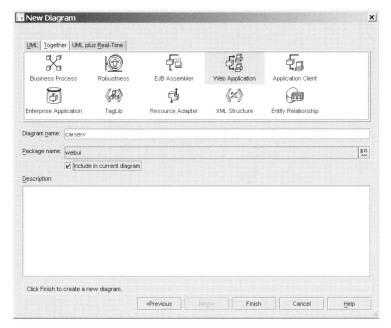

Figure 9–9
The Web application diagram is one of a number that support the development of J2EE applications.

There is no explicit support for indicating prerequisite JAR files (e.g., to connect to a database). However, the Web files icon can be used, since any files underneath are just added to the final Web application archive (the "WAR" file).

So, to specify prerequisite JARs,add a Web file icon (e.g., the "Carserv jar files") and point it to a path that contains the following structure:

```
WEB-INF\
   lib\
      x.jar
      y.jar
      z.jar
```

If you are following along, then you will find a `webjar` directory under the `CarServ` directory project. The "Carserv jar files" Web files icon points to this directory, though the actual `webjar\WEB-INF\lib` directory is empty. Copy the three Cloudscape JAR files (`client.jar`, `cloudscape.jar`, and `RmiJdbc.jar`) into this directory.

The file name for the Web application archive is taken from the "module name" property of the Web application diagram (Figure 9–11). This also defines the context root.[45] Other Web application information can also be specified here.

---

45. We think that it is a mistake that a context root property can be specified, since the root is not part of the deployment descriptor (`web.xml`), but rather the servlet container environment (as typified by `server.xml`). In fact, the value of this property does seem to be ignored!

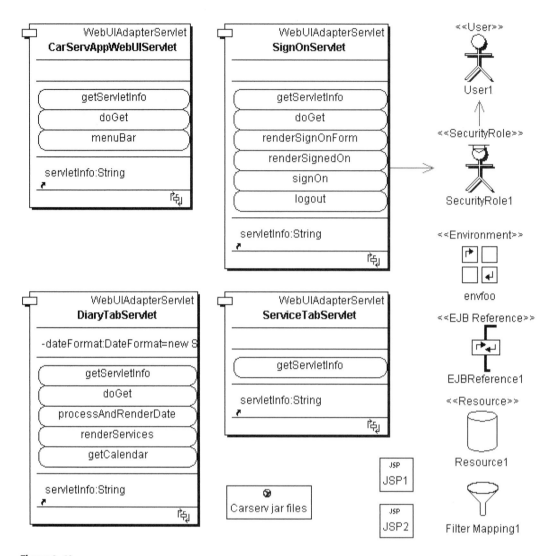

Figure 9–10

The Web application diagram is a graphical representation of a Web application deployment descriptor.

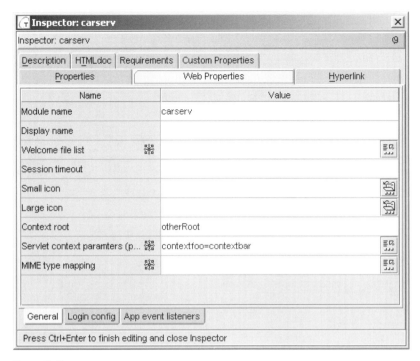

Figure 9–11
Web application diagram properties.

Packaging

To package the Web application, the EJB deployment expert is used, from *Deploy* → J2EE *Deployment Expert*. This should be run from the Web application diagram. Use the values shown in Figure 9-12. There are two further pages in the deployment expert; just select the defaults.

The deployment descriptor information is taken from both the Web application diagram and from the JavaDoc tags in the servlet source code previously discussed. If the appropriate tick box is selected in the expert, the packaging process opens up an XML editor to allow fine tuning of the deployment descriptor, as shown in Figure 9-13.

The result of this will be a WAR file in the directory specified in the expert. Incidentally, if you view the contents of the WAR file (using `jar tvf` or Win-Zip), then you will see the Cloudscape JAR files embedded within the WAR file. You should also be able to see the `web.xml` deployment descriptor.

Deploying and Running

To deploy the WAR file to Tomcat, just dump it in the `$TOMCAT_HOME\webapps` directory. To start Tomcat, use `$TOMCAT_HOME\bin\startup`. Figure 9-14 and Figure 9-15 show a Web browser connecting to Tomcat now running our Web application externally. Note that the context root is now `"carserv"` (rather than being the default context, as it was when we deployed to the bundled Tomcat).

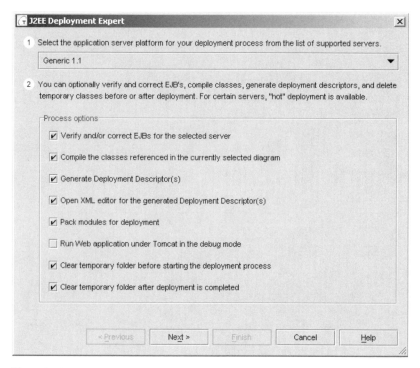

Figure 9–12
The EJB deployment expert is also used to deploy Web applications.

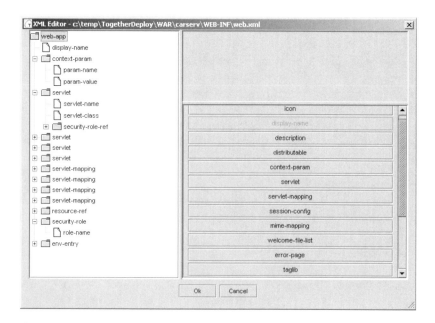

Figure 9–13
The XML editor can be used to fine tune the deployment descriptor.

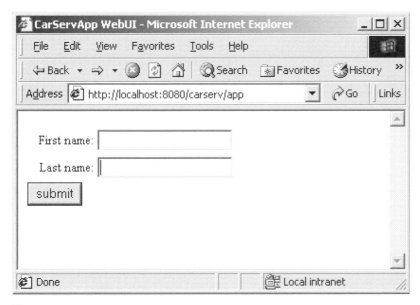

Figure 9–14
The Web application deployed externally.

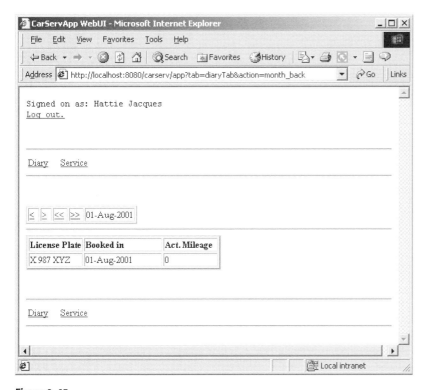

Figure 9–15
The *CarServ* Web application running externally.

Incidentally, this changing of context root (from the default context to `"carserv"`) might well point out some bugs in your code; it did with us. Specifically, if you use the `RequestDispatcher` object to forward or include the output from other servlets, then the URL pattern should be used (that is, prefixed with `"/"`). On the other hand, if you are simply generating `<a href="xxx">xxx</a>` tags on a Web page, then the hyperlink reference should be relative and so should *not* be prefixed with `"/"`. You'll find that using a `"/"` prefix in both situations means that the code runs when the context root is the default context but not otherwise.

Remote Debugging

The EJB deployment expert (shown in Figure 9-12) has an option "Run web application under Tomcat in debug mode." This is effectively the same as deploying the application to the bundled Tomcat, and indeed the context root reverts back to being the default rather than `"carserv"`. The only difference is that the additional deployment information in the Web application diagram is used to construct the deployment descriptor.

In a system test environment, what is more likely to be required is a mechanism to debug the application in situ. This is easy enough to do. First, edit the `tomcat.bat` script in `$TOMCAT_HOME\bin` and add the following line (if running under UNIX, edit `tomcat.sh` and make the equivalent change):

```
set TOMCAT_OPTS=-classic -Xms64m -Xmx128m -Xdebug -Xnoagent
 -Djava.compiler=NONE
 -Xrunjdwp:transport=dt_socket,address=8787,server=y,suspend=n
```

This should all be on a single line. Also, make sure that the `$JAVA_HOME/bin` is on your `$PATH`, to pick up a required shared library (on Windows, `runjdwp.dll`).

With this change made, start Tomcat in the usual way.

To actually debug the Web application, use *Run → Attach to Remote Process*. This is shown in Figure 9-16.

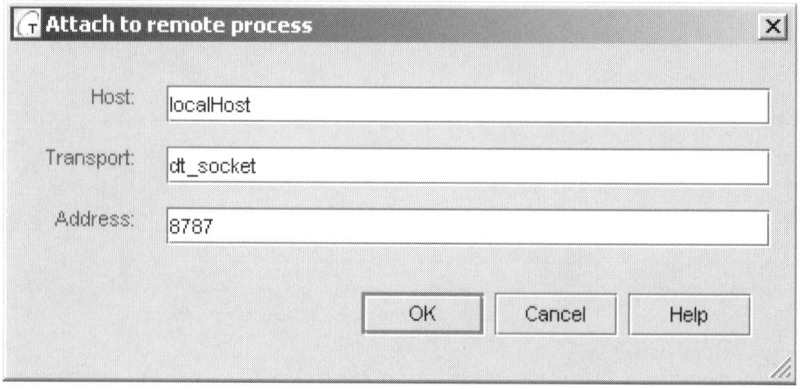

Figure 9–16
Attaching to a remote process (such as Tomcat) puts it under Together's control.

The Web application can then be debugged as per usual, with break-points and so on.

When you have finished your debug session, press the stop button in the *Run/Debug* tab. Make sure you answer "No" to the dialog box presented (shown in Figure 9-17).

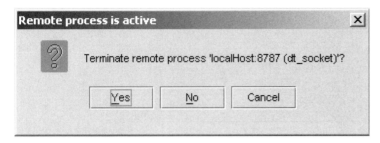

Figure 9–17
Don't accidentally kill the remote process when finishing debugging. Select "No".

If you go through the above steps, then you will notice that Tomcat becomes significantly slower once Together has attached to it. This is because the program execution within Tomcat is under Together's control, with multiple interprocess interactions going on all the time. Therefore, this technique should only be used with extreme caution if debugging code running in the production environment.

Other J2EE Support

In addition to the Web application diagram, Together has an EJB assembler diagram and an Enterprise application diagram. The first of these corresponds very closely to the Web application diagram; it is for constructing the deployment descriptor for an EJB or set or EJBs to be bundled up into an EJB-JAR file.[46] The second of these tools is for taking WAR files and EJB-JAR files and creating an Enterprise Archive, or EAR, file. This is appropriate for middle-tier applications that use both servlets and EJBs.

Together also provides patterns to build EJBs (session, entity, or message) and can reverse engineer existing databases into entity EJBs. Also, EJBs are treated as first class citizens in class diagrams. In other words, all their respective parts (the remote interface, the home interface, the bean itself as the primary key class for entity beans) can be manipulated using a single visual representation.

Together also allows JSPs to be developed using a built-in JSP editor, and even allows breakpoints to be defined on JSP source code—a clever trick considering that the actual code being executed is a servlet created at runtime from the JSP code.

---

46. Indeed, the use of deployment descriptors and WAR files for Web applications is based on the deployment process originally developed for EJBs.

Testing

In Chapter 6, "The Continuous Step: Measure the Quality" we discussed how JUnitX can be used to perform unit testing and functional testing of code. When testing servlets (and JSPs), this approach fails because the servlet is only called indirectly via the servlet container.

Luckily, though, there are a number of frameworks that aim to simplify the testing of servlets. These are based on, extend, or at least have similarities with JUnit and they are integrated with and supported by Together's testing framework. It's our intention just to highlight those frameworks rather than provide a thorough overview:

- HttpUnit is a framework that emulates a Web browser. It provides classes to manage a WebConversation (with a request and response object) such that JUnit tests can be written that inspect the state of those objects. There are helper methods that allow the easy development of tests of tables, forms, and frames. See *http://httpunit.sourceforge.net*.
- ServletUnit is a companion framework to HttpUnit. It emulates a servlet container, allowing testing of individual methods within a servlet. Again, JUnit is used to actually write the tests. Again, see *http://httpunit.sourceforge.net*.
- Apache's Cactus provides a framework for writing client-side JUnit tests (using classes that extend from JUnit) while actually testing them running within a target servlet container. In other words, it offers a similar granularity to ServletUnit, without having to simulate being a servlet container. Proxies are used to redirect the test invoked on the client side over to the server side. Cactus can use HttpUnit to develop client-side assertions. See *http://jakarta.apache.org/cactus/*.

Mock Objects is a generic approach (mentioned previously in Chapter 6) that creates classes that both emulate real functionality and enforce assertions about the behavior of our code. See *http://mockobjects.sourceforge.net*.

We leave you to explore the respective Web sites to determine which framework works best. The Apache Cactus Web site does a comparison of each of the above, and (in the order that we have presented them) ranks them from high-level functional testing through mid-level integration testing to very fine-grained unit testing. See if you agree.

Of course, the J2EE architecture means more than just servlets; there may also be EJBs. It is possible to develop client-side test harnesses that use JUnit directly, but one issue is that every test will incur a network call. This could make the tests take a prohibitively long time to execute.

The JUnitEE framework instead allows servlets to be developed to test your EJBs. The advantage is that the servlet will run in the same process space as the EJB under test, reducing the amount of time needed to execute the tests. Moreover, it is often the case that the client of an EJB will be a servlet, so this more accurately emulates the overall environment under test. As with most of the other frameworks, it works in conjunction with JUnit. For more information, see *http://junitee.sourceforge.net*.

In Summary

Together provides numerous features that support the development of J2EE-based applications. In this overview we have focused primarily on servlet development, but there is support too for EJBs and JSPs. The bottom line is that these features mean it is easier to identify problems with the code; that is, to keep the feedback loop tight.

There are a lot of powerful facilities that Together ControlCenter opens up to the developer, as we have seen, but J2EE development still isn't "easy." Don't get us wrong: most of the technology is there—it's just that the design issues need to be understood. So, let's see why.

Tiered Architectures

The J2EE architecture defines four tiers: presentation, application, domain, and data management. You may be more familiar with a three-tier architecture, where the application and domain layers are just termed "business logic." But it *is* worth splitting that business logic layer into two, because the domain objects within your organization are probably accessed through multiple applications

It's really quite a discipline to separate out presentation from business logic. In fact, there's a good example in the *CarServ* case study of how *not* to do it. If you open up the `ui` package, you'll see a whole bunch of listener interfaces; different bits of the UI notify other bits when a domain object has changed so that they can refresh themselves. Of course, those listener interfaces should have been defined in the `domain` package, not the `ui` package (see sidebar for a further discussion on this). But having made that mistake, how difficult would it be to get the budget to perform the required refactoring? Very, we think.

The tiers described above are logical; we aren't saying anything about which process space these objects exist in. For example, in *CarServ*, they all reside in just one process space. But with the EJB architecture, this is done differently. In Chapter 8, "The Macro Step: Architecture," we discussed implementing a `System` class—a class that acts as a façade to the application—and found that there were a number of candidates. So, one of the appealing aspects of the EJB architecture is that there is a ready-made candidate for this role, namely the session EJBs. In other words, there is a one-to-one mapping from the architectural abstraction to the physical code.

There are a couple of archetypal EJB deployments. The first is a Web-based approach, with the presentation layer being handled by the Web browser, servlets, JSPs, or all three, the application layer by session EJBs, and the domain layer by entity EJBs. The data management layer is a back-end JDBC connection to a relational database. An alternative deployment has the presentation layer entirely with a FAT client (usually Swing), with application, domain, and data management layers as above.

Presentation Layer Issues

Let's count the network connections in our Web-oriented EJB deployment. There will be one from the Web browser to the application server, and one from the application server to the relational database management system (RDBMS). What of network connections for the alternate Swing-oriented solution? Still two. But here, it's important to make sure that the communication between the presentation and application layers is efficient, because every such communication would be across the wire.

This difference in cost of communication means that developing multiple front-end presentation layers is not quite as simple as plug-and-play. The best example we have of this is when the presentation layer interacts with an entity EJB. What the presentation layer actually has is a reference to a remote object (as in one that implements `java.rmi.Remote`). When the presentation layer is in a different process space to the domain layer, any method call (`getName()`, `getPrice()`, etc.) is going to go across the wire. However, if a servlet or JSP makes such a method call, it's going to be comparatively cheap.[47] The best solution to all this is generally to use value objects or structs that pass nice big chunks of information from the application/domain layer to the presentation layer. Effectively, we pass a description of the remote object back to the presentation layer, not

---

47. The EJB specification says that the "pass by value" semantics must be preserved; this means that the application server must clone the objects being passed, even if the caller and callee are in the same process space. However, commercial EJB servers allow this "pass by value" semantic to optionally be switched off, so the method invocation can often be no more expensive than a regular Java method call.

the remote object itself. This, after all, is all that a `java.sql.Result-Set` is in traditional client/server terms.[48] Or, the current favorite solution is to send the data as an XML document in either a text or DOMDocument representation.

Persistence Layer Issues

The other network link—from entity EJB in the application server to the relational database—can also cause us problems. Container-managed persistence—whereby the application server automatically accesses and updates the database using metadata provided during the deployment process—was, in EJB v1.1, almost hilariously naive. The EJB v2.0 specification improves matters somewhat, going some way to defining workable relationships between entity EJBs. Now, at least, vendors should be able to develop sophisticated EJB containers that are compliant with the EJB v2.0 specification but not hamstrung by it. Nevertheless, it will take time for some vendors to develop and implement efficient object-oriented/relational mapping technology to embed within their EJB containers and for developers to feel adept in wielding such complex technology.

One alternative is to use an object-oriented database management system (OODBMS), or even an Associative database (Williams, 2000), rather than an RDBMS as the persistence layer. Indeed, many of the old OODBMS vendors have repositioned their products as application servers, because effectively they have solved this problem—or large portions of it—already. However, while OODBMS have been deployed in production systems for a good many years, they are still to hit the mainstream. The associative model of data shows promise but is still relatively immature.

An interesting development that might advance and popularize the idea of storing objects is the introduction of JVMs within RDBMS products. All the major RDBMS vendors are involved with the SQL/J initiative, and some have implemented their solution by having a JVM running in the process space of the DBMS server. This at least offers up the idea of EJBs running within the database server.[49]

The ability to store Java objects within RDBMS also means that bean-managed persistence—"roll-your-own"—becomes much less onerous. Indeed, if we could somehow automate the generation of (at least the majority of) the bean managed persistence logic,then that would save some effort. Using SQL/J level 2 means that data can be stored as Java objects; in Sybase ASE 12.5 we can create tables using the syntax:

```
1   CREATE TABLE mdl_model
2   (
3     mdl_name VARCHAR(20) NOT NULL,
4     obj      com.bettersoftwarefaster.carserv.domain.Model
5              NOT NULL,
6     CONSTRAINT PK_mdl_model PRIMARY KEY (mdl_name)
7   )
```

---

48. In fact, Richard Monson-Haefel suggests passing back `ResultSets` (Monson-Haefel 2000).

49. Oracle and Sybase don't quite do this; they have an EJB application server that runs on the same box as the database server, with shared-memory communication to minimize the overhead.

You can also do something similar in Cloudscape 4.0:

```
1   CREATE CLASS ALIAS Model
2   FOR com.bettersoftwarefaster.carserv.domain.Model;
3
4   CREATE TABLE mdl_model
5   (
6     mdl_name VARCHAR(20) NOT NULL,
7     obj SERIALIZE Model obj NOT NULL,
8     CONSTRAINT PK_mdl_model PRIMARY KEY (mdl_name)
9   );
```

As you can guess from the Cloudscape syntax, the object is simply serialized to disk. This is nice, because vector attributes (cardinality > 1) can be stored away without introducing any detail tables. In *CarServ*, the `Model` class effectively contains a `ServiceSchedule`, which in turn holds a `List` of `RegularService` objects; we can persist this entire graph in a single statement. Crucially, the SQL is also trivially easy to generate:

```
PreparedStatement ps = conn.prepareStatement(
  "INSERT INTO mdl_model (mdl_name, obj) VALUES (?,?)");
ps.setString(1, model.getName());
ps.setObject(2, this);
```

In other words, we don't have to sweat the small stuff—we're not even in first normal form! On the other hand, unless there is a JVM in the process space of the RDBMS, it's going to be an expensive operation to deserialize that object and to interact with it.[50]

It isn't too difficult to imagine developing a Together pattern that would create a new `datamgmt` subclass of some `domain` object. This would effectively do little more than provide `load()` and `save()` methods, the implementation of which would be just to perform the appropriate SQL using objects. The pattern could even generate the DDL scripts to create the tables.

It's a State

In Chapter 8 we floated an idea that wizards, as beloved by word processor vendors and even present in Together itself, are the realization of use cases. There is a goal, and there is ongoing state (characterized by that *Next* button at the bottom of the pane) until the goal is accomplished (and you press the *Finish* button).

In a J2EE architecture, there are a couple of candidates for holding that ongoing state. The obvious choice is a stateful session EJB, and this works fine. But if you are using a Web UI, then an alternative is to put the state in a servlet layer, using the `HttpSession` class. If you only expect there to be a Web UI, then you could even omit the session EJB layer completely and hold state just in servlets.

---

50. Realistically, you'd also want to export some information into regular columns so that the DBA can define indexes. At this time, neither Sybase nor Cloudscape allow indexes to be defined on getter methods.

To be honest, we don't advocate doing this; you *should* use the session EJB layer for state, because it represents the logical application. But we do recognize that it would be a tricky task to justify the budget for refactoring a Web-based application that holds its state in `HttpSession` objects to move that state over to stateful session EJBs instead.

One other point on stateful matters: Only hold state in one place. Or, put another way, don't have a stateful object invoke services on another stateful object. The reason for this is timeouts. All stateful objects (either servlet sessions or stateful session beans) are deployed with a timeout, say, of 20 or 30 minutes. If stateful object A calls stateful object B, should A's timeout be longer or shorter than that for B? Well, let's try it:

1. Let's make A's timeout 30 minutes, and B's timeout 20 minutes. We call A at time t_1, and A in turn calls B to accomplish some processing. We then call A at time $t_2=t_1+29$, which attempts to call B; B has timed out and so the call to A fails.
2. Okay, let's make A's timeout 20 minutes, and B's timeout 30 minutes. Again, we call A at time t_1, which calls B. Now let's call A again at time $t2=t1+19$, where this time A doesn't need to call B to complete the work. Finally, we call A at time $t_3 = t_2+19 = t_1+38$, and now A needs to call B; B has timed out, so again we have a failure.

Whichever way we cut it, we could end up with a failure. If you know enough about your application to ensure that the second scenario never happens, you can safely make A's timeout less than B's timeout—but that sounds like pretty fragile code to us. So, instead, you'll have to hold the state in A and make B stateless. In a server-side environment, this is no bad thing, because stateless objects are inherently more scalable than stateful. Better to have a single stateful object per connected user than many stateful objects.

In Summary

So, have we depressed you or excited you? There is no doubt that a correctly implemented J2EE-based system has lots going for it, and the reason is that a good architecture will have been imposed on you. But if you don't have a couple of failed attempts before finally getting that implementation right, then you'll be doing well.

chapter 10

Parting Words

*To learn something and then to put it into practice at
the right time: is this not a joy?*
Confucius

*Computers in the future may have only
1,000 vacuum tubes and perhaps only weigh
one and a half tons.*
Popular Mechanics, 1949

Caution: Cape does not enable user to fly.
Batman costume warning label

*A book is a version of the world. If you do not like it,
ignore it; or offer your own version in return.*
Salman Rushdie

David walked away from the project meeting with a smile of satisfaction. He was leaving the project after a period of around 20 months in which the bank had alternatively praised and castigated him for the project's progress, but he was leaving with a sense of real satisfaction. The bank's Internet service had grown from strength to strength, and the new architecture—delivered later than expected but successfully and without negative impact on existing users—was proving its worth. Automation of previously manual parts of the system was delivering a better service at significantly lower cost, and new features that were tuned to both the needs of the users and the marketing department's desire to launch new services were either in operation or well on the road to successful implementation.

But David also realized that he was moving to a new project whose challenges were different but no less urgent. "We need you to do it again," his boss had said to him the previous day, "but it's a larger distributed team this time, and there are two subcontractors involved in the development."

He didn't mean that he wanted David to literally do the same thing as the previous project, but to produce results again. The lessons learned from yesterday will only ever take us part of the way on the next project. Thus, it

**We Need You
to Do it Again!**

wasn't so much David's gray hairs that were important (the symbol of years of experience and knowledge about what was done last time), it was his gray cells that were required, his ability to think about the new challenges and different situations that he would face on the next assignment.

We feel similarly that the end of this book is only another starting point. These ideas are not the end of our journey to find ways to make better software faster. They are, we hope, a staging post, but we have no doubt that they will be transformed by the experience of future endeavors and others' wisdom, so that in time we may look back on them and smile (or wince) at their insights. (Some computers do indeed weigh less than one and a half tons!) We hope, though, that these words contribute to your search for better processes, better tool support, and better architecture, and that indeed your projects may produce better software faster as a result.

Ideas on paper are often a world apart from the heat and dust of a real project, even though for the most part we have distilled them from real project experience. So, in effect, there's a warning label on this book, not unlike that on the Batman costume—"This book does not enable the reader to do the impossible!" The "death march" projects (Yourdon 2000) with impossible goals, deadlines, and politics will remain impossible, even if you take the advice of these pages.

Yet we have shared some thoughts that we hope will help improve software development. This closing chapter is aimed at summarizing the key ideas we have offered and at looking forward to the new lessons to be learned from their application.

A Simple Summary

Our practical advice has been focused on teams using Together Control-Center. But behind this, there are a number of ideas that apply to any development environment able to apply a similar approach, not just to Together. All these themes have been written about by others, but they are brought together here, we believe, for the first time. What are these general ideas? Here are four of them:

- Just One Single-Source Model
- The Minimum Metamodel
- The Perturbation Change Model
- Continuous Measurement of Quality

Just One Single-Source Model

Our starting point followed from the most remarkable characteristic of Together itself—LiveSource. When you have a development environment that can derive all its editable and viewable documents and diagrams from a single source of versioned files, significant advantages follow. However, as we have shown, it is possible to use LiveSource simply to improve the way in which multiple models are maintained within a relatively traditional development process. We believe that it is better to move directly to a single model from which views at different levels of abstraction (e.g., analysis, design, and implementation) are derived.

The single-model approach means that early versions of the domain model are transformed into the final design. Subsequently, analysis-level views can be derived from the implementation directly, meaning that there is only one model. Reviews may refer back to historical versions to confirm compliance with earlier work, but the single stream of change is applied to the model that includes implementation detail as well as requirements and business process information.

The Minimum Metamodel

A single model needs a metamodel to guide the identification of a consistent and complete model. The minimum metamodel described in this book looks for the simplest set of information that *must* be linked and kept consistent build by build. In effect, this boils down to four essential elements: requirements (for example use cases), tests (functional, nonfunctional, and unit tests), interaction design (often expressed in a sequence diagram), and implementation.

Simple rules follow from these elements of the minimum metamodel: Every requirement should have a fair test that passes; every requirement should have a design; every design should reference objects and messages that have implemented classes and operations; every operation should be tested by at least one unit test; and all unit tests should pass.

The Perturbation Change Model

While we haven't sought to introduce a new development process, we have tried to provide advice on software development and management within the framework of a generic change process, which we termed the perturbation change model. This is the evolutionary model of change where every generation of the product must be a stable realization, fulfilling the requirements of the minimum metamodel for consistency and completeness. Yet each generation is only a stepping stone to yet greater quality and/ or functionality in the next generation. The perturbation change model needs equilibrium as its starting point (a build of sufficient quality), a perturbation from equilibrium (such as accepting a new requirement into the build) as its driver, and, once again, equilibrium as its end point.

The perturbation change model is compatible with many of the named software development processes that we have discussed throughout the book. However, it does place a greater emphasis on the similarity of activities through the phases of a project, rather than emphasizing different activities in different phases. It is also at the heart of understanding feature-centric processes of management, which we discussed in Chapter 5, "The Controlling Step: Feature-Centric Management."

Continuous Measurement of Quality

Finally, we have stressed that to produce *better* software, you must be able to measure the quality of the software, and to do so continuously. This follows from a commitment to iterative development processes, since each build—even builds that are delivered to the end-users—are only interim points in the succession of builds leading to improvements for the users. While we have emphasized the role of automated and repeatable tests in measuring quality, audits, metrics, document generation, and inspection are also vital parts of this.

We have been discussing all of these themes in the context of a team using Together ControlCenter. This development platform and others like it that no doubt will appear on the market, are themselves evolving into ever more powerful environments for software teams. We have been writing about Together at a particular point in time, and so there are features and new ways of doing things that will appear in later versions.The products will change. The principles however will endure.

Now Over to You

So, now it is down to putting these ideas to the test. We hope that as you do so you will let us know how it goes. We look forward to hearing from you, through the book's Web site, *www.bettersoftwarefaster.com*, or through other means. Your feedback is vital to us in order that lessons applied in practice provide new lessons themselves.

Installing the
Case Study Software

To inspect and use the case study software that is released with this book, there are several simple steps to follow. These steps are described in this appendix.[51] You will need Internet access to obtain the software. Also, before you start, it is worth checking the book's website *www.bettersoftwarefaster.com* for updates to these instructions.

Before You Start

Here is a summary of the steps:

1. Download and install Together ControlCenter (and obtain an evaluation license from TogetherSoft if required)
    a. [optional] create directory structure
    b. set environment variables
    c. install
2. [Optional] Download the customization files
    a. copy the `.config` files
    b. set classpaths
    c. copy the QA modules
3. Download, install and start the Cloudscape client (the server, bundled with the Together download, must also be started)
4. Download the case study project software
5. Test the installation

If you do not already have Together installed, then you can download the current version from the TogetherSoft Web site (*www.togethersoft.com*). If you choose to download the version without a JVM, then you will also need to obtain one, for example, from Sun's Web site (*java.sun.com*).

Together Download and Install

TogetherSoft's download process includes obtaining a license for Together. Evaluation licenses are available—free of charge at the time of writing—and there are also special arrangements for educational establishments.

---

51. We've written these instructions for Microsoft Windows, but they are readily adaptable if you are using a different operating system.

Environment Variables

Together does not require environment variables to be defined, but we do recommend that you set some up—if only so that we don't need to hard-code paths in this book! If you have been trying out the custom modules described in the various sidebars throughout the preceding chapters, you will know that they require the %TOGETHER% environment variable to be defined to point to Together's home directory. We recommend for the %TOGETHER%[52] variable be version-specific, such as C:\Together-soft\Together6.0, as this simplifies support for multiple versions of Together. The full set of environment variables that you should define are shown in Table A–1. In Windows they can be set up from the *Control Panel* → *System* → *Advanced* dialog.

Table A–1

Environment Variables

Environment Variable	Description	Typical Value
TOGETHERSOFT	The location of all Together versions and customizations.	C:\TogetherSoft
TOGETHER	The location of the root Together directory.	C:\TogetherSoft\Together6.0
JAVA_HOME	The location of the Java virtual machine.	C:\TogetherSoft\Together6.0\jdk
J2EE_HOME	The location of the J2EE Reference Implementation bundled with Together; this in turn defines the location of the Cloudscape database server.	C:\TogetherSoft\Together6.0\bundled\j2ee

Managing Multiple Together Versions

If you use Together ControlCenter for a while, you'll soon notice that new releases of the product become available frequently. Judging by previous years, you can expect at least one major version annually, with one or even two minor releases. For example, between mid-2000 and mid-2002 Together-Soft released Together ControlCenter v4.0, v4.1, v4.2, v5.0, v5.5, and v6.0 with occasional bug fix releases as well.

52. The %TOGETHER% environment variable should have the same value as Together's own TGH variable used in its .config files.

What this means is that you can soon expect a number of different versions of Together to reside on your hard disk, and every time you install a new version, then you'll need to reapply all of your configuration and other customizations. Those customizations will mostly involve one or more types of change: new `.config` *files (see Appendix C for details of* `.config` *changes discussed in this book), new templates (see Appendix D), new modules (see Appendix E for a framework for writing module-based inspectors, and throughout the book for other modules mentioned), new audits and metrics (see Chapter 6), or indeed new patterns (discussed in Chapter 7).*

Clearly, reapplying configurations represents significant effort, so we thought we'd show you a few shortcuts. The directory structure we use is:

```
C:\
   TogetherSoft\
     my\
     config\
     modules\
     projects\
     templates\
   TogetherX.Y\
   TogetherX.Z\
```

Our custom modules reside in the `my\modules` *directory, our custom templates in the* `my\templates` *directory, and our custom* `.config` *files in the* `my\config` *directory. As you can see from Appendix C, we never edit the* `.config` *files shipped with Together directly.*

To get Together to pick up our customization, there are a couple of steps required. The first is to copy our `.config` *files into the appropriate version-specific* `config` *directory, for example,* `C:\Together- Soft\Together6.0\config`*. If you are running on a UNIX-based system, then you can use symbolic links instead.*

One of the `.config` *files we install (*`zzzBSwF.personalPrefer- ences.config`*) is used to point Together at our* `my\templates`*,* `my\mod- ules`*, and* `my\project` *directories. To point Together to our* `my\templates` *directory, it has the entries:*

```
;misc.config
template.root.2 = "C:/TogetherSoft/my/templates"

;navigator.config
VfsNavigator.root.6 = file("C:/TogetherSoft/my/templates")
```

To point Together at our `my\modules` *directory, it has the entries:*

```
;scriptloader.config
scriptloader.root.3 =
\ file("C:/TogetherSoft/my/modules/com/togethersoft/modules")
scriptloader.root.3.name = "Custom Modules"
```

*   The custom modules described in the book and downloadable from the website actu- ally install into `%TOGETHER%\modules`, rather than `%TOGETHERSOFT%\my\mod- ules`. We did this only so that our suggested directory structure remains that: a suggestion, not an absolute requirement. But to use our suggested directory struc- ture for custom modules, just change the `install.bat` scripts provided.

And, to point Together at our my\projects directory, it has the entries:

```
;general.config
project.new.locationDefault = C:/TogetherSoft/my/projects

;navigator.config
VfsNavigator.root.5 = file("C:/TogetherSoft/my/projects")
```

It is also necessary to start Together with a modified classpath so that our custom modules are picked up. This is most easily done by defining the environment variable TG_CLASSPATH to include the directory containing our custom modules, namely %TOGETHERSOFT%\my\modules. However, you must then start Together using its .bat command file, such as C:\Together-Soft\TogetherX.X\bin\together.bat. (Alternatively, you could perhaps just edit the system CLASSPATH, but we are generally reluctant to suggest that.)

One last thing. Unfortunately, at the time of this writing QA plug-ins are not picked up using this technique, so, you will need to manually copy any custom audits and metrics into the appropriate directory under %TOGETHER% (or use symbolic links if running under UNIX).

Cloudscape

The case study uses Cloudscape 4.0 as its persistent datastore. Cloudscape is a pure Java RDBMS written by Informix Corporation (now part of IBM). We have used Cloudscape for the database, since it is bundled with the J2EE RI, which in turn is bundled with Together.

Cloudscape can operate in either client-server or embedded mode. For the case study, we use the former,[53] which means that you do need to remember to start the Cloudscape server engine. You also need a network connection, but you can always install a software-only network adapter (such as the Microsoft Loopback Adapter on Windows).

In order to set up the case study, you will need to download the *Cloudview* client from *www.cloudscape.com*. This is a GUI that allows SQL to be submitted and the database to be queried. The files to download (for Cloudscape v4.0) are as follows:

- `cloudview40.jar`
- `jh.jar`

Place these into `%J2EE_HOME%\lib\cloudscape`. Next, edit the following line of `setenv.bat`, which you will find in `%J2EE_HOME%\bin`:

```
set CLOUDJARS=%CLOUDSCAPE_INSTALL%\RmiJdbc.jar;
    %CLOUDSCAPE_INSTALL%\client.jar
```

by appending both

---

53. In fact, the case study was developed to support either mode. The class data-mgmt.DatabaseSession can be edited to switch to embedded mode. However, we don't discuss the steps needed to setup the CLASSPATH for using embedded mode.

```
;%CLOUDSCAPE_INSTALL%\cloudview40.jar
```

and

```
%CLOUDSCAPE_INSTALL%\jh.jar
```

Create the following batch file `cview.bat` in `%J2EE_HOME%\bin`:

```
@call setenv.bat
%JAVA_HOME%\bin\java -classpath %CPATH%
                COM.cloudscape.tools.cview
```

If you want to save some typing, you'll find both `cview.bat` and `setenv.bat` are available for download from the book's Web site, *www.bettersoftwarefaster.com*.

To test that Cloudscape is working, create two consoles in `%J2EE_HOME%\bin`. In the first, start the Cloudscape server using the command `cloudscape -start`. You should see something like this (Figure A–1).

Figure A–1
Starting the Cloudscape server.

You can stop the server using the other console window.[54] The command is `cloudscape -stop`.

Now use the second console to start the *Cloudview* client using `cview.bat`. Got to the *Connection* tab, as shown in Figure A-2, and enter the following values:

- Prefix: `jdbc:cloudscape:rmi:`
- Driver class: `COM.cloudscape.core.RmiJdbcDriver`

Press the *Test Driver* button to make sure that your configuration is correct.

---

54. If you don't stop the server like this after use, the files may not be closed properly, and next time the server is started, it may have to recover the database.

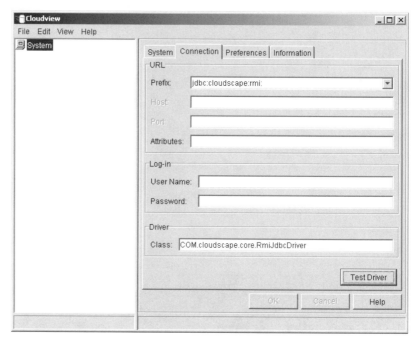

Figure A–2
Connection configuration for *Cloudview.*

Case Study Source Code

The case study files are obtainable from *www.bettersoftwarefaster.com*, and are delivered as a zip archive. This archive includes a Together project with separate subdirectories for source, diagrams, and classes. There are also a number of subdirectories that have non-Java software: batch files and SQL to set up the database.

The content of the zip archive is as follows:

```
projects\
  carserv\
    bin\         // location for binaries - empty
    classes\     // location for bytecode - empty
    diag\        // Together diagrams
        html\    // location for generated HTML - empty
         rtf\    // location for generated RTF - empty
    sql\         // SQL to build database
        src\     // Java source (and the .tpr project file)
    tests\       // test framework files
    webjar\      // jars to build webui

config\          // custom config files
modules\         // custom modules
templates\       // custom templates
```

Extract this to an appropriate directory. If you are following the recommendations of the previous sidebar, this would be the %TOGETHER-SOFT%\my directory.

The directories \src, \diag and \classes each contain the Java packaging structure of \com\bettersoftwarefaster\carserv.

The main project file carserv.tpr, is located in the ...\projects\carserv directory.

Set up Database

The last step for installing the case study is to set up the database. For this we will use the *Cloudview* client, configured earlier. Within *Cloudview*, choose *File* → *New* → *Database*.

In the resultant dialog box, enter the name *CarServ*DB, as shown in Figure A–3. Then hit *OK*. Note that you *must* use this name, since it is hardcoded into the actual case study. There's no need to change the directory— Cloudscape will create it under its own directory.

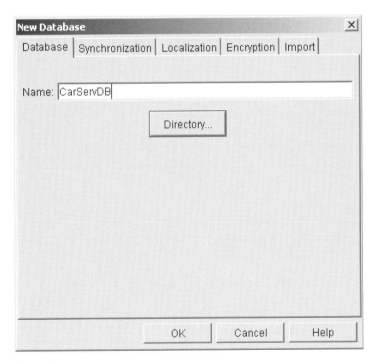

Figure A–3
The *Cloudview* client can be used to create databases.

All being well, *Cloudview* should be displaying the newly created database, as shown in Figure A–4.

Incidentally, to reopen a database already created, you can use *File* → *Open By Name*, and again type in *CarServ*DB, or find recently opened databases under the *File* menu.

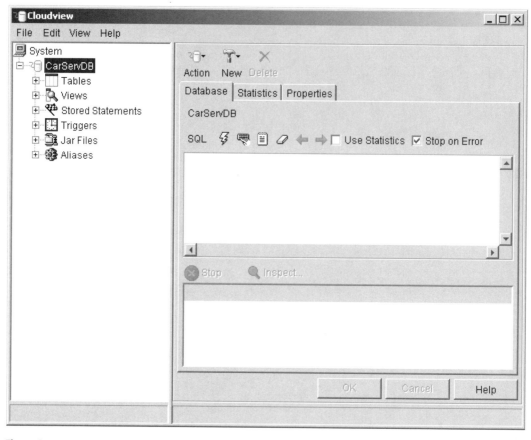

Figure A–4

Cloudview allows databases to be managed.

To create the database tables and populate those tables with data, use the SQL pane on the right-hand side of the user interface. The icon to load up the script is the "notepad."

In turn, load up and execute (the "lightning" icon) the following files from the case study's `sql` directory:

- `createTables.DDL`
- `populateReferenceTables.SQL`
- `addSampleData.SQL`

You are now done; the database is set up. If you ever need to reset the database, you can do this by dropping the tables by loading `dropTables.DDL`. Then, rerun the above three scripts.

As a quick test, open up the *Tables* node in the explorer pane of the *Cloudview* UI. You should see the newly created tables. Then, in the right-hand pane, execute the following SQL:

```
SELECT * FROM cst_customer
```

You should get back five rows, as shown in Figure A–5.

Now that you've got this far, you are ready to run through Chapter 2, "The Last Step: Deploy and Run!" and test the *CarServ* application.

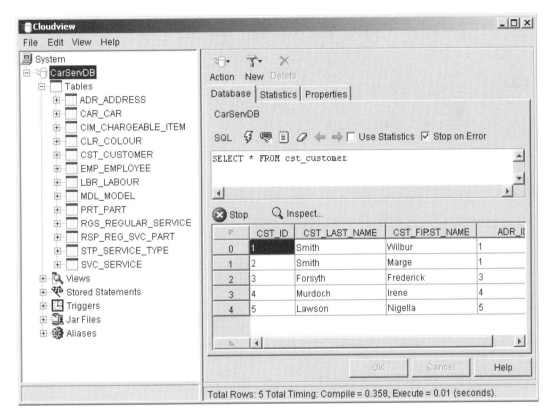

Figure A–5
The *CarServ*DB is populated and ready to use.

JUnit and JUnitX

There are, of course, many frameworks and third-party tools available to assist with unit testing, but the JUnit framework deserves special coverage. Three reasons:

- It is free and is open source.
- It is influential; JUnit was developed by Beck and Gamma (*www.junit.org*) and has spawned a whole set of similar toolsets.
- It is strongly supported within Together.

Underpinning Together's testing support is a set of patterns and templates that allow JUnit test cases to be quickly generated. Together also provides patterns and templates for the JUnitX framework, an extension to JUnit that allows package-local or protected features of a class to be tested. JUnitX uses the Java Reflection API to accomplish this.[55]

When unit test cases have been developed, they need to be organized. Together offers a number of options for doing this. For example, features of Together's Testing Framework (discussed in Chapter 6) allows the test cases to be quickly organized into test plans. Or, as was done for the CarServ case study, they can be organized into test suites. This can be done semi-automatically by applying the test suite pattern and editing the results.

Even so, no matter how many patterns and templates are provided within Together, at the end of the day it is still necessary to write the body of the unit test methods. This appendix aims to give some insight as to how this should be done.

To use the JUnit and JUnitX patterns, the Testing Framework feature must first be activated using *Activate/Deactivate Features*. When you then bring up the default or project options dialog, a *Testing Framework* section will be enabled to allow you to configure the feature as required. This is shown in Figure B–1.

You can accept most of the defaults. If you wish to use only standard JUnit features, then you can disable the JUnitX family; however, you will not

---

55. Together also has support for Cactus and HttpUnit testing frameworks, mentioned in Chapter 9.

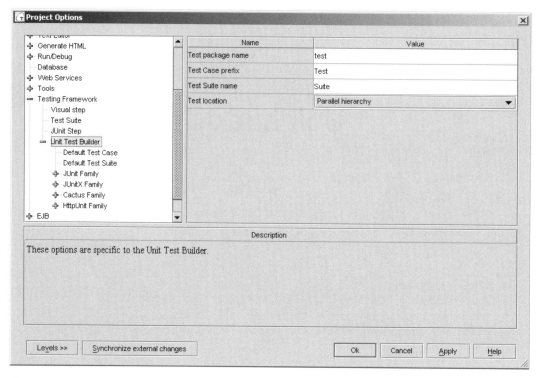

Figure B–1

Activating the Testing Framework features enables additional options to be configured.

be able to exercise the package-local or protected features of the class under test. Since JUnitX is deeply integrated into Together, and since the source code to the framework is freely available, we can't ourselves see any reason why you would want to disable it.

One configuration option that requires some consideration is the "Test location" property. This is used to determine the package where generated test cases should be created, and there are three choices:

- Same package: The test cases are generated in the same package as the classes under test.
- Subpackage: The `test` cases are generated in a subpackage called "test".
- Parallel hierarchy: The test cases are generated in a parallel test hierarchy.

This last means that for example the tests for classes in `com.better-softwarefaster.carserv.app` will be found in `test.com.better-softwarefaster.carserv.app`. You may find it helpful to use multiple project paths and package prefixes to physically separate the two trees; the case study does this.

Creating Test Cases

Together's Testing Framework allows unit tests to be created in one of two ways: either as a pattern or by using shortcuts on the speed menu. We recommend using the shortcuts, since all they do is apply the test case pattern, anyway.

    To create a skeleton test case for some class `Xyz` that you wish to test, select the class and then choose *Test* → *Default TestCase* from the speed menu. This will generate a standard JUnit test case. If you want to be able to test package-local features, then you will need to create a JUnitX test case. This can be done from the *Test* speed menu similarly (*Test* → *Generate* → *JUnitX* → *Private TestCase* in Together v6.0). A corresponding class called `TestXyz` will be created in the appropriate `test` package. If the `test` package didn't previously exist, it will be automatically created.

    For each method `abc()` in `Xyz`, a corresponding method `testAbc()` will be created. You then fill in the implementation of the `testAbc()` methods and call `assertXxx()` methods for conditions that should be true or `fail()` for conditions that represent a test failure. These methods are inherited from the `junit.framework.Assert` superclass, shown in Table B–1.

Table B–1

Assert Methods (Overridden in Various Ways)

Method	With msg parameter	No msg parameter	x, y as primitives	x, y as object	b as boolean
`assertTrue(msg, b)`	-	Y	-	-	Y
	Y	-	-	-	Y
`assertEquals(msg, x, y)`	-	Y	Y	-	n/a
	Y	-	Y	-	n/a
	-	Y	-	Y	n/a
	Y	-	-	Y	n/a
`assertSame(msg, x, y)`	-	Y	n/a	Y	n/a
	Y	-	n/a	Y	n/a
`assertNull(msg, x)`	-	Y	n/a	Y	n/a
	Y	-	n/a	Y	n/a
`assertNotNull(msg, x)`	-	-	n/a	Y	n/a
	-	-	n/a	Y	n/a

Creating a Test Proxy

    If the class being tested will have a unit test that tests the package-local or protected features of that class, then also create a `TestProxy`, using *Test* → *Generate* → *JUnitX* → *TestProxy* in the same package as the class to be tested. A JUnitX `PrivateTestCase` delegates tests that invoke package-local features to the `TestProxy`.

Creating Test Suites

Creating test cases is the most important part of the story; however, it's also necessary to somehow organize them. Chapter 6, "The Continuous Step: Measure the Quality," discusses one approach using Together's testing framework and test plans. Alternatively, you can organize the test cases into test suites. To do this, simply navigate to the package where the test cases have been created and right-click on the diagram to bring up its speedmenu. Choose *Test → Generate TestSuite* and a test suite class will be generated that automatically invokes all test cases within that package.

Running Your Tests

To run your tests, simply right-click on your test suite to bring up the speedmenu, and choose *Run Suite*.

The Framework Classes

Behind the Scenes

The Testing Framework's *Default TestCase* pattern creates a test case class that is a subclass of `junit.framework.TestCase`. If you selected the JUnitX *Private TestCase*, then the test case class will instead extend `junitx.framework.PrivateTestCase` (which in turn extends `junit.framework.TestCase`). The relationship of these classes with the rest of the JUnit framework is shown in Figure B–2.

The `TestCase` and `PrivateTestCase` classes implement the `junit.framework.Test` interface, which provides a single method `run(TestResult)`. The idea behind this method is to perform tests and write the result of the test (success, failure, or error) to the `TestResult` object. That said, the JUnit framework offers numerous ways to write tests, and the above approach of implementing `run()` is not the easiest approach. We will return to this topic shortly.

Unit tests can be organized into larger test suites through the `junit.framework.TestSuite` class. Since this implements the Composite pattern (Gamma et al. 1995), `TestSuites` can be built out of other `TestSuites` as well as leaf `TestCases`. In other words, a hierarchy of `TestSuites` can be built up. The `run()` method of `TestSuite` simply calls the `run()` method of all the `Tests` that it aggregates.

`TestSuites` are also needed to actually run the tests using the provided `TestRunners`. These take care of user interface issues, as well as manage the `TestResult` object. JUnit provides a number of different runners. By default, the defaut `TestSuite` created by the Testing Framework uses the `junit.swingui.TestRunner` class, but a different `TestRunner` can easily be used just by editing the suite's `main()` method. You may find the `junit.textui.TestRunner` useful when you have a requirement to keep documentary evidence that tests were passed, for example, before shipping code into production (though check out the more advanced features of Together's Testing Framework as described in Chapter 6 since they offer broader capabilities in this area).

In fact, the `TestRunner` classes are not passed an instance of a `TestSuite`, but rather the name of a class that is a `TestSuite`. The

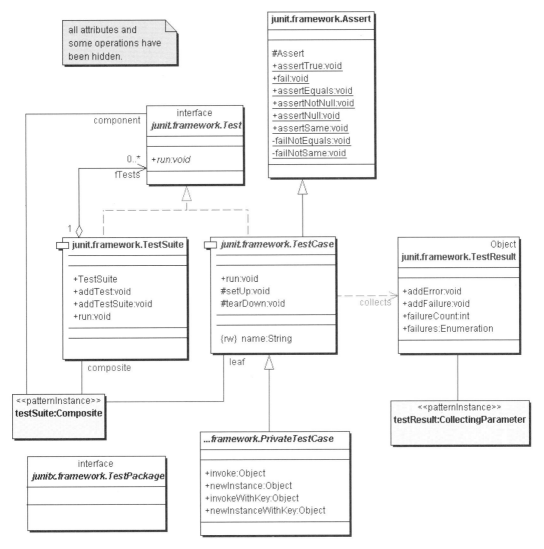

Figure B–2
The fundamental JUnit classes and interfaces.

TestRunner can be invoked either by its static main() method or by its static run() method; it amounts to much the same thing. The following fragments of code from the junit.swingui.TestRunner show how this works:

```
1   package junit.swingui;
2   public class TestRunner {
3     public static void run(Class test) {
4     String args[]= { test.getName() };
5     main(args);
6   }
7
8   public static void main(String[] args) {
```

```
 9        new TestRunner().start(args);
10      }
11
12    public void start(String[] args) {
13      String suiteName= processArguments(args);
14      setSuite(suiteName);
15      runSuite();
16    }
17
18    synchronized public void runSuite() {
19      final String suiteName= getSuiteText();
20      final Test testSuite= getTest(suiteName);
21      doRunTest(testSuite);
22    }
23
24    private void doRunTest(final Test testSuite) {
25      fRunner= new Thread("TestRunner-Thread") {
26        public void run() {
27          testSuite.run(fTestResult);
28        }
29      };
30      fRunner.start();
31    }
32  }
```

So that you can see what this gives you, Figure B–3 has a screen shot of the JUnit SwingUI TestRunner, running the test suite for the datamgmt package of *CarServ*.

As we noted above, in practice, unit tests are not written by actually overriding the run() method of TestCase or PrivateTestCase. The approach that takes the least amount of effort—and that adopted by the Testing Framework—is to simply write methods whose names begin with the word "test." The framework, on being handed such a test case, uses Java's Reflection API to determine which of its methods should be invoked. In this way, a single test case may provide many different test executions, as many as there are methods named testAbc().

This bit of magic is actually performed in the TestSuite constructor. A simplified version of this is shown below.

```
 1  public TestSuite(final Class theClass) {
 2    Constructor constructor = getConstructor(theClass);
 3    Class superClass= theClass;
 4    Vector names= new Vector();
 5    while (Test.class.isAssignableFrom(superClass)) {
 6      Method[] methods= superClass.getDeclaredMethods();
 7      for (int i= 0; i < methods.length; i++) {
 8        addTestMethod(methods[i], names, constructor);
 9      }
10      superClass= superClass.getSuperclass();
11    }
12  }
```

This constructor is passed a class that implements the TestCase; the addTestMethod() adds a Test for every public method named test-Abc().

Figure B-3
JUnitX's SwingUI TestRunner.

As noted earlier, when a `TestSuite` is generated, it references all the `TestCases` within that same package. This is probably best seen in code. Assuming two `TestCases` in a package `com.bswf.app`, one called `TestPqr` and the other `TestXyz`, the Testing Framework's *TestSuite* pattern will generate the following:

```
1   package test.com.bswf.app;
2
3   import junit.framework.*;
4   import junitx.framework.*;
5   import junit.swingui.*;
6
7   /** @stereotype test package */
8   public class Suite extends TestSuite {
9
10    public Suite() {
11      addTest(suite());
12    }
13    static public void main(String[] args) {
14      junit.swingui.TestRunner.run(Suite.class);
15    }
16
17    public static Test suite() {
```

```
18      TestSuite suite = new TestSuite("Test suite");
19      suite.addTestSuite(test.com.bswf.app.TestPqr.class);
20      suite.addTestSuite(test.com.bswf.app.TestXyz.class);
21      return suite;
22    }
23  }
```

The static `suite()` method is called by `TestRunner`'s `run()` method.

The `TestCase` class also defines two protected methods called `setUp()` and `tearDown()`. These are to set up and tear down what the JUnit authors call the *fixture*. The fixture is the test data and environment within which the unit test will run. The methods are called before and after each and every test, so that the tests are independent on each other.

Finishing off our tour of the JUnit/JUnitX framework classes, as noted above the `junitx.framework.PrivateTestCase` provides methods to invoke package-level or protected methods or constructors that would otherwise be unavailable.

Extensions

There are a number of extensions that make it easy to define additional tests, using the Decorator pattern (Gamma et al. 1995). They are:

- `RepeatedTest`: Runs some `Test` a number of times.
- `TestSetup`: Runs some `Test` (most likely a complete `TestSuite`) to be wrapped in its own fixture. Overrides the protected `setUp()` and `tearDown()` methods.
- `ActiveTestSuite`: run an entire `TestSuite` in its own thread. Normally JUnit runs `TestCases` (leaf `Tests`) in their own thread, but not the enclosing suite.

Figure B–4 shows the classes of the JUnit extension package.
To use these decorators, add a `Test` using `addTest()`. For example:

```
systemTestSuite.addTest(
  new SubSystemATestSetup(
     subSystemATestSuite   ) );
```

where `SubSystemATestSetup` subclasses `TestSetup` to provide a single fixture for all of the test in the `subSystemATestSuite`. Another example:

```
performanceTestSuite.addTest(
  new RepeatedTest(underlyingTest, 1000));
```

where `underlyingTest` is some `TestCase` or `TestSuite` that is to be run 1000 times.

The `ActiveTestSuite` decorator runs the test in a separate thread. When the test eventually completes, `TestResult` is updated as usual.

One slight disadvantage with these decorators is that they are not presented correctly in the Swing-based `TestRunner`; the structure hierarchy of the underlying test cases is not shown because it is hidden by the decorator. However, the tests *do* run correctly.

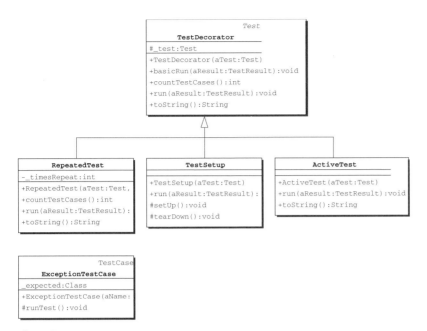

Figure B–4
JUnit Extensions package.

The extensions package also provides one other class, Exception-TestCase. This is used for checking that an Exception was thrown. However, in our opinion, it doesn't save that much effort. The normal way to check that an exception was thrown (without using ExceptionTestCase) is something like:

```
1  public class TestSomeClass extends TestCase {
2    public void testMethodThatShouldThrowAnException() {
3      try {
4        methodThatShouldThrowAnException();
5      } catch (SomeThrownException ex) {
6        return; // as expected
7      }
8      fail (
9        "Expected SomeThrownException to have been thrown");
10     }
11   }
12 }
13
14 // then, add to some appropriate test suite
15
16 someTestSuite.addTest(TestSomeClass.class);
```

Using `ExceptionTestCase`, this can be refactored into:

```
1   public class TestSomeClass extends ExceptionTestCase {
2
3   // constructor omitted
4
5     public void testMethodThatShouldThrowAnException()
6                 throws Throwable {
7       methodThatShouldThrowAnException();
8     }
9   }
10
11  // then, add to some appropriate test suite
12
13  someTestSuite.addTest(
14    new TestSomeClass(
15      "testMethodThatShouldThrowAnException",
16      SomeThrownException.class));
```

We don't really like this because (a) it relies on getting the name of the method correct (line 11), (b) the constructor of the `TestSomeClass` test case is more complex to write, and (c) the logic of the test is now split between the test case code and the code that adds the test case to the test suite.

Writing Tests in Practice

Okay, that's the theory, but what about in practice? In general, it works just as advertised, but there are one or two things of which to be aware. All of the following tips are based on the unit tests within *CarServ*, but there is other literature for your further reading—for example, A. Schneider's "JUnit Good Practices" (2000), a web article at *www.javaworld.com*.

tearDown

After a test has completed, the `tearDown()` method is called to tear down the fixture. This is done whether the test succeeds or fails. Then, the `setUp()` method will be called to set up the fixture for the next test.

The majority of tests will affect only the state of objects in memory; the system environment (databases and the like) will not be changed. For these cases there is little to be done, because new objects will be instantiated for the next test and the modified objects will just be garbage collected.

If a test changes a database, however, then it isn't so straightforward, because we have to remember that we don't know if the test succeeded or failed. A good example is in the `tearDown()` method of `TestCarDM` in `test.com.bettersoftwarefaster.carserv.datamgmt`. This performs direct SQL to repair the database.

Changing System.out

Sometimes, the expected result is that something should be printed to `System.out`. To capture the actual results for comparison, we can use the `System.setOut()` method.

The following code is taken from the `testExecute()` method of `TestPrintCommand` in `test.com.bettersoftwarefaster.carserv.infra`:

```
1   OutputStream testOut = new ByteArrayOutputStream();
2   System.setOut(new PrintStream(testOut));
3
4   command.execute("This is a test");
5   assertTrue(testOut.toString().
6       startsWith("This is a test") );
```

The `setUp()` method for this test should cache the value of `System.out` into an instance variable, and the `tearDown()` method should reinstate `System.out` to the value of this instance variable.

Testing Hidden Functionality (using TestProxy)

One problem with placing test cases in a separate package from the code being tested is that methods with package-level or protected visibility cannot be tested. The `junitx.framework.PrivateTestCase` superclass provides four methods that get around this problem. These are:

- `invoke(obj:Object, methodName:String, args:Object[])`
- `invokeWithKey(obj:Object, key:String, args:Object[])`
- `newInstance(className: String, args: Object[])`
- `newInstanceWithKey(className:String, key:String, args:Object[])`

The two `invoke` methods are to invoke a method on the specified object, whereas the two `newInstance` methods are to instantiate a new instance of the specified class.

Those methods *without* the `WithKey` suffix are for methods and constructors where all the arguments are primitives. The arguments themselves are wrapped up in the wrapper classes (`Integer`, `Float` and so on); `PrivateTestCase` uses reflection on the arguments to determine the required types.

To invoke a method or constructor that takes nonprimitive objects, the `WithKey` versions must be used. The "key" is a string that follows a certain format to provide the type information of the arguments (similar to the way in which a string is created for Java Native Interface). For example:

- The key for a method that accepts an `int`, `String`, `String`, and a `long` is
  `"_int_java.lang.String_java.lang.String_long"`.
- The key for a method that accepts an `int`, `String`, `String`, and a `com.bettersoftwarefaster.carserv.data-mgmt.AddressData` is
  `"_int_java.lang.String_java.lang.String_com.bettersoftwarefaster.carserv.data-mgmt.AddressData"`.

As you will have guessed, under the covers there are heavy doses of Java Reflection API in use. These methods won't work unless you have a `TestProxy` instance in the same package as the class under test. As you

now know, the Testing Framework feature can be used to quickly create the
`TestProxy`.

The `TestProxy` also represents a massive security hole, so make sure
that you do not ship a live copy of `TestProxy` in your production code. You
can download stubbed out versions of all the classes from *www.extreme-*
java.de. These allow the test code to compile but prevent the `TestProxy`
from being used by rogue software.

Unexpected Exceptions with TestProxy

We've already discussed how to handle exceptions. If the `TestProxy`
is in use, then there is an additional consideration, because the actual
method being called is that of `TestProxy`, not the class under test. Any
exception will therefore be wrapped in an instance of `TestAccessExcep-`
`tion`.

So, if using `TestProxy`, the easiest approach is to ensure that
`TestAccessException` is declared in the `throws` clause of the method.

If you want a little more detail, then you can catch `TestAccessEx-`
`ception` within the body of the test and try to determine the underlying
exception. Here's is a version of `testIsDatabaseConnectionValid()`
of `TestDomainSessionManager` in the `test.com.bettersoft-`
`warefaster.carserv.domain` package:[56]

```
1  boolean isValid = false;
2  try {
3    isValid = ((Boolean)invoke(getCarServApp(),
4      "isDatabaseConnectionValid", new Object[] { }
5    )).booleanValue();
6  } catch(TestAccessException ex) {
7    Exception reason = ex.getReason();
8    if (reason instanceof
9        java.lang.reflect.InvocationTargetException) {
10     fail(
11   ((java.lang.reflect.InvocationTargetException)reason).
12     getTargetException().getMessage() );
13   } else {
14     fail( reason.getMessage() );
15   }
16  }
17  assertTrue("database connection is valid.", !isValid);
```

If an exception is caught, then the test will fail (line 10 or line 14), showing the underlying problem (lines 8 through 12), if possible.

Threading

We've already briefly mentioned the `ActiveTestSuite` extension;
this runs the test in a separate thread. But what about the case when the
method under test uses a thread internally—that is, it has asynchronous

56. The version that we shipped doesn't do any of this; it just throws `TestAccessEx-`
     `ception`. The exception was unexpected, after all.

semantics? The fact that the method returns does not mean that the required action has been complete, and if we were to check for our expected results, then we most likely would not find them.

So, it is important that the test of the asynchronous method accounts for this. There should be some way for the test to determine when the underlying piece of asynchronous work has been completed, for example, by using `join()` on the underlying thread.

In *CarServ*, the sign-on command is asynchronous, so the test cases have been written to take account of this. Here is the `testExecuteCurrentUser()` method of `TestSignOnCommand` in the `test.com.bettersoftwarefaster.carserv.app` package:

```
1   public void testExecuteCurrentUser()
2        throws AppException, InterruptedException {
3   signOnLanceCommand.executeSelf();
4   signOnLanceCommand.getThread().join();
5   assertNotNull("app", getCarServApp());
6   assertNotNull("current user",
7   getCarServApp().getCurrentUser());
8   }
```

We have to admit that using this `join()` on the underlying thread is not attractive. A more common approach would be to install some sort of listener and use that to determine whether the command has completed. Indeed, the `SignonCommand` does provide a `CommandCompletionListener`.

The problem, though, is that until we test it, we do not know whether the `CommandCompletionListener` works! Here is the code that tests this functionality (also in `TestSignOnCommand`):

```
1    public void testExecuteCommandCompletionListener()
2         throws AppException, InterruptedException {
3    signOnLanceCommand.addCommandCompletionListener(
4    this.commandCompletionIndicator);
5    signOnLanceCommand.executeSelf();
6    signOnLanceCommand.getThread().join();
7    assert(signOnLanceCommand.getMessage(),
8    signOnLanceCommand.allAsExpected());
9    assertTrue("listener",
10     commandCompletionIndicator.isComplete());
11   }
```

So, it seems to us that you will need access to the underlying thread one way or another. The only improvement to the above code that we can think of is that the `getThread()` method ought to have only package-level visibility and then be accessed using the `TestProxy`.

Customizing Together with .config Files

This appendix summarizes the various customizations performed using `.config` files within the body of the book. To install any of these customizations, simply copy the corresponding file into `%TOGETHER%/config`, where `%TOGETHER%` is the home directory for Together, e.g., `C:\Together-Soft\Together6.0`.

There is some trickery going on with these files; it is worth appreciating it so that you use the same tricks when developing your own `.config` customizations. There are five `.config` files discussed in this appendix:

- Bean Properties
- Documenting Patterns Instances
- Colored Notes
- Before-and-After Object Diagrams
- Documenting Package Dependencies

File Names

The names of all the files begin "zzz." This means that when Together loads up the files, they will be loaded last because Together processes the files alphabetically. This is important because it means that they replace any default configuration in the shipped files loaded first.

Adding, Not Overriding

In several places we want only to supplement the existing `.config`, not replace it. A good example is with coloring of icons. In these cases, we use a new config key value where the condition is by default guaranteed to be true. For example, consider the key of

```
view.map.*.DependencyLink.( hasPropertyValue("$shapeType",
"DependencyLink") )
```

The expression `hasPropertyValue("$shapeType", "DependencyLink")` will, by definition, always by true for dependency links, but the key itself is different from that found in the shipped `view.config`, namely:

```
view.map.*.DependencyLink.true
```

Therefore, both `.config` files will be processed and the new `.config` will act as an addendum.

Bean Properties

In Chapter 3, "The First Step: The Model Domain," we showed how to configure JavaBeans so that JavaBean properties would be annotated {r}, {rw}, or {w} for read-only, read/write, or write-only respectively. The `.config` file that performs this is `zzzBSwF.beanProperties.config`, which has the following entries:

```
1   ;view.config
2   view.map.*.BeanProperty.( hasPropertyValue(
    "$shapeType", "BeanProperty")) =
3   \ prepend("} ");
4   \ setter =
5   \   findElement(getProperty("$setterUniqueName"));
6   \ getter =
7   \   findElement(getProperty("$getterUniqueName"));
8   \ if ( setter != null &&
9   \ setter->hasProperty("$public"),
10  \ prepend("w"));
11  \ if ( getter != null &&
12  \ getter->hasProperty("$public"),
13  \ prepend("r"));
14  \ prepend("{")
```

Documenting Pattern Instances

In Chapter 6, "The Continuous Step: Measure the Quality" we suggested a technique for documenting pattern instances (UML collaborations) as objects. The `.config` file that is needed to allow associations to be drawn between objects and classes, and to color in the pattern instances correctly, is `zzzBSwF.patternInstances.config`. This has the following entries:

```
1   ;model.config
2   model.constraint.link.AssociatesLink.both.14 =
3   \ !(
4   \  ((%dst%->hasPropertyValue(
5   \     "$shapeType", "Class" )              )&&
6   \   ( (%src%->hasPropertyValue(
7   \       "$shapeType", "Object") )&&
8   \    !((%src%->hasPropertyValue(
9   \      "stereotype","patternInstance") ) ||
10  \      (if(%src%->hasProperty(
11  \        "$instantiatedClass"),
12  \      class = findElement(
13  \        %src%->getProperty("$instantiatedClass"));
14  \      if (class != null,
15  \        class->hasPropertyValue(
16  \        "stereotype", "pattern"),
17  \        false ),
```

```
18  \         false        ) ) ) )                    ) ||
19  \  ((%src%->hasPropertyValue(
20  \      "$shapeType", "Class")              )&&
21  \    ( (%dst%->hasPropertyValue(
22  \        "$shapeType", "Object") )&&
23  \     !((%dst%->hasPropertyValue(
24  \       "stereotype", "patternInstance") ) ||
25  \      (if(%dst%->hasProperty(
26  \          "$instantiatedClass"),
27  \       class = findElement(
28  \          %dst%->getProperty("$instantiatedClass"));
29  \        if (class != null,
30  \         class->hasPropertyValue(
31  \           "stereotype", "pattern"),
32  \         false ),
33  \        false)      ) ) ) )
34  \ )
35  model.constraint.link.AssociatesLink.both.14.message =
    "Association can not be drawn between Class and
    Object (unless Object is a pattern instance)."
36
37  ; view.config
38  view.map.*.Class.hasPropertyValue(
    "stereotype","pattern") =
39  \ setBackground(RGB(204,255,255))
40
41  view.map.*.Object.hasPropertyValue(
    findElement(getProperty("$instantiatedClass")),
    "stereotype","pattern") =
42  \ setBackground(RGB(204,255,255))
43
44  view.map.*.Object.hasPropertyValue(
    "stereotype", "patternInstance") =
45\ setBackground(RGB(204,255,255))
```

In Chapter 6 we also discussed a `.config` to color in notes. This helps them stand out on diagrams. The `.config` file that is needed is `zzzB-SwF.coloredNotes.config`, which has the following entries:

```
1  ;view.config
2  view.map.*.Note.(
   isOnTopLevelDiagram() &&
   hasPropertyValue("$shapeType", "Note") ) =
3  \ setBackground(RGB(204,204,255))
```

In Chapter 7, "The Micro Step: Design and Implement," we discussed the technique from the Catalysis method (D'Souza & Wills 1998) to draw example object diagrams representing before-and-after object configurations. Paul Field contributed a `.config` to *www.togethercommunity.com*, and the `.config` file `zzzCatalysis.beforeAfter.config` is based on his original idea. It has the following entries:

```
 1   ;inspector.config
 2   inspector.node.element.*.AssociatesLink.item.Link.
     item.lifetime =
 3   \  ChoiceField(
 4   \     {
 5   \        values := { "noChange", "destroyed",
 6   \                    "new", "transient" },
 7   \        names := { "no change", "destroyed",
 8   \                    "new", "transient" }
 9   \     }
10   \  )
11   inspector.node.element.*.AssociatesLink.item.Link.
     item.lifetime.name =
12   \  Lifetime
13   inspector.node.element.*.Object.item.Properties.
     item.lifetime =
14   \   ChoiceField(
15   \      {
16   \         values := { "noChange", "destroyed",
17   \                     "new", "transient" },
18   \         names := { "no change", "destroyed",
19   \                     "new", "transient" }
20   \      }
21   \   )
22   inspector.node.element.*.Object.item.Properties.
     item.lifetime.name =
23   \  Lifetime
24
25   ;view.config
26   view.map.*.AssociatesLink.hasProperty("lifetime") =
27   \  icon = addLabelIcon(
28   \         "{"+getProperty("lifetime")+"}",
29   \         "AbòveLeftCenter");
30   \  icon->setInplaceEditor({property:="lifetime",
31   \                          default:="noChange"})
32
33   view.map.*.AssociatesLink.hasPropertyValue(
                         "lifetime", "new") =
34   \  setForeground(red)
35   view.map.*.AssociatesLink.hasPropertyValue(
                         "lifetime", "destroyed") =
36   \  setForeground(gray)
37   view.map.*.AssociatesLink.hasPropertyValue(
                         "lifetime", "transient") =
38   \  setLineStyle("dashed")
39
40
41   view.map.*.Object.hasProperty("lifetime") =
42   \  if (!hasPropertyValue("lifetime", "noChange"),
43   \     lifetimeLabel = addToCompartment(
44   \  label("{"+getProperty("lifetime")+"}"), "Names");
45   \     lifetimeLabel->setInplaceEditor(
46   \                   {property:="lifetime"});
47   \     lifetimeLabel->setFont(%defaultFontName%,
48   \                   "Plain", %defaultFontSize%);
49   \     lifetimeLabel->setAlignment("Left");
50   \     lifetimeLabel->setLayoutConstraints(
```

```
51  \                           preferredHeight(16),
52  \                           fixedHeight(true))
53  \   )
54
55  view.map.*.Object.hasPropertyValue(
                "lifetime", "new") =
56  \ setForeground( red );
57  \ shadow=getViewProperty("2DLook");
58  \ if (hasOption("option.shadows") && shadow==null
59  \     || shadow=="3D",
60  \   setShadow(3, RGB(128,0,0))
61  \ )
62
63  view.map.*.Object.hasPropertyValue(
                "lifetime", "destroyed") =
64  \ setForeground( gray );
65  \ shadow=getViewProperty("2DLook");
66  \ if (hasOption( "option.shadows") && shadow==null
67  \     || shadow=="3D",
68  \   setShadow(3, RGB(128,128,128))
69  \ )
70
71  ;this one doesn't work.
72  ;view.map.*.Object.hasPropertyValue(
                "lifetime", "destroyed") =
73  ;\ setLineStyle("dashed");
```

In Chapter 8, "The Macro Step: Architecture," we talked about some `.con-figs` to help manage and color dependencies. This file sets dependency checking options, colors the links, and adds a `<<constraint>>` label if the dependency is drawn rather than discovered from the code. It also alters the filter applied when dependencies are hidden on a diagram. The `.con-fig` file that is needed is `zzzBSwF.dependencyLinks.config`, which has the following entries:

Documenting Package Dependencies

```
1   ;;;;;;;;;;;;;;;;;;;;;;;;;;;;;;;;;;;;;;;;;;;;;;;;;;;;;
2   ; color dependency links
3   ;;;;;;;;;;;;;;;;;;;;;;;;;;;;;;;;;;;;;;;;;;;;;;;;;;;;;
4
5   ;view.config
6   view.map.*.DependencyLink.(hasPropertyValue(
                "$shapeType", "DependencyLink") ) =
7   \ if(hasProperty("automatic"),
8   \   setForeground(RGB(180,0,0)),
9   \   (
10  \     setForeground(RGB(0,180,0));
11  \     memberLink=findElement(getProperty(
12  \                         "$uniqueName"));
13  \     source=memberLink->getSource();
14  \     destination=memberLink->getDestination();
15  \     if(%diagram%->hasPropertyValue(
16  \             "$shapeType", "ClassDiagram") &&
17  \       source->hasPropertyValue(
18  \             "shapeType","ClassDiagram")     &&
19  \       destination->hasPropertyValue(
```

```
20  \                              "shapeType","ClassDiagram") &&
21  \              !memberLink->hasProperty("stereotype"),
22  \           if(hasProperty("reverse"),
23  \              icon=addIcon(
24  \                  "OpenTriangle", "OnSource" ),
25  \              icon=addIcon(
26  \                  "OpenTriangle", "OnDestination" )
27  \           );
28  \           icon->setBackground(RGB(0,180,0));
29  \           addLabelIcon(
30  \              "<<constraint>>","AboveLeftCenter")
31  \       )
32  \    )
33  \ )
34
35  ;;;;;;;;;;;;;;;;;;;;;;;;;;;;;;;;;;;;;;;;;;;;;;;;;;;;;;;
36  ; always show explicitly drawn dependencies
37  ;;;;;;;;;;;;;;;;;;;;;;;;;;;;;;;;;;;;;;;;;;;;;;;;;;;;;;;
38
39  ;filter.config
40  filter.j = hasPropertyValue(
41  \           "$shapeType", "DependencyLink" ) &&
42  \           !hasProperty("$pure")
43
44  ;;;;;;;;;;;;;;;;;;;;;;;;;;;;;;;;;;;;;;;;;;;;;;;;;;;;;;;
45  ; enable implicit dependency checking
46  ;;;;;;;;;;;;;;;;;;;;;;;;;;;;;;;;;;;;;;;;;;;;;;;;;;;;;;;
47
48  ;viewManagement.config
49  option.dependencyLinks.showBetweenClasses = true
50  ;option.dependencyLinks.showBetweenClasses = diagram
51  option.dependencyLinks.inDeclarationsOnly = false
52  option.hyperLinks.showSeeAsHyperlinks = true
```

Customizing Together's Templates

Suppose you wanted to add an association between two classes. Together provides three ways to associate classes:

- Use the simple *Association* toolbar icon.
- Just write the code.
- Use the *Link by Pattern* command.

If you choose the *Association* toolbar icon, then the corresponding code automatically generated will support a maximum multiplicity of 1, because a simple scalar instance variable is generated. You can adorn this link with a multiplicity greater than 1 (e.g., "0..*"), but the underlying code won't support that multiplicity. So, whenever the system is actually being implemented, the actual type of the instance variable will need to be changed.

If you choose to write the code, then it will be as you wish. For a single multiplicity, Together will automatically draw a link between the two classes, but for multiple multiplicities (Lists or Vectors, etc.), Together won't know which class is being aggregated, and no link will be drawn.

However, if you use the *Link By Pattern* command, then you get the best of both worlds. From the dialog box, you can choose to implement the link using an ArrayList, HashMap, or other such collection class.

Knowing what's going on behind the scenes is worthwhile here. Both the *Association* toolbar icon and the *Link By Pattern* command actually use a template. These are just snippets of Java code, supporting a number of macros. They can be manipulated directly or through Together's *Code Template Expert* (*Tools* → *Code Template Expert*).

For example, we have modified the Default_Association.link file %TOGETHER%\templates\JAVA\LINK (where %TOGETHER% is the home directory for Together, e.g., C:\TogetherSoft\Together6.0) to be as follows:

```
1   /**
2    * @clientCardinality   1
3    * @supplierCardinality 0..1
4    */
5   private %Dst% %Name%;
```

When we draw the link, Together automatically adorns the line with the two cardinalities. This reminds us to correct it immediately or to delete it. For example, if we are early in analysis, we might have no idea what the cardinalities are, so we should delete the adornments. On the other hand, if we are moving into implementation, we might know that the supplier cardinality should be 0..*. In this case, we are reminded that we should have created the link in a different way (for example, using one of the templates that follow).

Each template also has a corresponding properties file. This stores a couple of pieces of information. First, it provides a description of the template; this appears on the dialog box. It also identifies which existing tags of the code feature should not be kept (that is, should be deleted) when the template is applied.

Collections API Templates

We have used templates to create our own versions of the Collections API classes. We keep our versions directly in the TGH\templates\JAVA\LINK directory so that they're nice and easy to get at. Our custom versions do the following:

- Specify appropriate cardinalities for client and supplier.
- Specify a supplierRole that matches the name of the instance variable implementing the association.
- Add OCL constraint(s) to indicate the semantics of the collection class chosen. For Lists, and arrays it is {ordered}; for Sets and Maps it is {unique} and for TreeSets and TreeMaps it is {sorted}.
- Add a qualifier for Maps.
- Use a concrete class (such as java.util.ArrayList) to instantiate the collection object, but refer to that object through the appropriate interface (such as java.util.List). See for example Bloch (2001) for further discussion on this idiom.

You can view all of these through the *Code Template Expert*, though note that the wizard does not seem to support more than one doNotKeepTag entry (which indicates the tags that should be removed when the template is applied) in the properties file. This is needed for our custom templates, to remove the qualifier and constraint tags, for example. We just edited the properties file directly.

Our collections templates also assume that java.util.* has been imported. We make sure that it has with a quick customization of the default class template. (%Name%.java in %TOGETHER%\templates\JAVA\CLASS).

The templates listed in Table D–I are available from the Web site at *www.bettersoftwarefaster.com* as `BSwF.linkTemplates.zip`. To install, extract into `%TOGETHER%`.

Templates

Table D–1

Custom Templates

Template Type	Name	Implementation
Java Link	Aggregation_as_ArrayList	```/** * @link aggregation * @associates <{%Dst%}> * @clientCardinality 1 * @supplierCardinality 0..* * @supplierRole %Name% * @constraint {ordered} */ private List %Name% = new ArrayList();```
	Aggregation_as_LinkedList	```/** * @link aggregation * @associates <{%Dst%}> * @clientCardinality 1 * @supplierCardinality 0..* * @supplierRole %Name% * @constraint {ordered} */ private List %Name% = new LinkedList();```
	Aggregation_as_Array	```/** * @link aggregation * @associates <{%Dst%}> * @clientCardinality 1 * @supplierCardinality %Supplier_Cardinality% * @supplierRole %Name% * @constraint {ordered} */ private %Dst% [] %Name% = new %Dst% [%Supplier_Cardinality%];```
	Aggregation_as_HashSet	```/** * @link aggregation * @associates <{%Dst%}> * @clientCardinality 1 * @supplierCardinality 0..* * @supplierRole %Name% * @constraint {unique} */ private Set %Name% = new HashSet();```
	Aggregation_as_TreeSet	```/** * @link aggregation * @associates <{%Dst%}> * @clientCardinality 1 * @supplierCardinality 0..* * @supplierRole %Name% * @constraint {unique} * @constraint {sorted} */ private Set %Name% = new TreeSet();```

Customizing
Together's Templates

301

Customizing
Together's Templates

301

Table D–1

Custom Templates

Template Type	Name	Implementation
	Aggregation_as_HashMap	```/** * @link aggregation * @associates <{%Dst%}> * @clientQualifier %Qualifier% * @clientCardinality 1 * @supplierCardinality 0..* * @supplierRole %Name% * @constraint {unique} */ private Map %Name% = new HashMap();```
	Aggregation_as_TreeMap	```/** * @link aggregation * @associates <{%Dst%}> * @clientQualifier %Qualifier% * @clientCardinality 1 * @supplierCardinality 0..* * @supplierRole %Name% * @constraint {unique} * @constraint {sorted} */ private Map %Name% = new TreeMap();```
	Default_Association	```/** * @clientCardinality 1 * @supplierCardinality 0..1 */ private %Dst% %Name%;```
Java Class	Default_Class	```import java.util.*; public class %Name%{ }```

Customizing Together's Inspectors

Properties can be associated with any element in the repository by using the property inspector *Properties* from the speed menu or just *Alt-Enter*. But what if the information we would like to capture is not defined as a property?

If the element is code-based (a class or an interface), then it's possible to capture the property using a JavaDoc tag. However, this approach does not let us define a list of valid values (as typified by the stereotype property), nor does it allow for conditional properties (where the value for a property can be set only if some other property has such-and-such a value). Moreover, JavaDoc tags cannot be added to non-code elements.

Together provides three different ways to configure custom properties and—more importantly—inspectors to change the values of those custom properties. Two are `.config` based, and the last uses Together's open API.

Motivation

Together provides inbuilt support for adding user-defined properties using the *Inspector Property Builder*, as shown in Figure E–1. (Note that this feature is an activatable feature of Together so if the *Inspector Property Builder* is not available from the *Tools* menu, select *Activate/Deactivate Features* instead and then ensure *Custom Properties* is checked.)

The inspector allows additional properties to be defined for the type of element that is selected in the diagram (in this case Object).

The inspector builder also shows any existing properties; in Figure E–1 it is showing the *lifetime* property configured from the Catalysis before/after `.config` described in Appendix B. Figure E–2 shows how this property appears on the property inspector.

Convenient though this technique is, it does not support properties that have dropdown list boxes and does not provide for conditional properties.

Inspector Property Builder

Figure E–1

Together provides an inspector property builder.

Figure E–2

The property inspector shows the additional property.

The config-based inspector must be enabled using the options dialog and then *Tools* → *Options* → *Project Level* then under *General*, ensure *Support user-defined inspector* is checked. Then, either edit the `inspector.config` file or, better, create a file named something like `zzzBSwF.inspector.config` to define the property (see Appendix C for discussion as to why to use such a file name). Use *Project* → *Synchronize with External Changes* to pick up the changes (if you edited `inspector.config`) or restart Together (if you created your own file).

If you use this approach, the properties you define are also shown as (read-only) properties within the inspector property builder dialog box previously discussed; effectively then, the inspector property builder is just a user interface to these configuration files. However, editing the `.config` files directly will enable features such as dropdown list boxes, not available through the UI.

So, to define a page called `MyProperties`, add the following line:

```
inspector.node.element.*.*.item.MyProperties.view.UI =
                    treeTableNodeUI
```

To define a property `MyStringProperty` on this page:

```
inspector.node.element.*.*.item.MyProperties.item.
                    MyStringProperties = StringField
```

The full syntax for a property page is as follows:

$$
inspector.node.element.\begin{Bmatrix} java \\ cpp \\ * \end{Bmatrix}.\begin{Bmatrix} ActivityDiagram \\ Actor \\ AssociationLink \\ Attribute \\ BusinessProcessDiagram \\ Class \\ ClassDiagram \\ ComponentDiagram \\ DependencyLink \\ DeploymentDiagram \\ ERDiagram \\ GeneralizationLink \\ Hyperlink \\ ImplementationLink \\ Note \\ Operation \\ Package \\ SequenceDiagram \\ StateDiagram \\ UseCaseDiagram \\ * \end{Bmatrix}.item.XYZview.UI = treeTableNodeUI
$$

where:

- `{java, cpp, *}` indicates the language supported.
- `{ActivityDiagram, Actor, … *}` indicates what types of elements the property page applies to.
- `XYZ` is the name of the property page.

An asterisk (*) is a wildcard meaning "all."
The syntax of the properties themselves is similar:

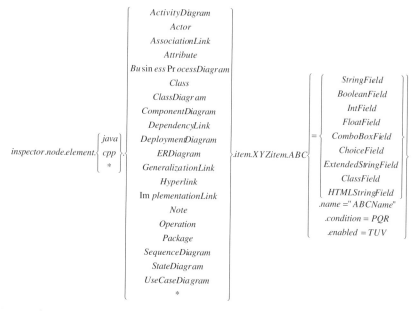

where:

- XYZ is the name of the property page on which the property is to appear.
- ABC is the name of the property itself.
- {StringField, BooleanField, … HTMLStringField} is the property type. Some of these take parameters (see below).
- ABC Name is the name that appears on the property page UI.
- PQR is a boolean expression that determines whether the property appears.
- TUV is a boolean expression that determines whether the property is enabled to edit.

Note that property names beginning with $ are reserved for Together's internal use, so don't use them.

The property types that take parameters are ComboBoxField, ChoiceField and ClassField. The first two of these are almost identical, both offering dropdown list boxes. The main difference is that a ComboBoxField provides a list but allows users to specify their own value (similar to the stereotype property), whereas the ChoiceField provides a list but does *not* allow user-defined values.

The syntax for a ComboBoxField is as follows (we have used wildcards for language and for element type):

```
inspector.node.element.*.*.item.XYZ.item.ABC = ComboBoxField
{
\ values := { "choice1", "choice2", … "choiceN" },
\ icons := {"choice1.gif", "choice2.gif", … "choiceN.gif"}
\ } )
```

It isn't necessary to specify icons, but if they are specified, then they need to reside in `lib\gifs.zip` in Together's home directory, something that complicates the deployment of the customization to all team members. (If you *do* do this, it's good practice to place your gifs in a subdirectory such as `com.mydomain\choice1.gif`).

The simplified syntax for a `ChoiceField` (again, with wildcards for language and element type) is almost the same, though it also provides a names parameter:

```
1  inspector.node.element.*.*.item.XYZ.item.ABC =
2  ChoiceField({
3  \ values := { "choice1", "choice2", … "choiceN" },
4  \ icons := {"choice1.gif", "choice2.gif", … "choiceN.gif"}
5  \ names := { "choice 1", "choice 2", … "choice N" },
6  \ } )
```

The names are shown in the UI, and the values are used in the repository.

The `ClassField` property allows classes (or interfaces) to be selected from the repository. This is used by Together itself in numerous places, e.g. defining the superclass or the interfaces that a class implements. The syntax is:

```
1  inspector.node.element.*.*.item.XYZ.item.ABC =
2  ClassField (
3  {
4  \ title := "Dialog title",
5  \ class_filter := PQR,
6  \ display_filter := TUV,
7  \ } )
```

where:

- `title` is the title that will be shown on the dialog.
- `PQR` is a boolean expression that indicates whether each class is selectable in the dialog box.
- `TUV` is a boolean expression that indicates whether each class is displayed in the dialog box.

For the `PQR` and `TUV` expressions, the macro `%class%` can be used for each element candidate. The macro `%element%` is also defined, meaning the element whose properties are being set.

The expressions that we have been mentioning hint at the power of the config-based approach. The `inspector.config` file has some example properties that show some sample expressions. For example, here is an expression for the `ClassField`'s `display_filter` parameter:

```
1  \ display_filter :=
2  \   if ( %class%->isPackage(),
3  \     true,
4  \     if ( %class%->isDiagram(),
5  \       true,
6  \       %class%->hasPropertyValue("$shapeType", "Class") &&
7  \       %element% != %class% &&
8  \       if ( hasProperty("$interface"),
```

```
 9   \              %class%->hasProperty("$interface"),
10   \              !%class%->hasProperty("$interface")
11   \          )
12   \        )
13   \    )
```

Let's see if we can work out what this expression yields. First, this expression will return true for all packages. Line 2 is the start of an if-then-else construct, with line 3 as the "then" component (true), and lines 4 through 12 as the "else" component. Similarly, it will return true for all diagrams. Line 4 is the start of an embedded if-then-else construct, with line 5 as the "then" component, and lines 6 through 11 as the "else" component. If the selected element is a class, it will return true for all classes (but not interfaces) except the element itself, whereas if the selected element is an interface, it will return true for all interfaces (but not classes) except the element itself. Within .config files, classes and interfaces are distinguished by the fact that interfaces evaluate hasProperty("$interface") to true, whereas classes do not. So, line 6 checks for if the selected element is a class or interface, and line 8 checks if it is actually just an interface. Bringing all of this together, then, this is actually the display filter for packages, diagrams and the generalization relationship.

However, this power of expression is also an impediment, because the syntax is proprietary to Together and is only sparsely documented. Many of the functions are similar to those found in the open API, but not all, it seems. The only real way to learn the config syntax is to study the config files.

These points go some way to explaining why TogetherSoft at one point deprecated the config-based approach. Now their preference (and ours) is to use the open API. It is just as powerful, is written in Java, and is (reasonably) well documented. So, let us now look at this final approach.

Open API

Using the open API offers the most control, but—inevitably—it is the most complex. Before we plunge in, some background might help.

Together's inspector is implemented as a module and resides in the inspector directory under modules\com\togethersoft\modules in Together's home directory. It is possible to modify Together's own shipped inspectors, and Togethersoft makes available the original source code to make this easier to do. It is also a good way to allow us (the would-be customizers) to learn how inspectors work. You can certainly glean some useful information from these source files, though perhaps a few more comments in the code might have been useful. To deliver a modified inspector this way, the code must be compiled and then the new version replace the original in inspector.jar (also in the inspector directory); not difficult conceptually, but a little fiddly. And it feels like we're hacking the product, potentially creating lots of problems for ourselves when upgrade time comes around.

An alternative approach—and the one we will use here—is to provide additional "bolt-on" inspectors that supplement the built-in inspectors with additional properties, et cetera. We prefer this approach because it isolates our changes from Together's own code.

To simplify the implementation, we have developed a framework that we will present first, followed by a small project to demonstrate its use. The framework is broadly comparable to the config-based approach, additionally allowing easy set up of properties of type multiple string, URL, Color, and inversed boolean,[59] and omitting just the `HTMLStringField` property type.

The open API uses registered `InspectorBuilder` objects to build up the properties page. Our framework thus has two objectives:

**Inspector
Framework**

- Allow `IdeInspectorBuilder` objects to be easily developed, providing support for the various property types.
- Register the `IdeInspectorBuilder` object with Together.

To do this, we've created an abstract class `IdeInspectorBuilder-Adapter` that defines most of the common `IdeInspectorBuilder` behavior, with well-defined hooks for subclasses to do—well, whatever they need to do. Moreover, this abstract superclass also provides the startup registration method. As you might have spotted, we've used the Adapter and Template patterns (Gamma et al. 1995).

This superclass defines a number of helper `addXxxProperty()` methods to make subclasses easier to implement. For each of this family of methods, the first two parameters are the page on which to add the property and the name of the property itself. Note that if the property already exists on that page, then it will be replaced. For each of these `addXxxProperty()` methods, there is also an overridden equivalent that takes an additional `Condition` object, which indicates whether the property should be displayed.

Figure E–3 shows the relationships (expressed in terms of instances of design patterns) between the `IdeInspectorBuilderAdapter` and the Together API interfaces.

The `IdeInspectorBuilderAdapter` class implements both the `IdeInspectorBuilder` interface (meaning that instances of it can be registered as a builder of inspectors) and `IdeStartup` (meaning that it can self-register if specified in a manifest file).

Together calls the `buildInspector()` method. This saves away the `context` an `rwiElements[]` array (represents the current item or items selected on the diagram) and an `inspector` object (represents the inspector in the process of being built) into instance variables. It then checks the characteristics of the selected element (or elements), and calls a hook method `buildXxxInspector()` accordingly. For example, if a class had been selected, then `buildClassInspector()` would be called.

Each hook method would typically call the various `addXxxProperty()` helper methods. If there is no appropriate helper method for the particular type of property to be added, the underlying `context` and `rwiElements[]` are still available to create any new type of property.

If the property is conditional (should only be displayed in certain circumstances), then a `Condition` object is required. To construct a `Condition` object, you can use code such as:

---

59. The inversed boolean property returns false if checked, true if unchecked.

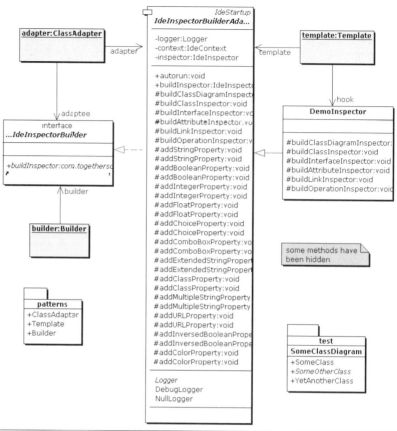

Figure E-3
InspectorBuilder adapter / template class.

```
1  new Condition() {
2    public boolean execute(IdeContext context) {
3      return RwiElementsUtil.checkProperty(
4      context, "myBooleanProperty", true);
5    }
6  }
```

The `RwiElementsUtil` class is a Together open API class. If this `Condition` were passed in to the overloaded version of an `addXxxProperty()` method, then the property would only appear if the selected elements have a property called `myBooleanProperty`. This technique can be used with any of the helper methods.

The Demo Inspector

The `DemoInspector` class is an example inspector that simply creates a new properties page `Demo` and adds a property of each of the supported types to that page. To keep the demo simple, the same set of properties are added no matter what the selected element type.

The Inspector Support framework is available from the Web site at *www.bettersoftwarefaster.com* as the zip `inspectorsupport.zip`. This will extract to:

```
inspectorsupport\
  inspectorsupport.tpr    // Together project file
  src\                    // source
  diag\                   // diagrams
  classes\                // compiled code
  manifest\               // manifest to describe demo modules
  bat\                    // batch files (buildjar & install)
```

To build the project, just load up `inspectorsupport.tpr` and rebuild. It's also necessary to install the project so that Together will pick up the demo modules. To install the modules, first make sure that the `%TOGETHER%` environment variable is set to Together's home directory (e.g., `C:\Together-Soft\Together6.0`), and then run `bat\install.bat`.

Because this is a framework, we also need to create a JAR file to support any inspectors we write using the framework. To create the JAR file, run `bat\buildjar.bat`. This will create a JAR file in `%TOGETHER%\modules\inspectorsupport.jar`. We'll add this to our classpath later.

To try out the demo inspector, restart Together and load up any project. The `inspectorsupport` project itself has a `test` package with some simple classes, so use that if you wish. Open up the properties inspector in the usual way (*Alt-Enter*) and navigate to the *Demo* tab, as shown in Figure E–4.

Name	Value
String property	a string
Boolean property?	✔
Integer property	3
Float property	33.0
Choice property	choice3
ComboBox property	comboBoxValue2
Extended string property	an extended string□□over several lines.
Class property	com.togethersoft.modules.inspector.bettersoftwarefas...
multiStringProperty	multiString1,multiString2,multiString3
URL property	http://www.bettersoftwarefaster.com
Inversed boolean property	
Color property	
Show conditional string?	✔
Conditional string property	a conditional string

Press Ctrl+Enter to finish editing and close Inspector

Figure E–4
User-defined properties can be added using the Inspector Support framework.

These demo properties appear due to the presence of the manifest file which contains:

```
1   Name = Demo InspectorSupport framework.
2   MainClassName=com.togethersoft.modules.inspector.
    bettersoftwarefaster.inspectorsupport.DemoInspector
3   Time = Startup
```

This is installed by the `install.bat` script into the `inspector\bettersoftwarefaster\inspectorsupport` directory under `%TOGETHER%\modules\com\togethersoft\modules`. If using the framework for your own properties, you won't want these demo properties. To make sure that they don't appear, just remove the manifest file.

Worked Example

To illustrate how the framework is used in practice, here is a small project that formalizes some of the user-defined properties that we have suggested previously in the book.

- For class diagrams, classes and interfaces, define:
  - a "represents" property that offers "domainModel", "domain-Model, and Implementation" or "implementation" as a dropdown list.
- For attributes representing links, define:
  - a "constraint" property, allowing multiple constraints (for example, {ordered} and {set}) to be defined. This ties in with the custom templates in Appendix D.

In this little example, we would also like to demonstrate user-defined properties for operations. To do this, we will add some properties so that Together can more fully support the Object Constraint Language (OCL). Consulting Warmer and Kleppe (1999), we see that the following properties are needed for operations:

- An `isQuery` meta-attribute is needed, indicating that the operation does not modify the state of the object.
- An «oclOperation» stereotype is required, indicating that an operation is synthetic and exists only to make an OCL construct simpler to phrase.

The Custom Inspector is available from the Web site at *www.bettersoftwarefaster.com* as the zip `custominspector.zip`. This will extract to:

```
custominspector\
  custominspector.tpr    // Together project file
  src\                   // source
  diag\                  // diagrams
  classes\               // compiled code
  manifest\              // manifest to describe demo modules
  bat\                   // batch files (install & installjar)
```

To build the project, load up `custominspector.tpr` and rebuild. To install the custom inspector, run the `bat\install.bat` (to copy the class files under `%TOGETHER%`) and restart Together.

When you reopen the project (or any other project), you should now see a new `BSwF` property page appearing for classes, class diagrams, links, and operations. The stereotypes property for operations should also have a new value, `oclOperation`.

Here's the code that does the work:

```
 1  protected void buildOperationInspector() {
 2    addBooleanProperty("BSwF", "isQuery", "is query?");
 3    addComboBoxProperty("Properties",
 4      "stereotype", "stereotype",
 5      new String[] { "query", "constructor", "update",
 6                     "external", "oclOperation" } );
 7    }
 8  protected void buildLinkInspector() {
 9    addMultipleStringProperty("BSwF",
10    "constraint", "constraints");
11  }
12  protected void buildClassDiagramInspector() {
13    addChoiceProperty(
14      "BSwF", "represents", "represents", dropDownList);
15  }
16  protected void buildClassInspector() {
17    addChoiceProperty(
18      "BSwF", "represents", "represents", dropDownList);
19  }
20  protected void buildInterfaceInspector() {
21    addChoiceProperty(
22      "BSwF", "represents", "represents", dropDownList);
23  }
24  String[] dropDownList = new String[] {
25    "implementation", "spec & impl", "domain model"
26  };
```

One thing that we noticed when developing the framework (and which we confirmed was also the case for config-based inspectors) is that modifying properties for existing property pages can be unpredictable. For example, you will find that it is okay to add properties to existing pages for classes and operations, but attempting to do so for links or for class diagrams results in only your new properties appearing. We can only surmise that this is down to the order in which the builders (Together's own and the custom ones) are installed. So, to be safe, always add a new property page to hold your user-defined properties. If you absolutely have to have your property on an existing page (or you want to modify an existing property), then the only safe way to do this is to edit Together's own inspectors, as previously mentioned.

Another point. You will find that if you delete the class files for the inspector framework (under `inspector\bettersoftwarefaster\inspectorframework` in `%TOGETHER%\modules\com\togethersoft\modules`), then you will find your custom inspector will stop working. In other words, the `inspectorsupport.jar` file is being used only during compile and development time, not during runtime.

The solution to this is to deploy the custom inspector as a JAR file rather than a set of classes files. We can use the manifest file (called manifest.mf rather than `manifest.def`) to point to the `inspectorsupport.jar` file at runtime.

To try out this approach, delete the entire `bettersoftwarefaster` directory under `%TOGETHER%\modules\com\togethersoft\modules\inspector`). Now, install the custom inspector using `bat\installjar.bat` (rather than `bat\install.bat` that you used before). This simply runs the `jar` command with an appropriate manifest and creates a file `custominspector.jar` in the `inspector` directory, with a manifest that points back to the `inspectorsupport.jar` under `%TOGETHER%\modules`. Restart Together to check that this has worked correctly. Lovely!

Finally, a note on debugging. Like any open API module, debugging custom inspectors can be tricky. One fallback is to use old-fashioned `System.out.println()` to trace the calls, but if you do this, remember that the output will go to Together's own console—so start it from a batch file or console window (e.g., on Windows run `together.bat` rather than `together.exe`).

To Conclude

Table E–1 compares the three approaches to implementing inspectors.

Table E–1

Comparison of Approaches for Implementing User-Defined Properties

	Property Builder	inspector.config	Open API
Implementation type	Through user interface; changes written to `changes.config`	Together's own configuration script	Java
Implementation effort	Low effort	Medium effort	Medium effort (with appropriate infrastructure)
Property types?	Some types supported	All types supported	All types supported
Conditional properties?	No	Yes	Yes
Possible values for drop-down list boxes	Not supported	Hardcoded into the config file	Dynamic; could be calculated on the fly or read from a database
Deployment	Mixed into `changes.config`; more tricky to manage in team-based environment	Mixed into `inspector.config`; more tricky to manage in team-based environment	Simple to manage; can be packaged into a jar or well-defined subdirectory under modules.

The *RwiSupport* Framework

To assist in developing modules that iterate over the RWI[59] part of Together's repository (as opposed to the audit modules that iterate over the lower level SCI part of its repository), we have developed a framework that simplifies such development considerably.

The framework is put to practical use in Chapter 6, "The Continuous Step: Measure the Quality," and Chapter 8, "The Macro Step: Architecture." The framework itself comes with two demo modules so that you can see it in use.

Figure F–1 shows the main classes in the *RwiSupport* framework.

`RwiVisitorDispatcher` is the workhorse of the framework, iterating over each of the different element types in turn. It passes an implementation of `com.togethersoft.openapi.rwi.RwiVisitor` to each element, provided that the corresponding method in `RwiVisitorFilter` returns true. If you are familiar with the Visitor pattern (Gamma et al. 1995) you will know that it relies on a well-defined class structure; in this case we're talking about the organization of the different elements within Together's repository. Figure F–2 shows those elements in the `openapi.rwi` package. The elements that we iterate over are packages, diagrams, nodes (e.g., classes and interfaces), and members.

There are two designs for passing a `RwiVisitor` and a `RwiVisitorFilter` to the `RwiVisitorDispatcher`. The first is to subclass `RwiVisitorSupport`. This class also has support for displaying message pages (through the helper `RwiMessagePage` class). This design approach is used in the demo module `DemoSubclassModule`. Alternatively, a module can delegate to an instance of `RwiVisitorSupport` (obtaining the message page support functionality) and pass in specific instances of `RwiVisitor` and `RwiVisitorFilter`. This is the approach used in the demo module `DemoDelegatorModule`.

---

59. RWI is Together's Read/Write Interface, and SCI is the Source Code Interface. The RWI gives access to all code and non-code elements.

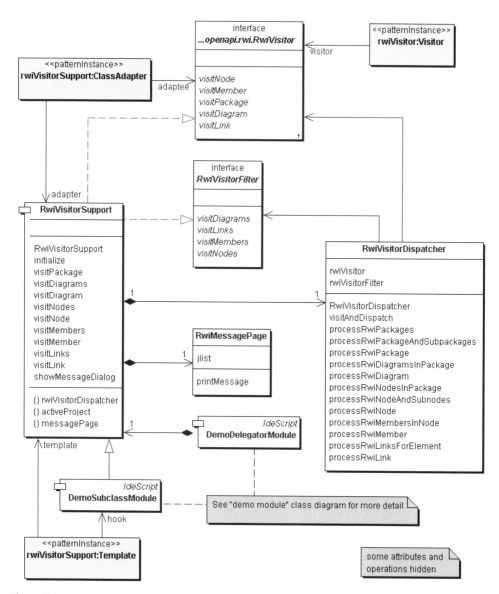

Figure F–1

The *RwiSupport* framework allows auditing of non-code based elements.

The RWI Support framework is available from the Web site at *www.better-softwarefaster.com* as the zip `rwisupport.zip`. This will extract to:

```
rwisupport\
   src\              // source and Together project file
   diag\             // diagrams
   classes\          // compiled code
   manifest\         // manifest to describe demo modules
   bat\              // batch files (buildjar & install)
```

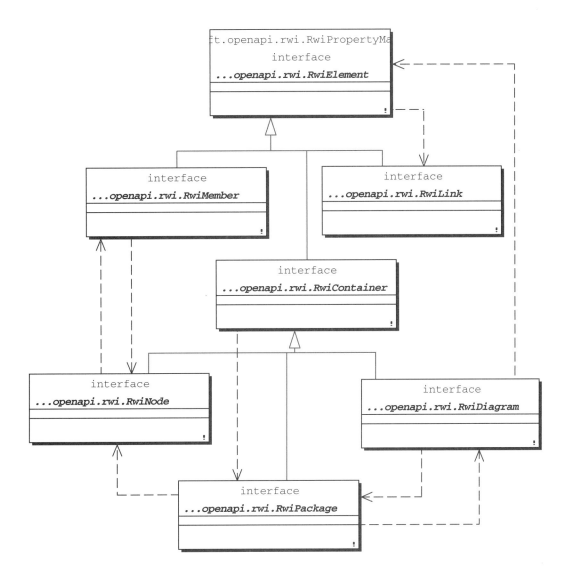

Figure F-2
Rwi Model elements form a class hierarchy.

To build the project, just load up `rwisupport.tpr` and rebuild. It is also necessary to install the project so that Together will pick up the demo modules. To install the modules, set the `%TOGETHER%` environment variable to Together's home directory (e.g., `C:\Together-Soft\Together6.0`) and then run `bat\install.bat`.

Because this is a framework, we also need to create a JAR file to support any modules we develop that use the framework. To create the JAR file, run `bat\buildjar.bat`. This will create a JAR file in `%TOGETHER%\modules\rwisupport.jar`. We'll add this to our classpath later for modules that use the framework.

To try out the demo modules, restart Together and load up a project, and then go to the modules tab. You can run the module from the speed menu, as shown Figure F–3.

If you run either of these modules, you'll find that they just print out how many items (packages, diagrams, classes, operations, and attributes) there are in the project.

Figure F–3
The *RwiSupport* demo modules.

Possible Enhancements

Although the *RwiSupport* framework is already quite powerful, there are several ways in which it could be enhanced. Given that the framework is the basis for custom modules, it would make sense to provide the facility to compose all modules into a single module. You'd probably need to create some interface (`Composable`, say) for supporting multi-pass modules; the composite visitor would keep dispatching the visitors until all composed visitors indicated that they had completed all of their passes. The Composable interface might also be used to define a mechanism for querying the leaf visitors; alternatively, a Collecting Parameter pattern could be used. But we don't want to have all the fun—we'll leave those enhancements as an exercise for the reader (we've always wanted to say that!).

You are of course welcome to use the *RwiSupport* framework for your own modules (please acknowledge copyright if you do so).

CarServ Case Study

This Appendix contains some of the key diagrams from the case study project, *CarServ*:

- Figure G-1 is an overview class diagram showing a number of the key classes and dependencies between them.
- Figure G-2 is as summary diagram of the domain model classes omitting the details of class properties and operations.
- Figure G-3 is an implementation level class diagram to show the interaction between `Car` and `Service` objects.
- Figure G-4 shows a sequence diagram for the operation `BookIn.doExecute()` which is carried out when a car is brought in for servicing.
- Figure G-5 is a package diagram for the application showing dependencies between the packages and classes within the packages.
- Figure G-6 shows the database schema for the application.

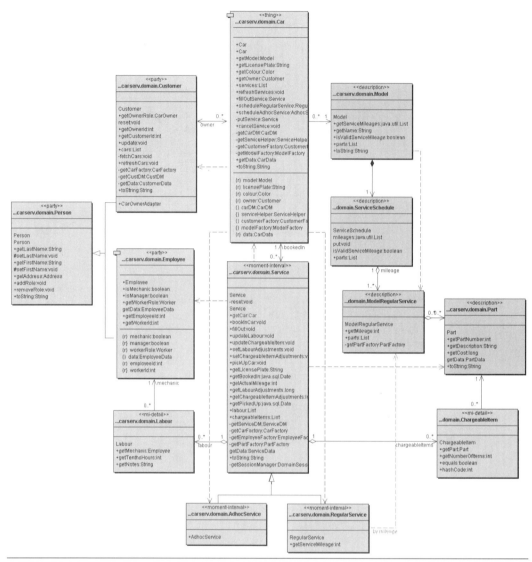

Figure G–1

Overview class diagram.

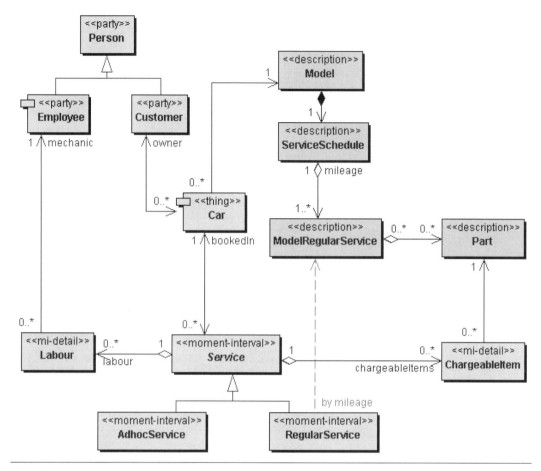

Figure G–2
Overview class diagram, detail omitted.

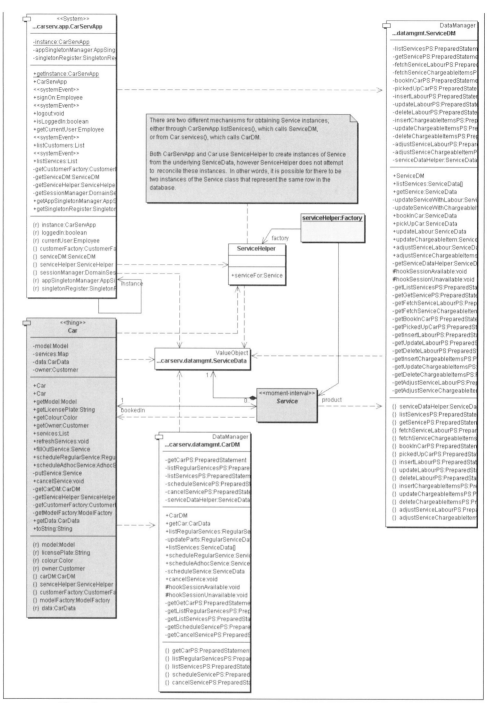

Figure G-3

Car and Service Implementation class diagram.

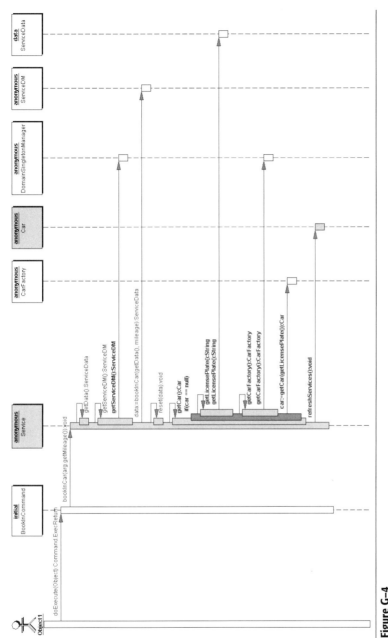

Figure G–4

BookIn.doExecute() sequence diagram.

CarServ Case Study

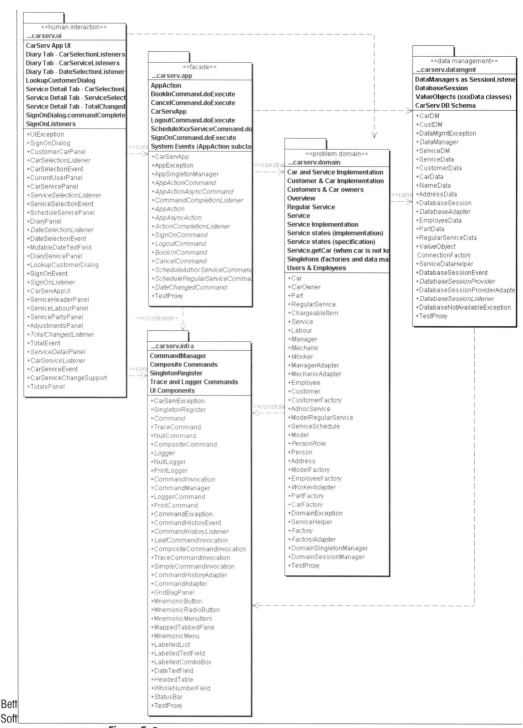

<<human interaction>>
...carserv.ui

CarServ App UI
Diary Tab - CarSelectionListeners
Diary Tab - CarServiceListeners
Diary Tab - DateSelectionListener
LookupCustomerDialog
Service Detail Tab - CarSelectionL
Service Detail Tab - ServiceSelect
Service Detail Tab - TotalChanged
SignOnDialog.commandComplete
SignOnListeners

+UiException
+SignOnDialog
+CustomerCarPanel
+CarSelectionListener
+CarSelectionEvent
+CurrentUserPanel
+CarServicePanel
+ServiceSelectionListener
+ServiceSelectionEvent
+ScheduleServicePanel
+DiaryPanel
+DateSelectionListener
+DateSelectionEvent
+MutableDateTextField
+DiaryServicePanel
+LookupCustomerDialog
+SignOnEvent
+SignOnListener
+CarServAppUI
+ServiceHeaderPanel
+ServiceLabourPanel
+ServicePartsPanel
+AdjustmentsPanel
+TotalChangedListener
+TotalEvent
+ServiceDetailPanel
+CarServiceListener
+CarServiceEvent
+CarServiceChangeSupport
+TotalsPanel

<<facade>>
...carserv.app

AppAction
BookInCommand.doExecute
CancelCommand.doExecute
CarServApp
LogoutCommand.doExecute
ScheduleXxxServiceCommand.do
SignOnCommand.doExecute
System Events (AppAction subcla

+CarServApp
+AppException
+AppSingletonManager
+AppActionCommand
+AppActionAsyncCommand
+CommandCompletionListener
+AppAction
+AppAsyncAction
+ActionCompletionListener
+SignOnCommand
+LogoutCommand
+BookInCommand
+CancelCommand
+ScheduleAdhocServiceCommand
+ScheduleRegularServiceComma
+DateChangedCommand
+TestProxy

<<data management>>
...carserv.datamgmt

DataManagers as SessionListene
DatabaseSession
ValueObjects (xxxData classes)
CarServ DB Schema

+CarDM
+CustDM
+DataMgmtException
+DataManager
+ServiceDM
+ServiceData
+CustomerData
+CarData
+NameData
+AddressData
+DatabaseSession
+DatabaseAdapter
+EmployeeData
+PartData
+RegularServiceData
+ValueObject
ConnectionFactory
+ServiceDataHelper
+DatabaseSessionEvent
+DatabaseSessionProvider
+DatabaseSessionProviderAdapte
+DatabaseSessionListener
+DatabaseNotAvailableException
+TestProxy

<<problem domain>>
...carserv.domain

Car and Service Implementation
Customer & Car Implementation
Customers & Car owners
Overview
Regular Service
Service
Service Implementation
Service states (implementation)
Service states (specification)
Service.getCar (when car is not kr
Singletons (factories and data ma
Users & Employees

+Car
+CarOwner
+Part
+RegularService
+ChargeableItem
+Service
+Labour
+Manager
+Mechanic
+Worker
+ManagerAdapter
+MechanicAdapter
+Employee
+Customer
+CustomerFactory
+AdhocService
+ModelRegularService
+ServiceSchedule
+Model
+PersonRole
+Person
+Address
+ModelFactory
+EmployeeFactory
+WorkerAdapter
+PartFactory
+CarFactory
+DomainException
+ServiceHelper
+Factory
+FactoryAdapter
+DomainSingletonManager
+DomainSessionManager
+TestProxy

...carserv.infra

CommandManager
Composite Commands
SingletonRegister
Trace and Logger Commands
UI Components

+CarServException
+SingletonRegister
+Command
+TraceCommand
+NullCommand
+CompositeCommand
+Logger
+NullLogger
+PrintLogger
+CommandInvocation
+CommandManager
+LoggerCommand
+PrintCommand
+CommandException
+CommandHistoryEvent
+CommandHistoryListener
+LeafCommandInvocation
+CompositeCommandInvocation
+TraceCommandInvocation
+SimpleCommandInvocation
+CommandHistoryAdapter
+CommandAdapter
+GridBagPanel
+MnemonicButton
+MnemonicRadioButton
+MnemonicMenuItem
+MappedTabbedPane
+MnemonicMenu
+LabelledList
+LabelledTextField
+LabelledComboBox
+DateTextField
+HeadedTable
+WholeNumberField
+StatusBar
+TestProxy

Figure G–5

Implementation Packages (showing classes).

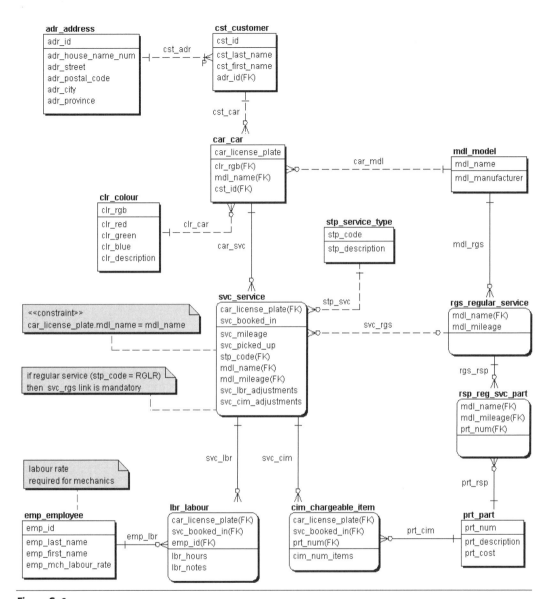

Figure G–6
Database schema.

bibliography

Alexander, C. (1977). *The Timeless Way of Building.* Oxford University Press, Oxford, UK.

Ambler, S., and L. L. Constantine (2000). *The Unified Process Inception Phase.* CMP Books, Lawrence, KS.

Anderson, B. (1994). "Patterns: Building Blocks for Object-Oriented Architectures." *Software Engineering Notes,* January, ACM.

Armour, F., and G. Miller. (2000). *Advanced Use Case Modeling.* Addison-Wesley, Reading, MA.

Astels, D., R Miller and M. Novak, (2002). *A Practical Guide to eXtreme Programming.* Prentice-Hall, Englewood Cliffs, NJ.

Beck, K., and W. Cunningham. (1989). "A Laboratory for Teaching Object-Oriented Thinking." OOPSLA 1989 Conference Proceedings, republished at *http://c2.com/doc/oopsla89/paper.html.*

Beck, K., and R. Johnson. (1994). "Patterns Generate Architectures." Proceedings of ECOOP '94, M. Tokoro and R. Pareschi (Eds.), LNCS 821, pp. 139–149, Springer-Verlag, Italy.

Beck, K. (2000). *Extreme Programming Explained: Embrace Change.* Addison-Wesley, Reading, MA.

Beck, K., and M. Fowler (2001). *Planning Extreme Programming.* Addison-Wesley, Reading, MA.

Bloch, J. (2001). *Effective Java Programming Language Guide.* Addison-Wesley, Reading, MA.

Booch, G. (1993). "Patterns." *Object Magazine,* SIGS Publications, New York.

Booch, G. (1996). *Object Solutions.* Addison-Wesley, Reading, MA.

Brooks, F. P., Jr. (1974). *Mythical Man Month: Essays on Software Engineering.* Addison-Wesley, Reading, MA.

Brown, W. J., R. C. Malveau, W. H. Brown, H. W. McCormick, and T. J. Mowbray. (1998). *AntiPatterns.* Wiley & Sons, New York.

Bulka, D. (2000). *Java Performance and Scalability, Volume 1: Server-Side Programming Techniques.* Addison-Wesley, Reading, MA

Buschman, F., R. Meunier, H. Rohnert, P. Sommerlad, and M. Stal. (1996). *Pattern-Oriented Software Architecture, Volume 1: A System of Patterns.* Wiley & Sons, New York.

Carmichael, A. R. (1994a). "Toward a Common Object-Oriented Meta-Model for Object Development." in A. R. Carmichael (Ed.), *Object Development Methods.* Cambridge University Press, Cambridge UK.

Carmichael, A. R. (1994b). "Quality...in a Class of Its Own." Report on Object-oriented Analysis and Design (ROAD)., Vol. 1, No. 3, SIGS Publications, New York.

Carmichael, A. R., and M. J. Swainston-Rainford. (2000). "Features Game—A Game for up to 24 Players Based on Feature-Driven Development." OT2000 Conference, BCS-OOPS, Oxford, UK.

Cheesman, J., and J. Daniels. (2000). UML *Components: A Simple Process for Specifying Component-Based Software* (*The Component Software Series*). Addison-Wesley, Reading, MA.

Coad, P. (1992). "Object-Oriented Patterns." *Communications of the* ACM, 35(9), 152–159. ACM.

Coad, P., D. North, and M. Mayfield. (1997). *Object Models: Strategies, Patterns and Applications.* 2nd ed., Prentice-Hall, Englewood Cliffs, NJ.

Coad, P., E. Lefebvre, and J. De Luca. (1999). *Java Modeling in Color.* Prentice-Hall, Englewood Cliffs, NJ.

Cockburn, A. (1997). "Structuring Use Cases with Goals." JOOP Sep/Oct 1997 and Nov/Dec 1997. Republished at *members.aol.com/acockburn/papers/usecases.htm.*

Cockburn, A. (2000). *Writing Effective Use Cases.* Addison-Wesley, Reading, MA.

Cooper, A. (1999). *The Inmates Are Running the Asylum : Why High Tech Products Drive Us Crazy and How To Restore The Sanity.* SAMS, Indianapolis, IN.

Coplien, J. O. (1992). *Advanced C++ Programming Styles and Idioms.* Addison-Wesley, Reading MA.

DeMarco, T., and T. Lister. (1987). *Peopleware: Productive Projects and Teams,* 2nd ed. 1999, Dorset House, New York.

Dikel D.M., D. Kane and J. R. Wilson (2001). *Software Architecture: Organizational Principles and Patterns.* Prentice-Hall, Englewood Cliffs, NJ.

D'Souza, D. F., and A. Wills. (1998). *Objects, Components, and Frameworks With UML : The Catalysis Approach.* Addison-Wesley, Reading MA.

Fagan, M. E. (1976). "Design and Code Inspections to Reduce Errors in Program Development." IBM *Systems Journal,* 15(3), 182—211.

Fowler, M. (1997). *Analysis Patterns.* Addison-Wesley, Reading, MA.

Fowler, M. (2000a). UML *Distilled,* 2nd ed. Addison-Wesley, Reading, MA.

Fowler, M. (2000b). *Refactoring.* Addison-Wesley, Reading, MA.

Gamma, E., R. Helm, R. Johnson, and J. Vlissides, (1995). *Design Patterns: Elements of Reusable Object-Oriented Design.* Addison-Wesley, Reading, MA.

Gilb, T. (1989). *Principles of Software Engineering Management.* Addison-Wesley, Reading, MA.

Gilb, T., and D. Graham. (1993). *Software Inspection.* Pearson Education Ltd. London, UK.

Gilb, T. (1997). "The Evolutionary Project Managers Handbook." Evo Manuscript Distribution Edition 0.1, *http://home.c2i.net/result-planning/Pages/2ndLevel/gilbdownload.html.*

Gilb, T. (2002). *Competitive Engineering: A New Systems Engineering Approach for Controlling Complexity, Communicating Clearly, and Challenging Creativity.* The Planguage Series, Vol. I. Addison-Wesley, Reading, MA.

Graham, I., B. Henderson-Sellers, and H. Younessi. (1997). *The Open Process Specification.* Open Series, Addison-Wesley, Reading, MA.

Haywood D., M. Bond, and P. Roxburgh. (2002). *Teach Yourself J2EE in 21 Days,* SAMS, Indianapolis, IN.

Halstead, M. H. (1977). *Elements of Software Science.* Operating, and Programming Systems Series, Vol. 7. Elsevier, New York.

Hammer, M. (1990). "Reengineering Work: Don't Automate, Obliterate." *Harvard Business Review,* 90, 104–12.

Henney, K. (1999). "Mutual Registration Pattern." Proceedings of the 4th European Conference on Pattern Languages of Programming, EuroPLOP 99, Irsee, Germany.

Highsmith, J. A. (1999). *Adaptive Software Development: A Collaborative Approach to Managing Complex Systems.* Dorset House, New York.

Hunt, J. (2000). *The Unified Process for Practitioners: Object Oriented Design, UML and Java.* Practitioner Series. Springer-Verlag, London, UK.

Jacobson, I. , M. Ericsson, A. Jacobson. (1994). *The Object Advantage: Business Process Reengineering with Object Technology.* Longman Higher Education.

Jacobson, I., G. Booch, and J. Rumbaugh. (1999). *Unified Software Development Process.* Addison Wesley, Reading, MA.

Jennings, J., and L. Haughton. (2001). *It's Not the Big that Eat the Small...It's the Fast that Eat the Slow.* Harper Collins, New York.

Johnson, R. (1992). "Documenting Frameworks Using Patterns". OOPSLA Conference Proceedings, October 1992, pp. 63–76, ACM.

Johnson, J. (1995, July). "Creating Chaos." *American Programmer,* Cutter Consortium, MA.

Johnson, S. (2001). *Emergence.* Scribner, USA. Allen Lane, The Penguin Press, London, UK.

Kan, S. K. (1995). *Metrics and Models in Software Quality Engineering.* Addison-Wesley, Reading, MA.

Kruchten, P. (1998). *The Rational Unified Process: An Introduction.* Addison-Wesley, Reading, MA.

Langr, J. (1999). *Essential Java Style,* Prentice-Hall, Englewood Cliffs, NJ.

Larman, C. (1998). *Applying UML and Patterns.* Prentice-Hall, Englewood Cliffs, NJ.

Liskov, B., with J. Guttag. (2001). *Program Development in Java.* Addison-Wesley, Reading, MA.

McConnell, S. (1996). *Rapid Development: Taming Wild Software Schedules.* Microsoft Press, Richmond, WA.

Martin, R. C. *Designing Object-Oriented C++ Applications Using the Booch Method.* Prentice-Hall, Englewood Cliffs, NJ.

Martin, R. C. (1996). "Dependency Inversion Principle." Article from C++ *Report*, republished at *www.objectmentor.com/publications/dip.pdf*.

Martin, R. C. (1996). "Granularity." Article from C++ *Report*, republished at *www.objectmentor.com/publications/granularity.pdf*.

Monson-Haefel, R. (2000). *Enterprise JavaBeans*. O'Reilly, Sebastopol, CA.

Norman, R., and D. Kranz. (In press). *A Practical Guide to Unified Process*. Prentice-Hall, Englewood Cliffs, NJ.

Palmer, S., and M. Felsing. (2002). *A Practical Guide to Feature-Driven Development*. Prentice-Hall, Englewood Cliffs, NJ.

Parnas, D. L. (1979). "Designing Software for Ease of Extension and Contraction." IEEE *Transactions on Software Engineering*, SE-5(2).

Pitt, R., and A. R. Carmichael. (2000). "Measuring the Effect of Refactoring." 6th International Conference on Object Oriented Information Systems, Springer-Verlag, London.

Putnam, L. H., and W. Myers. (1992). *Measures for Excellence: Reliable Software on Time, Within Budget."* Prentice-Hall, Englewood Cliffs, NJ.

Royce, W. W. (1970). "Managing the development of large software systems: concepts and techniques." Proceedings of WESCON 1970, pp. 1–9.

Royce, W. (1998). *Software Project Management: A Unified Framework*. Addison-Wesley, Reading, MA.

Schneider, A. (2000). "JUnit Good Practices." Web article at *http://javaworld.com/javaworld/jw-12-2000/jw-1221-junit_p.html*.

Slater, N. (2000). *Appetite: So What Do You Want to Eat Today?*. Fourth Estate Ltd., London, UK.

Simonyi, C., and M. Heller. (1991, August). "The Hungarian Revolution." BYTE, 131–38.

Stapleton, J. (1997). DSDM. Addison-Wesley, Reading, MA.

Warmer, J., and A. Kleppe. (1999). *The Object Constraint Language*. Addison-Wesley, Reading, MA.

Warren, N., and P. Bishop. (1999). *Java in Practice*. Addison-Wesley, Reading, MA.

Williams, S. (2000). *The Associative Model of Data*. Lazy Software Ltd, High Wycombe, UK.

Yourdon, E., and L. Constantine. (1979). *Structured Design: Fundamentals of a Discipline of Computer Program and Systems Design*. Yourdon Press, Englewood Cliffs, NJ.

Yourdon, E. (2000). *Death March: The Complete Software Developer's Guide to Surviving 'Mission Impossible' Projects*. Yourdon Computing Series, Prentice-Hall, Englewood Cliffs, NJ.

Online Resources

Beck, K., and E. Gamma: *www.junit.org* "Java Unit Testing framework" – open source & documentation

Brown, W., R. Malveau, H. McCormick, and T. Mowbray: *www.antipatterns.com*. A site dedicated to the discussion of Anti-patterns and the books from these authors.

Cactus: *http://jakarta.apache.org/cactus/*. A simple test framework for unit testing server-side Java code (Servlets, EJBs, Tag Libs, etc.).

Carmichael, A. R., and D. Haywood: *www.bettersoftwarefaster.com*. The Web site for this book and source for the example Together project and source code.

Cloudscape: *www.cloudscape.com*. Download the database used in the case study from here.

Cockburn, A.: *members.aol.com/acockburn*. Download articles and insights on use case modeling and other software engineering topics.

Cunningham and Cunningham: *http://c2.com*. A discussion site on many software topics, including XP.

Gilb T.: *http://home.c2i.net/result-planning/Pages/2ndLevel/gilbdownload.html*. Books, articles, slides, etc. by Tom Gilb and others.

Globetrotter Inc.: *www.globetrotter.com* Suppliers of FlexLM software.

Heilwagen, A.: *www.extreme-java.de*. "JUnitX 4.0 & XPTest."

Hillside Group: *www.hillside.net/patterns*. A source for information about all aspects of software patterns and pattern languages.

JUintEE: *http://junitee.sourceforge.net*. An extension to JUnit that allows tests to be run from within a J2EE application server.

JavaWorld: *www.javaworld.com*. IT news and Java resources.

Merriam-Webster's Collegiate® Dictionary: *www.m-w.com*. An American English dictionary.

MockObjects: *http://mockobjects.sourceforge.net*. A generic unit testing framework.

ObjectMentor: *www.objectmentor.com*. Includes a number of useful articles from Robert Martin.

SEI, Software Technology Review: *www.sei.cmu.edu/str*. Review of many aspects of software engineering, including software metrics.

HttpUnit: *http://httpunit.sourceforge.net*. A framework for automated Web site testing

Standish Group: *www.standishgroup.com*. Project management surveys and services.

Together Community: *www.togethercommunity.com*. Web site for exchanging news, views, and plug-ins with other Together users.

TogetherSoft: *www.togethersoft.com*. Corporate Web site.

index

Properties, classes, 59, 60–61
PVCS, 11

Q

Qualified associations, 202–3
Quality:
continuous measurement of, 267–68
document generation, 145–61
design patterns, 153–56
hyperlinking, 146–52
Together's document generation, 156–58
inspections, 158–61
measuring, 111–61
black-box measurement, 114–15
steps in, 112–14
testing, 115–32
white-box measurement, 114–15
reviews, 158–61
testing, 115–32
functional testing, 115, 116–17
nonfunctional testing, 115, 117–18
unit testing, 115, 119–20
Quality monitoring, 14–16
audits, 14
document generation, 15
metrics, 15

R

Ratio, 15
"Rational Design Process: How and Why to Fake It, A" (Parnas/Clements), 19
Realization links, 146–48
recalcTotal attribute, 50
Receive Payment use case, 79–80
Record Work Done use case, 77–78
Reenskaug, Trygve, 163
Refactoring, 205–8
for attributes, 207
for classes and interfaces, 206–7
for information purposes, 206–7
object of, 205
for operations/methods, 207
for information purposes, 207

Refactoring costs, 107–8
Refactoring (Fowler), 119
Reference HttpServlet pattern, 242, 244
RegularService class, 53
Release management, 237–39
Release quality, 113
removeXxxListener(), 199
RepeatedTest decorator of the JUnit framework, 118
RepeatedTest extension, 286
represents property, 194
Requirements, 17–18
accepting into the build, 165–68
on/off states, 22
requirements package, single-source model, 31–33
Requirements specification, *See* Specification of requirements
Reverse engineering, 41–44
Reverse Link Direction, 62
Reviews, 158–61
of the build against the initial design, 160
RFC (Response For Class), 134
Rich Text Format (RTF), 15, 38–40, 157
Root package diagram, 31–32
single-source model, 31, 35
Roth, Bill, 241
Run -> Run/Debug Run Configurations, 27, 123, 246
Rushdie, Salman, 265
RwiSupport framework, 145, 209, 315–18
enhancements, 318
framework classes, 315–18
motivation, 315

S

Saint-Exupery, Antoine de, 163
Sales Manager role, 77
Same package choice, Test location property, 280
Save set As, 138
Scenarios, documenting, 80–81
Schedule Service use case, 77
Schneider, A., 288
Security implementations, 81–82
Self-reviews, 158

Types:
  domain model, 56–57
  modeling as classes, 57–63

U

ui package, 168, 232
  single-source model, 31
UML activity diagrams, 8
UML diagrams, 66–69
Unified Modeling Language (UML), 4
  and component diagrams, 221
  and functional requirements, 87
  message types, 190–92
  navigability in, 61–62
  and nonfunctional requirements, 87–88
  qualifier, 202–3
  stereotypes, 59
  types in, 56–57
Unified Process (UP), 93
Unit testing, 129–33
Unit tests, 17–18, 282
Unmodified code, testing, 22
Unqualified quality level, 113–14
UP, xix
Update Package Dependencies, 224
Use case diagrams, 73–74
  benefit of, 214
Use cases, hyperlinking, 152
User interaction, designing, 169–72
User reviews, 158

V

Value object class pattern, 209
Version control, 237–39
  moving/renaming model elements under, 238–39

View -> Editor, 35
View Management -> Dependencies -> Show between Classes = true, 179, 195
View Management -> JavaBeans/C++ properties, 59
View Management -> Show -> All Members = false, 195
View Management -> Show -> Dependencies = false, 195
View Management -> Show -> Dependencies = true, 195
View -> Services, 29
view.config file, 154
Visual tests, 128

W

Walkthroughs, 158
Waterfall-style development process, 8–9, 18–19
Web application archive (WAR file), 251
webui package, 242
  single-source model, 31
web.xml file, 249
Weighted Methods Per Class (WMPC2), 129, 131
White-box measurement, 114–15
withCallback() method, 191–92

X

XP (Extreme Programming), xix, 93, 159

Y

YAGNI, 107–8, 214

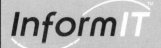